THE

# MYSTERIES OF MASONRY.

BEING THE OUTLINE OF A UNIVERSAL PHILOSOPHY
FOUNDED UPON THE RITUAL AND DEGREES
OF ANCIENT FREEMASONRY.

By L. E. REYNOLDS, P. M., P. H. P.

**British Library Cataloguing-in-Publication Data**
A catalogue record for this book is available from
the British Library

# PRELIMINARY.

## THE ORIGIN AND PROGRESS OF FREEMASONRY.

ANY inquiry into the symbolism and philosophy of Freemasonry must necessarily be preceded by a brief investigation of the origin and history of the institution. Ancient and universal as it is, whence did it arise? What were the accidents connected with its birth? From what kindred or similar association did it spring? Or was it original and autochthonic, independent, in its inception, of any external influences, and unconnected with any other institution? These are questions which an intelligent investigator will be disposed to propound in the very commencement of the inquiry; and they are questions which must be distinctly answered before he can be expected to comprehend its true character as a symbolic institution. He must know something of its antecedents before he can appreciate its character.

But he who expects to arrive at a satisfactory solution of this inquiry must first — as a preliminary absolutely necessary to success — release himself from the influence of an error into which novices in Masonic philosophy are too apt to fall. He must not confound the doctrine of Freemasonry with its outward and extrinsic form. He must not suppose that certain usages and ceremonies, which exist at this day, but which, even now, are subject to extensive variations in different countries, constitute the sum and substance of Freemasonry. " Prudent antiquity," says Lord Coke, " did for more solemnity and better memory and observation of that which is to be done, express substances under ceremonies." But it must be always remembered that the ceremony is not the substance. It is but the outer garment which covers and perhaps adorns it, as clothing does the human figure. But divest man of that outward apparel, and you still have the microcosm, the wondrous creation, with all his nerves, and bones, and muscles, and, above all, with his brain, and thoughts, and feelings. And so take from Masonry these external ceremonies, and you still have remaining its philosophy and science. These have, of course, always continued the same, while the ceremonies have varied in different ages, and still vary in different countries.

The definition of Freemasonry that it is " a science of morality, veiled in allegory, and illustrated by symbols," has been so often quoted, that, were it not for its beauty, it would become wearisome. But this definition contains the exact principle that has just been enunciated. Freemasonry is a science — a philosophy — a system of doctrines which is taught, in a manner peculiar to itself, by allegories and symbols. This is its internal character. Its ceremonies are external additions, which affect not its substance.

Now, when we are about to institute an inquiry into the origin of Freemasonry, it is of this peculiar system of philosophy that we are to inquire, and not of the ceremonies which have been foisted on it. If we pursue any other course we shall assuredly fall into error.

Thus, if we seek the origin and first beginning of the Masonic philosophy, we must go away back into the ages of remote antiquity, when we shall find this beginning in the bosom of kindred associations, where the same philosophy was maintained and taught. But if we confound the ceremonies of Masonry with the philosophy of Masonry, and seek the origin of the institution, moulded into outward form as it is to-day, we can scarcely be required to look farther back than the beginning of the eighteenth century, and, indeed, not quite so far. For many important modifications have been made in its rituals since that period.

Having, then, arrived at the conclusion that it is not the Masonic ritual, but the Masonic philosophy, whose origin we are to investigate, the next question naturally relates to the peculiar nature of that philosophy.

Now, then, I contend that the philosophy of Freemasonry is engaged in the contemplation of the divine and human character; of GOD as one eternal, self-existent being, in contradiction to the mythology of the ancient peoples, which was burdened with a multitude of gods and goddesses, of demigods and heroes; of MAN as an immortal being, preparing in the present life for an eternal future, in like contradiction to the ancient philosophy, which circumscribed the existence of man to the present life.

These two doctrines, then, of the unity of God and the

immortality of the soul, constitute the philosophy of Free-masonry. When we wish to define it succinctly, we say that it is an ancient system of philosophy which teaches these two dogmas. And hence, if, amid the intellectual darkness and debasement of the old polytheistic religions, we find interspersed here and there, in all ages, certain institutions or associations which taught these truths, and that, in a particular way, allegorically and symbolically, then we have a right to say that such institutions or associations were the incunabula — the predecessors — of the Masonic institution as it now exists.

With these preliminary remarks the reader will be enabled to enter upon the consideration of that theory of the origin of Freemasonry which I advance in the following propositions : —

1. In the first place, I contend that in the very earliest ages of the world there were existent certain truths of vast importance to the welfare and happiness of humanity, which had been communicated, — no matter how, but, — most probably, by direct inspiration from God to man.

2. These truths principally consisted in the abstract propositions of the unity of God and the immortality of the soul. Of the truth of these two propositions there cannot be a reasonable doubt. The belief in these truths is a necessary consequence of that religious sentiment which has always formed an essential feature of human nature. Man is, emphatically, and in distinction from all other creatures, a religious animal. Gross commences his interesting work on " The Heathen Religion in its Popular and Symbolical Development" by the statement that " one of the most remarkable phenomena of the

human race is the universal existence of religious ideas —
a belief in something supernatural and divine, and a
worship corresponding to it." As nature had implanted
the religious sentiment, the same nature must have directed it in a proper channel. The belief and the worship must at first have been as pure as the fountain whence
they flowed, although, in subsequent times, and before the
advent of Christian light, they may both have been cor-
rupted by the influence of the priests and the poets over
an ignorant and superstitious people. The first and second propositions of my theory refer only to that primeval
period which was antecedent to these corruptions, of
which I shall hereafter speak.

3. These truths of God and immortality were most
probably handed down through the line of patriarchs
of the race of Seth, but were, at all events, known to
Noah, and were by him communicated to his immediate
descendants.

4. In consequence of this communication, the true
worship of God continued, for some time after the sub-
sidence of the deluge, to be cultivated by the Noachidæ,
the Noachites, or the descendants of Noah.

5. At a subsequent period (no matter when, but the
biblical record places it at the attempted building of the
tower of Babel), there was a secession of a large number
of the human race from the Noachites.

6. These seceders rapidly lost sight of the divine truths
which had been communicated to them from their common ancestor, and fell into the most grievous theological
errors, corrupting the purity of the worship and the
orthodoxy of the religious faith which they had prima-
rily received.

7. These truths were preserved in their integrity by but a very few in the patriarchal line, while still fewer were enabled to retain only dim and glimmering portions of the true light.

8. The first class was confined to the direct descendants of Noah, and the second was to be found among the priests and philosophers, and, perhaps, still later, among the poets of the heathen nations, and among those whom they initiated into the secrets of these truths. Of the prevalence of these religious truths among the patriarchal descendants of Noah, we have ample evidence in the sacred records. As to their existence among a body of learned heathens, we have the testimony of many intelligent writers who have devoted their energies to this subject. Thus the learned Grote, in his "History of Greece," says, "The allegorical interpretation of the myths has been, by several learned investigators, especially by Creuzer, connected with the hypothesis of *an ancient and highly instructed body of priests*, having their origin either in Egypt or in the East, and communicating to the rude and barbarous Greeks religious, physical, and historical knowledge, *under the veil of symbols.*" What is here said only of the Greeks is equally applicable to every other intellectual nation of antiquity.

9. The system or doctrine of the former class has been called by Masonic writers the " Pure or Primitive Freemasonry" of antiquity, and that of the latter class the " Spurious Freemasonry" of the same period. These terms were first used, if I mistake not, by Dr. Oliver, and are intended to refer — the word *pure* to the doctrines taught by the descendants of Noah in the Jewish

line, and the word *spurious* to his descendants in the heathen or Gentile line.

10. The masses of the people, among the Gentiles especially, were totally unacquainted with this divine truth, which was the foundation stone of both species of Freemasonry, the pure and the spurious, and were deeply immersed in the errors and falsities of heathen belief and worship.

11. These errors of the heathen religions were not the voluntary inventions of the peoples who cultivated them, but were gradual and almost unavoidable corruptions of the truths which had been at first taught by Noah ; and, indeed, so palpable are these corruptions, that they can be readily detected and traced to the original form from which, however much they might vary among different peoples, they had, at one time or another, deviated.   Thus, in the life and achievements of Bacchus or Dionysus, we find the travestied counterpart of the career of Moses, and in the name of Vulcan, the blacksmith god, we evidently see an etymological corruption of the appellation of Tubal Cain, the first artificer in metals. For *Vul-can* is but a modified form of *Baal-Cain*, the god Cain.

12. But those among the masses — and there were some — who were made acquainted with the truth, received their knowledge by means of an initiation into certain sacred Mysteries, in the bosom of which it was concealed from the public gaze.

13. These Mysteries existed in every country of heathendom, in each under a different name, and to some extent under a different form, but always and everywhere with the same design of inculcating, by allegorical and

symbolic teachings, the great Masonic doctrines of the unity of God and the immortality of the soul. This is an important proposition, and the fact which it enunciates must never be lost sight of in any inquiry into the origin of Freemasonry; for the pagan Mysteries were to the spurious Freemasonry of antiquity precisely what the Masters' lodges are to the Freemasonry of the present day. It is needless to offer any proof of their existence, since this is admitted and continually referred to by all historians, ancient and modern; and to discuss minutely their character and organization would occupy a distinct treatise. The Baron de Sainte Croix has written two large volumes on the subject, and yet left it unexhausted.

14. These two divisions of the Masonic Institution which were defined in the 9th proposition, namely, the pure or primitive Freemasonry among the Jewish descendants of the patriarchs, who are called, by way of distinction, the Noachites, or descendants of Noah, because they had not forgotten nor abandoned the teachings of their great ancestor, and the spurious Freemasonry practised among the pagan nations, flowed down the stream of time in parallel currents, often near together, but never commingling.

15. But these two currents were not always to be kept apart, for, springing, in the long anterior ages, from one common fountain, — that ancient priesthood of whom I have already spoken in the 8th proposition, — and then dividing into the pure and spurious Freemasonry of antiquity, and remaining separated for centuries upon centuries, they at length met at the building of the great temple of Jerusalem, and were united, in the instance of the Israelites under King Solomon, and the Tyrians

under Hiram, King of Tyre, and Hiram Abif. The spurious Freemasonry, it is true, did not then and there cease to exist. On the contrary, it lasted for centuries subsequent to this period; for it was not until long after, and in the reign of the Emperor Theodosius, that the pagan Mysteries were finally and totally abolished. But by the union of the Jewish or pure Freemasons and the Tyrian or spurious Freemasons at Jerusalem, there was a mutual infusion of their respective doctrines and ceremonies, which eventually terminated in the abolition of the two distinctive systems and the establishment of a new one, that may be considered as the immediate prototype of the present institution. Hence many Masonic students, going no farther back in their investigations than the facts announced in this 15th proposition, are content to find the origin of Freemasonry at the temple of Solomon. But if my theory be correct, the truth is, that it there received, not its birth, but only a new modification of its character. The legend of the third degree — the golden legend, the *legenda aurea* — of Masonry was there adopted by pure Freemasonry, which before had no such legend, from spurious Freemasonry. But the legend had existed under other names and forms, in all the Mysteries, for ages before. The doctrine of immortality, which had hitherto been taught by the Noachites simply as an abstract proposition, was thenceforth to be inculcated by a symbolic lesson — the symbol of Hiram the Builder was to become forever after the distinctive feature of Freemasonry.

16. But another important modification was effected in the Masonic system at the building of the temple. Previous to the union which then took place, the pure Free-

masonry of the Noachites had always been speculative, but resembled the present organization in no other way than in the cultivation of the same abstract principles of divine truth.

17. The Tyrians, on the contrary, were architects by profession, and, as their leaders were disciples of the school of the spurious Freemasonry, they, for the first time, at the temple of Solomon, when they united with their Jewish contemporaries, infused into the speculative science, which was practised by the latter, the elements of an operative art.

18. Therefore the system continued thenceforward, for ages, to present the commingled elements of operative and speculative Masonry. We see this in the *Collegia Fabrorum*, or Colleges of Artificers, first established at Rome by Numa, and which were certainly of a Masonic form in their organization; in the Jewish sect of the Essenes, who wrought as well as prayed, and who are claimed to have been the descendants of the temple builders, and also, and still more prominently, in the Travelling Freemasons of the middle ages, who identify themselves by their very name with their modern successors, and whose societies were composed of learned men who thought and wrote, and of workmen who labored and built. And so for a long time Freemasonry continued to be both operative and speculative.

19. But another change was to be effected in the institution to make it precisely what it now is, and, therefore, at a very recent period (comparatively speaking), the operative feature was abandoned, and Freemasonry became wholly speculative. The exact time of this change is not left to conjecture. It took place in the reign of

Queen Anne, of England, in the beginning of the eighteenth century. Preston gives us the very words of the decree which established this change, for he says that at that time it was agreed to " that the privileges of Masonry should no longer be restricted to operative Masons, but extend to men of various professions, provided they were regularly approved and initiated into the order."

The nineteen propositions here announced contain a brief but succinct view of the progress of Freemasonry from its origin in the early ages of the world, simply as a system of religious philosophy, through all the modifications to which it was submitted in the Jewish and Gentile races, until at length it was developed in its present perfected form. During all this time it preserved unchangeably certain features that may hence be considered as its specific characteristics, by which it has always been distinguished from every other contemporaneous association, however such association may have simulated it in outward form. These characteristics are, first, the doctrines which it has constantly taught, namely, that of the unity of God and that of the immortality of the soul ; and, secondly, the manner in which these doctrines have been taught, namely, by symbols and allegories.

Taking these characteristics as the exponents of what Freemasonry is, we cannot help arriving at the conclusion that the speculative Masonry of the present day exhibits abundant evidence of the identity of its origin with the spurious Freemasonry of the ante-Solomonic period, both systems coming from the same pure source, but the one always preserving, and the other continually corrupting, the purity of the common fountain. This is also the necessary conclusion as a corollary from the propositions advanced in this essay.

There is also abundant evidence in the history, of which these propositions are but a meagre outline, that a manifest influence was exerted on the pure or primitive Freemasonry of the Noachites by the Tyrian branch of the spurious system, in the symbols, myths, and legends which the former received from the latter, but which it so modified and interpreted as to make them consistent with its own religious system. One thing, at least, is incapable of refutation; and that is, that we are indebted to the Tyrian Masons for the introduction of the symbol of Hiram Abif. The idea of the symbol, although modified by the Jewish Masons, is not Jewish in its inception. It was evidently borrowed from the pagan mysteries, where Bacchus, Adonis, Proserpine, and a host of other apotheosized beings play the same rôle that Hiram does in the Masonic mysteries.

And lastly, we find in the technical terms of Masonry, in its working tools, in the names of its grades, and in a large majority of its symbols, ample testimony of the strong infusion into its religious philosophy of the elements of an operative art. And history again explains this fact by referring to the connection of the institution with the Dionysiac Fraternity of Artificers, who were engaged in building the temple of Solomon, with the Workmen's Colleges of Numa, and with the Travelling Freemasons of the middle ages, who constructed all the great buildings of that period.

These nineteen propositions, which have been submitted in the present essay, constitute a brief summary or outline of a theory of the true origin of Freemasonry, which long and patient investigation has led me to adopt. To attempt to prove the truth of each of these propositions in its order by logical demonstration, or by historical evidence, would involve the writing of an elaborate treatise. They are now offered simply as suggestions on which the Masonic student may ponder. They are but intended as guide-posts, which may direct him in his journey should he undertake the pleasant although difficult task of instituting an inquiry into the origin and progress of Freemasonry from its birth to its present state of full-grown manhood.

But even in this abridged form they are absolutely necessary as preliminary to any true understanding of the symbolism of Freemasonry.

- The Symbolism of Freemasonry,
Albert G. Mackey, M. D.

# CONTENTS

# CONTENTS

# THE ARGUMENT.

Every one that has received the degrees of Ancient Freemasonry, is aware that they represent the building of a spiritual Temple, not made with hands; eternal in the heavens.

Are these symbolic representations arbitrary? Or do they exist in the nature of things? These are questions that must arise to every reflecting Mason. If they exist in the nature of man, the degrees of Masonry must be, not only a likeness of the natural formations of the human body; but, of the universe itself; and the opening of the degrees and their ceremonies, must refer to the orderly changes of the mind, and the progress of creation.

The reflecting mind may at once see, that all created things run in series and degrees, as end, cause and effect; that the effect, when carried into uses, becomes the foundation of other causes and effects. Thus, that the universe is a system of uses, causes and effects, consisting of a series of three, six, nine and twenty-seven; with their attendant orders of three, five and seven, in likeness of the degrees of Ancient Masonry. The object of the present work, is to unfold a knowledge of these degrees in the creation of the universe; and the regeneration of man agreeably to the principles of science, as far as they have been developed.

Where these have failed, the author has relied upon the highest probabilities of science. If he has ascended into the regions of the vast and unknown, and unlocked and brought forth their hidden mysteries, it has been because the foot-prints of Masonry have led him in that direction, and its symbols have furnished a ready key to unlock their wonders; for which he claims the indulgence of the Craft.

THE AUTHOR.

# INTRODUCTION.

As the earth is cold in winter, but revives under the genial sun of spring, bringing forth her love flowers as a token of divine favor; so the heart, when chilled by self-love, is a dreary waste, and darkness is upon the face of the deep. But when the heavenly spirit of charity moves upon the waters, the heart is warmed, and the understanding is illuminated by a divine light. A thousand principles of latent truth spring forth to quicken and elevate the imagination to view, with reverence and awe, the unfoldings of those principles handed down to us through the golden age of man, concealed in correspondential semblances, locked like a precious casket, and sealed with seven seals, which the Divine Hand will only open to a loving heart and faithful breast.

To the selfish man, masonry is a dreary road, strewed with unmeaning ceremonies and the dry husks of the past. God is love, and warms the

1*

breasts of his children with mutual love, and charity is the fruit. "An honest man is the noblest work of God." Honesty springs from love, and is not the work of policy. The empire of charity is the counting house and workshop, through which she dispenses her blessings. The judge who condemns the guilty, has performed an act of love to humanity. A kind and sympa- thetic spirit, and a liberal hand, governed by a judicious head, are tokens of a loving heart; a blind sympathy may be the impulse of a depraved heart suggested by an unlawful end. Charity is the work of principle and sympathy. The heart and the head must join in the act. Our affections are best protected by an enlightened understand- ing. Without it, the work of the heart may be used to pervert order, and, what we intended as a good, may become the greatest evil. Faith and charity cannot be separated. The love of use to the human family ever seeks the truths of a living faith. Whatever is good, is also true, and *vice versa.* The mind, that loves truth for the sake of truth, loves good. These are inseparably blended, like light and heat, in the rays of the sun. Hence charity is equally as much the work of truth as it is of love. Love is the soul of truth, and truth is the body of love. Therefore he, who is in charity, is also in truth and love.

To teach the truth and inculcate the precepts of charity, for the sake of a divine life, are the sole ends and objects of masonry. Hence, all the instructions given in the Masonic Lodge, are representative of a true and universal system of religious doctrines, constituting a universal faith in God and the sacred Scriptures, charity being the end or life. Thus faith and charity are both adjoined, making the true Mason, either one, alone, being dead. Therefore, we must look to the ritual of Masonry for the true doctrines of the sacred Scriptures, and to the life of the Mason for true charity or a heavenly life. Masonry is explanatory of the life and doctrines of the church.

No. 2. Ancient Masonry is a life of charity, agreeable to a certain system of natural, moral and spiritual truth, correspondentially and representatively given in three discrete degrees, each degree consisting of three continuous degrees. Hence, they are termed three, and three times three, or nine. The instruction is natural, when it relates to our duty to ourselves; moral, when it relates to our neighbor; and spiritual when it

teaches our duty to God.  Instruction is conferred, when it is given through a correspondential
and representative ceremony, and communicated,
when orally explained.

Representation is the substitution of natural
objects and ceremonies, to represent spiritual substances and acts, in which the mind sees the parallelism.  Correspondence is the agreement and
parallelism that exist between the principles and
qualities of natural things and the truths and affections of the spiritual.  Thus light corresponds
to truth, and heat to love.  Correspondence and
representation are not mere comparisons, to be
used at the discretion of the speaker, but arise
from fixed and positive laws of parallelism and
agreement, that exist between mind and matter,
or the natural and spiritual worlds, which are
discrete or distinct substances, that can in no wise
be compounded, but are parallel by agreement of
uses.  So that the spiritual world rests in and
upon the natural, and every natural substance
and quality serves as a vessel and base for the
spiritual world or world of mind : and yet the
substances of each are distinct.  The parallelism
between natural and spiritual objects does not take
place by any agreement of form or geometrical

principle; but arises alone from uses—the parallelism being between the uses in the two worlds of mind and matter. When objects in the natural world perform certain uses to the body and natural things, we must reflect and discover what mental ideas and substances perform the same use in the world of mind, and the correspondence and representative will be complete.

There are no such things as literal truths in Masonry. Every word, action or substance represents a rational idea or spiritual truth. The working tools and implements of Masonry are symbols or representatives of spiritual operations and truths. Hence, in order to understand the spiritual world, we must first comprehend the natural. The desire of spiritual knowledge, first culminates in the natural, then ascends to the spiritual; so that the natural is the base of spiritual thought; and just in proportion as we understand the laws and uses of this world, we are prepared to comprehend those of the next. The great use of uses is the progression, growth and regeneration of the spiritual man, which are the object and end of Masonry. But our motives and ends govern our reasoning and train of thought. If other motives be uppermost in the mind, we

have but little care and thought upon the subject
of regeneration.   Man must first feel the necessity of being saved.   This, in Masonic language,
is called the desire of light.   The Holy Bible is
the great light of Masonry, but this can best be
understood by doctrinals, which are taught in the
symbols of Masonry.

No. 3. In comtemplating the three discrete degrees of Masonry, we behold the trinity of God,
the order of the heavens, and the three-fold life
of man.   In the natural man, there are formed,
in the successive order of his creation, three receptive planes of will, understanding and action.
These are the first stages of the creation, in which
the man's powers are altogether natural, relating
only to the gratification of his desires and the preservation of life. If his creation were arrested here,
his desires would grow into an unrestrained selflove, and love of the world.   Earth would become
his empire of thought and affection.   He would
regard all things as proceeding in the order of creation, from the solid to the fluid and gaseous forms;
thus the order of creation would be reversed.   He
would regard God as a principle, and himself its
highest manifestation, and hence the Pantheistic
idea of Gods many.   This state, in Masonic lan-

guage, is a state of darkness : "and the earth was without form and void, and darkness was upon the face of the deep."

The next stage of creation consists of three successive states of implantation of truth ; first, in the memory, secondly, in the understanding, and lastly in the will, which corresponds to the initiation, passing and raising of the candidate. Then follows the comfirmation of these truths, by work, in the three several higher degrees, by which he makes them his own, interwoven into a divine life of charity, by which he becomes a man-angel, and stands in the presence of his Maker. These six successive states are the Masonic days of creation. The seventh is a day of rest. These are spiritual states of regeneration or the perfecting of the intellectual principle ; then follow the six states of implantation and confirmation of the affections, which are represented in the higher degrees of Ancient Masonry.

There is a natural body, and there is a spiritual body, 1. Cor. 15, 44. The natural body is first, afterwards the spiritual, 1. Cor. 15, 46. The corporeal and sensual body is purely animal, and composed of substances belonging to this world, and to the natural sun. The spiritual body is composed of spiritual substances, and belongs entirely to the spiritual world. Between these two worlds, there is a parallelism. They adjoin by agreement of uses, and not by infusion of substances.

Masonry treats of the formation of the spiritual man, which is represented by the building of Solomon's Temple; and each mason is represented, as building to himself a spiritual house, not made with hands, but eternal in the heavens. We cannot, therefore, treat of the formation of that house, without first explaining the formation of the natural body and its correspondential and receptive degrees.

No. 4. Altogether the mineral, vegetable and animal kingdoms rise in discrete degrees, with lofty, mental grandeur, above each other, yet they occupy a world of effects, far below the commencement of the Masonic creation. One is a state of ultimation of natural substances, the other of mental creation. They are separated by a discrete degree. No sublimation of ultimate matter can ever elevate it to a thought, substance of the human mind. The mind surveys, with a pure and serene light, the world below. But the natural mind, without the opening of the spiritual, can never contemplate the spirit, and any essay to arise terminates in a negation that places spirit in the dust beneath its feet, as the offspring of matter.

All things live and subsist from an interior principle, by discrete degrees, yet more and more interior, until they terminate in an infinite will and understanding, in which the past, present and future join as in a circle, in a simultaneous and progressive order, like the instantaneous conception of a mighty problem in the mind, where all the operations are present, yet to be out-worked in progressive states. That Being is not a combination of effects, but the First Cause, existing in three discrete degrees, in his manifestations of will, understanding and action; yet in himself, he is distinctly one. He has no law in common with other substances, no more than the cause can operate in common as the law of the effect. He is therefore distinctly a a person, having no law or principle in himself common to any other person. From his divine good flows forth his creative fiat, through his divine Wisdom or Word, in endless successive order, like a mighty sun of causes, through discreted suns, into worlds of ultimate effects, clothed with the three kingdoms of nature for the reception of man.

2

No substance of these three kingdoms can become a part of any living organism without decomposition, and a regrowth, under the direct influence and laws of the organism in which they are incorporated; the new growth being in a certain likeness of the animal, vegetable and mineral kingdoms. Thus all things proceed in series of life and death, running through three discrete and six continuous degrees, in likeness of the degrees of Masonry which we shall now proceed to unfold as contained in the natural organism of man.

Physiology is a world in itself. We therefore can give but a rapid sketch of the degrees in the physical system, and advance to the more important unfolding of the parallelism that exists between the symbols of Masonry and the mental states and conditions of the mind, or, in other words, the parallelism that exists between mind and matter. Natural objects and actions are the resting points of thought, and no man can reflect upon spiritual things without natural objects as his starting point; and then he cannot proceed without a knowledge of the laws of correspondence and representation, which are the spiritual language of nature, contained in the symbols of Masonry. The mind cannot be elevated into the sphere of life and comprehend its laws, without the aid of the science of correspondence and representation. All the natural sciences treat of the arrangement and qualities of natural objects, that come under the notice of the senses and may be demonstrated by observation.

By the laws of chemistry, we may follow the affinities of the elements through their various changes; but whenever they become subject to an organism or germ of life, they pass beyond our reach and become the subjects of death again, before we can apply the analytical powers of chemistry. It is true that we may analyse the various substances of an organism, and ascertain what elements have entered into its composition ; but it is beyond the skill of the chemist to produce a like organized substance. We may infer many things relative to' the process of the growth of plants and animals, which are of great use, but the law of life can only be comprehended and understood through the science of correspondence and representation.

We shall therefore proceed to the consideration of the degrees contained in the body, and afterwards to the degrees of the spirit, and finally to the changes that take place in the progressive states of regeneration, taught through the correspondential and representative ceremonies of Masonry.

# OF THE DEGREES IN MAN.

No. 5. All things move by a mysterious cause. We behold the elemental world tending to the animal, vegetable and mineral kingdoms of nature, with an unerring certainty, through chemical combinations. Hence we are irresistibly led to infer that all of the elements, in their solid, liquid and gaseous forms, have been previously prepared and arranged under three distinct spheres of chemical affinities, with a view to their ultimate combination in the body of man, and for his express and immediate wants. We are also led to the conclusion, with equal force, that every combination of the elements, as well as the elements themselves, are referrable to one or the other of these kingdoms; and, that every particle of nature has its seed-germ planted within it; and, so far as science has unfolded the causes, we are directed to light, heat and electricity, in their discrete degrees, as the great workers in the laboratory of nature. There is no combination, action or decomposition in nature without their excitation. They constitute a trinity of three, and three times three.

There are three rays of light, the red, yellow and blue, containing three discrete rays of heat, of different refractive and chemical power, susceptible of demonstration from the thermometer and prism. In the great field of nature, they excite positive, negative and animal electricity in their respective kingdoms. In the mineral, it is electric; in the vegetable, it is aromal; and in the animal, it is magnetic. In their continuity and unity, they form the substance of the animal spirit in its three kingdoms of primates, with its throne in the base of the brain, with all the animal affections, powers and appetites; whence the animal spirit descends through the nerves, and presses on every molecule of the body, and pervades the great laboratory of the blood in the three kingdoms of its red globules, fibrine and albumine, which agree with the electric fluids of the three kingdoms of nature. The electric and magnetic fluids, which reside in the red globules and fibrine, are positive and negative to each other; but unite their common power in the albumine. The blood globules, like little earths, are lighted and vivified

as from a great central sun. Being freshly coated
with a deep alluvial soil from the decomposed kingdoms of food, through the chyle, in passing the
lungs, they are oxidized and warmed from the atmosphere ; whence they are again returned to the
heart, where they are magnetised by the heart
through the white blood.

The red globules are thrust forth into the
arteries in the spring of their orbits, in little
groups of globules, in their three, five and seven
fold order. In this state, the vitalizing and fecundating influence first commences upon a single
particle, which brings forth its metallic and
mollusca tribes. Upon the adjoining globule next
spring forth from its coating, in order, all the varie-
ties of the vegetable formation, shooting forth as
little trees, plants and shrubs. In successive order
of formation, there follows, upon the adjoining
globule, every beautiful form of the infusoria tribes,
in the type of the animal creation. These operations are reversed in the aged ; the order of the
animal creation coming forth first. These little
form substances, which have grown in likeness of
the three kingdoms, have their instantaneous day
of life and die ; decomposition follows, and they
are expelled from the red globules, and taken up

by the white blood that immediately surrounds the globules, which has been electrified by the white and red globules and formed into lymph, which acts as a vehicle receptive of the form particles that have been cast off from the globules. The fibrine of the blood slightly contracts, drawing the red globules to the centre, throwing the lymph and white globules to the surface, along the walls of the arteries. The red globules now repel each other, and, as the arteries branch in a thousand directions to their final destination, the red globules pass single into the capillaries, being held together by the fibrine, the lymph, containing the nutrition derived from the growth and death of the three kingdoms, that takes place upon the globules heretofore described, passes through the walls of the capillaries by exceedingly minute vessels, passing directly into the glands and cellular tissue. The red globules, and white blood after it is deprived of its nutriment, passing onward in the capillaries through the glandes, enter into the veinous capillaries, where they give off their surplus light and heat. The fibrine and red globules, contracting, reject portions of the serum and watery substances of the blood, which, in a normal state, passes in a gaseous, insensible perpiration.

If the temperature of the system be suddenly raised, the blood contracts more violently, and ejects its watery substances as sensible perspiration. Each secretory organ has its own peculiar electric motion which contracts the blood, causing it to eject such portions as may be required by the organ, until the oxygen and vitalizing gases, together with the nutritous substances, are exhausted from the blood. The blood at this point becomes absorbent, and takes on a sheet of electric light from the nerves and surrounding electricity, and returns with its surplus of carbon, through the veins, towards the heart, while the lymph, derived from the white blood which passed off through the walls of the arterial capillaries, conveying its nutriment, from the growth in the blood of the three kingdoms of nature has conveyed its richly laded substances to every tissue and pervaded every cell with its vitalizing influence, taking on such substances from the glands as may be required for the blood, and is collected into the small lymphatic vessels, and returns by the throracic duct towards the heart. Having been supplied and refreshed by the decomposed substances derived from the food, through the decomposing fires of nature, it ascends and again is united with the veinous blood just before

it reaches the heart. .The arterial blood, ascending to the head, gives off its lymph in the manner
heretofore described, the brain being supplied with
vitalized blood by four large arteries ; namely, the
two carotids, and the two vertebrals. These ascend, dividing into innumerable small branches,
ramifying the *dura mater*, from which the arterial
capillaries descend dipping in to the great cortical
substances of the brain, giving off its lymph, which
is taken up by a class of cells arranged in the tissues in a glandular form. There being three cells
of a primitive character, the walls of which are
composed of smaller cells, the walls of these again
are composed of a third class of a still finer tex-
ture. The membranes or coatings of the cells are
continued and formed into cerebral tubules in a
three, six and nine fold order.

Thus the lymph is sifted and strained, as it passes
inwardly to the substances of the brain, giving off
its vital forces of light, heat and electricity in their
continuous degrees, the states of which are represented by the nine colors of the positive and negative spectrums, which will be hereafter treated of
when we come to speak of the nine portions of
the brain. The finer portions of the lymph are
consumed in the operations of the brain and

nervous system ; the serous portion of the lymph being collected by the ventricles, and used for the softening of the tissues of the brain. The lymph of the scalp, neck, face, and upper portion of the chest, is collected and returned to the veinous circulation by the right throracic duct. Thus it is that the blood is the seat of life, and any part or organ of the body, deprived of arterial blood, becomes immediately paralized and dead. The three kingdoms of nature hold a distinct or discrete relation to each other; yet they compound, by their continuous degrees, in a three, six and nine fold principle. From these again arise a series of orders which follow as three, five and seven, which will be explained when we come to treat of these numbers in Masonry.

The mechanical manifestations of the blood, in external uses, take place by corresponding organs and parts of the body, which are directly adapted to the wants and uses of life in the external world. The first elementary organs or tissues, which composed the whole and entire bodily form, are three, namely: the nervous, vascular and cellular tissues; from these again are derived the white and yellow fibres, which compound, with considerable variety, in an areolar tissue, which is receptive of the cells, glands and follicles. These nine degrees of the bodily formation compound in the soft and hard tissues, which consist of muscles, membranes and tendons, cartilages, bones and ligaments, sacs, tubules and glands. These are manifested and grouped in the human body in a series of three, six and nine parts; namely, the head, chest and abdomen, the fore-arm, arm and hand; the femur, leg and foot. These consist of groups which are in themselves articulated agreeably to their order, which will be treated of when we speak of the subject of orders. The nine groupings of the form are duplicated in the right and left sides.

The interior organs, also, consist of nine groupings, namely: the brain, heart and lungs, the liver, stomach and bowels, the spleen, kidneys and organs of generation. Thus the groupings of the human form are twenty-seven, being a multiplication of three and three times three, which being again multiplied by three, give twenty-seven, which is the full number of cryptic Masonry.

The great uses of the human system are nine, expressed by nine groups in the body; namely, the heart, lungs and stomach with their appendages; the mucles, bones and excretory system; the integumentary, or skin, and generative organs.

These are all harmoniously arranged, and inductively acted upon by the nervous system, the centre of which is the brain, it being the great centre or seat of life and sensation, through which the blood charges the system with its vital forces or animal spirits, ultimately accumulated and reworked in the nine lobules of the testes, and elaborated into a minute form or principle of the human brain.

The soul-germ takes upon itself a fœtal body in the womb from the blood of the mother. When all the organs are formed, the blood, which exists in the arteries and veins at the time of birth, receives an independent motion by the inflowing of forces from the external world through the medium of respiration and the skin. The heart is stimulated to action, and an independent circulation of the blood is produced, with its laboratory of chemical forces for the future growth of the body and mind. The forces of the human system are derived from the same source as those of the animal, vegetable and mineral kingdoms, which are light, heat and electricity.

There are three degrees or rather separate atmospheres, each having an elemental formation or composite. The atmospheric air is composed of gases mingled together, within which exists an etherial atmosphere, consisting of caloric and ether, the active force of which is electricity in its continuous degrees. Within these, again, reside the most subtle forces of the sun. The decomposition, or separation of caloric into its continuous degrees, produces the manifestation of the different heat rays. The decomposition of ether, is induced by the active forces of caloric, which produce the sensation of light, the electric force being the combined result of each.

The decomposition of electricity into its discrete degrees, gives rise to the electric, magnetic and aromal forces as they exist in the kingdoms of nature, which will be hereafter illustrated. The positive and negative electricities are the result of decomposition or division into their respective degrees, the recombination of which give rise to the phenomena of attraction and repulsion. A decomposition of the electric forces also takes place by passing a current at right angles to a different conductive body, producing an inductive current, which is always at right angles to the motive force. The atmosphere acts as a lens, decomposing the light and heat of the sun, producing the inductive, elec-

tric and magnetic currents of the earth, which are
similar to the nervous forces in man.

There are three degrees or rather separate atmospheres, each having a composite elemental formation. The atmospheric air is composed of gases
mingled together. Within this, exists an etherial
atmosphere, consisting of caloric and ether, the
active force of which is electricity in its continuous
degrees. Within these, again, reside the most subtle forces of the sun. The decomposition, or separation of caloric into its continuous degrees, produces the manifestation of the different heat rays.
The decomposition of ether is induced by the active forces of caloric, which produce the sensation
of light, the electric force being the combined result of both.

No. 6. There are nine groupings of the brain
which are receptive of the forces of the blood;
three of which are primitive and discrete in their
character, the others are compound and inductive ;
neither of these groups can induce action by itself.
It requires at least three of the groups, on both
sides of the brain, to induce co-ordinate action in
the body. Every act of life, to be truly rational,
must partake of the entire forces of the brain.

Hence, there is a great circuit of the mental forces through the commissures of the brain and oblongata, descending to the body. Animal life, perception and order are located in these basular lobes on either side of the base of the encephalon; namely, the cerebellum, anterior and middle lobes. The cerebellum is the seat of the animal will, and receives, by influx, all the laws of natural order, relating to procreation and civil life. The anterior lobes are 'perceptive in their character, and receive by influx all the forces and powers of special sense. The middle lobes of the brain are the true seat of action, and are both compound and inductive in their character, receiving the vital forces of the cerebellum and anterior lobes, which they first present for approval and support to all the other groups, collecting the combined action and forces of the three basular lobes, on either side of the brain, passing them upward by the middle cornues along the hippocampus major. The electric forces of the upper posterior lobes are brought forward along their cornues by the commissures of the hippocampus minor, extending forward and downwards to the floor of the lateral ventricles, passing forward through their commissures; they receive the forces of the ra-

tional faculties by the commissures of the anterior
cornues; and are collected by the corpus callosum.
Passing upward and backward, they descend to
the body by the six commissures of the oblongata and spinal cord.

The inceptive forces of the cerebellum are pulsatory, which continue in their life currents as
described, by the hippocampus major, fornix and
corpus callosum; where they receive, by the cross
commissures, another pulsatory motion which
flows in through the superior hemispheres of the
brain, uniting the forces of the middle respiratory, central lobes on either side of the lateral
ventricles, which flow into the pulsation of
the cerebellum during their passage through the
commissures of the corpus callosum.

It is important to the life-actions of the body
and mind, that these two pulsatory motions
should exactly agree as to time, so as to unite
their combined efforts in all the operations of
life. The respiratory motions of the brain take
place, in a normal condition, about every fourth
pulsation. The brain swells and the corpus callosum rises, with a gentle motion, at each respiration. As these currents and forces are constant
in their operation, they are provided with three

sets of fibres, one of which proceeds from the middle basular lobes, one from the cerebellum, and one from the superior hemispheres. Thus, the day, with the regenerate man, who stands in divine order, is divided into three equal parts; giving eight hours for the avocations of life, eight for the relief of a worthy distressed brother, and eight for refreshment and sleep; the cerebellum standing watch by night, and holding the reins of life, the perceptive faculties watching by day during the common avocations, and the superior hemispheres of the brain holding the control during the hours of devotion. These necessities will be more apparent when we come to speak of sleep.

In the unregenerate man, the influxes of the upper brain are weak and feeble, so that they are unperceived in the mind and body; but, as regeneration takes place, these influxes increase, until they are seen and felt by the higher faculties of the mind, when they assume a full and complete control of the entire being.

There are fibres entering the nervous system from each degree of the brain; but, in general, there are three great systems of nerves, arising from the lobes in the base of the brain; namely,

3*

the nerves of special sense, and the motor and involuntary nerves. The involuntary nerves have their centres in the cerebellum. The motor nerves take their rise in the middle lobes, and the nerves of special sense derivé their power from the influxes of the anterior lobes of the brain. Fibres, from each of these systems, enter the ganglionic, which, in the main, is involuntary, its great office being to decompose, allot and partition the nervous forces agreeably to the wants of the human system, manifested in the different organs. The nerve fibre of the brain does not extend into the organs, but acts upon their forces by decomposition and induction, producing chemical action by their recombination.

No. 7. The cerebellum acts as a ganglion upon the forces of the spinal cord during the wakeful state of the mind. The nerves of special sense, collected in the medulla oblongata, are positive to the cerebellum and the ganglionic system; so that a third part of their fibres, or tubules are entirely at rest; yet they receive a passing current that restores the wear and tear of the night; also the frontal perceptive powers of the brain are entirely at rest, the same being the case with the motor fibres of the central lobes.

When these portions of the brain become weary and require resuscitation, the cerebellum becomes active, and produces a positive power on the nerve fibres of the spinal cord and ganglionic system. Embracing the head of the medulla oblongata close in the folds of the pons-verolii, it sends around it a spiral band of electric currents, and sends down the spinal cord a flow of inductive electricity. The ganglionic system becomes generally active and positive to the nerves, giving off by the spinal column. The electric forces of the brain extending down the spinal cord, proceed no further than the root of the branching nerve to be affected, passing round the root. It decomposes the electricity of its centre, thereby producing an inductive current in the nerve branch, and returns again to the brain. The inductive current, in the branching nerve, becomes positive, again decomposing the electric current of the ganglion, sending off an inductive current to the muscles and bodily organs, as the case may require, and *vice versa* with the returning current.

The nerve forces of light, heat and electricity, which are set at liberty by the blood in the heart, body and limbs, are separated by a discrete

degree, acting upon each other by induction, produced by chemical change of the molecules of
the forces in their decomposition and recombination, acting upon each other by loop nerves and
ganglia. The blood of the throrax and abdomi-
nal regions makes a great circuit through the
lungs to the heart, another through the spleen
and bowels, returning by the liver; and a third
by the kidneys, throwing off its lymph to the viscera and organs, and setting at liberty its vital
forces of light, heat and electricity, by chemical
changes that take place in the blood.

The nerve forces, thus liberated, supply the
ganglionic system, being decomposed and separated into discrete and continuous degrees by the
ganglions, which produce such inductive currents
as are required for the chemical operations in the
motion of the organs. The current of the blood,
through the limbs, sets at liberty the electric degree of the nervous forces which are confined to
the extremities and the muscular tissues of the
limbs, being partitioned by ganglia peculiar to
its own system.

The nerve forces of the head or brain are decomposed into discrete and continuous degrees
for the nine groupings of the brain. Thus, there

is a complete system of action and reaction of the nervous forces, one degree inducing action in another. The whole nervous system decomposing and setting at liberty, in the chemical changes, the forces of light, heat and electricity, which flow in their appropriate currents, induced by the cardiac and pulmonary actions of the brain, being induced by general influxes of efforts which flow in, through the spiritual world, from the Divine mind.

The cardiac action of the cerebellum contains all the principles of divine order, relating to generation and civil life. The pulmonary motion of the superior brain contains the principles of divine Providence, relating to the perservation of man, in which the soul resides. The cardiac motions of the superior and inferior brains, together with the motions of the heart, are derived from the three continuous degrees of divine love. The pulmonary motions of the superior and inferior brain, together with the motions of the lungs, are derived, through the spiritual world, from the three degrees of divine truth. The cardiac motion of the cerebellum flows forth into the right and left inferior middle lobes of the brain, where it is vitalized through the pulmonary motion of the influxes, de-

rived from divine truth, and where it receives the
outward influxes of the world through the medium
of the senses; being carried upward just above
the ear, forward and downward to the floors of the
lateral ventricles. It rises upward and backward,
being again vitalized by the cardiac and pulmonary
motions of the superior hemispheres. It passes
downward by the medulla oblongata being decomposed. The forces of the light, heat and electricity are distributed by induction to the organs and
tissues of the body. Passing outward to the skin,
and inward to the bones, it returns along the gela-
tinous nerves of the skin, pericardium and muscles by inductive currents of the vital organs and
brain, having sensed the surrounding world and
internal tissues.

The pulmonary motions of the lungs are in complete harmony with the actions of the body and
mind, adjusting themselves to them in speaking,
thinking and muscular movements; receiving
their currents directly from the pulmonary motion
of the brain by both voluntary and involuntary
nerves, by which the muscular currents are
induced, reversed, altered and changed to suit
the slightest mental perception of the mind; the
pulmonary action stimulating, vivifying and pro-

ducing chemical changes in the cardiacal currents of the cerebellum ; so that, there is a complete flux and reflux, action and reaction between the two producing a complete intercourse between the will and the understanding. With the regenerate man, the cardiac and pulmonary actions are opened in the superior hemispheres of the brain, and, with it, a perception and understanding of the laws of divine Providence, from which arise celestial faith and science by perception.

The foregoing hypothetical statements account for the widest range of physical and psychological facts known to man. Their principles and science will be fully illustrated in the following pages, when we come to treat of the degrees and order in masonry, and the correspondence and symbols. Mathematics is only an expression of the degrees and order that exist in the mental and physical world. Without these degrees and orders, the universe would be a complete chaos ; but through the degrees of the divine mind, there is action and reaction, harmony and beauty in all things. The key to unlock the mysteries of the universe, is found in the numbers, three, five and seven, three six and nine, and two, four, eight and twelve. These numbers correspond to the laws contained in the ·numeral digits ; ten and twelve being the fulness of affections and truths. The principles contained in these numbers are the foundations of all science and knowledge, and have ever been held in high estimation among Masons. All the operations of the physical and mental man, who stands in divine order, being in likeness of the Lodge, Chapter and Council, as will be shown when we treat of the opening of these bodies.

## OF THE TEMPERAMENTS.

No. 8. The ultimate kingdoms of nature, in their discrete and continuous degrees, compose the blood which gives off its forces of light, heat and electricity, which are interwoven into the substances of the animal spirit. Therefore, as the blood is, so is the temperamental quality of the tissues; a similar series of degrees running through the temperaments, giving harmony of action, and manifestation of mind. If the law of the temperaments be perfectly understood, the form and quality of all the parts may be known, from the development of any organ or tissue. The nine groups of the brain are developed in an exact ratio to their corresponding parts of the body.

Hence, there are three qualities or temperaments, with their continuous degrees, which agree with the animal, vegetable and mineral kingdoms, run-

4

ning throughout the brain and tissues. These exist separately and yet simultaneously in the brain. The grosser and more corporeal degrees of the temperaments are located in the base of the brain; the more intellectual degrees of the temperaments are located in a horizontal belt or stratum, occupying the middle portion of the head. The more refined and subtle degrees of the temperaments are located in the superior lobes of the hemispheres. These are divided perpendicularly by the anterior, middle and posterior lobes. Thus the hemispheres, upon either side of the head, are divided into nine groups or three great columns of brain. The inferior lobes, namely, the cerebellum, anterior and middle lobes, on both sides are the seat of animal life, which is possessed of three powers; namely, desire or will, perception and action.

The intellectual or spiritual life of the man resides in the central belt of the head, occupying three groups of organs upon both sides; namely, the rational faculties, the semi-intellectual and social, which have corresponding powers of intellectual thought, affection and action; namely, the affections of social life, rationality and judgment. The celestial principles of the mind reside in the superior hemispheres of the brain; the peculiar qualities of which are dignity, sympathy and devotion. To these nine principles of the human mind, in general, are referrable all the motives, ends, thoughts and affections of the soul, spirit and body. All the activities of the mind reside in the central columns of the brain; the affection in the posterior, and the intellectual in the frontal.

We shall now proceed to describe the temperaments and their marks and indications in the head and body. From the foregoing article, it will be perceived that the temperaments cannot be referred to the tissues, but to the blood, from which they have their origin, and any attempt to derive them from the tissues would mislead the mind. Yet the temperaments are marked in all the bodily formations. It is not our purpose to treat on phrenology. We shall, therefore, follow the subject of the temperaments no further than they relate to the degrees. If the mineral substances of the blood prevail, the osseous and muscular systems are strongly developed. If the vegetable kingdom predominates, the nutritive system, consisting of the elementary canal and lymphatics, are strongly marked. When the animal kingdom in the blood prevails, there is a chemical activity of all the parts derived from the lungs and arterial blood. The movements are quick and sprightly, and the pulsations of the heart are rapid. Thus the combined qualities culminate in three temperaments; namely, the bilious, lymphatic and sanguine, with their continuous degrees. The bodily tissues of these discrete temperaments react, and produce the cellular, vascular and nervous systems, which interblend in continuity in all the ultimate tissues of the body, as described in article 5.

The cerebellum gives rise to the heart and arterial system, controlled and governed by the sympathetic or ganglionic system of nerves. The lymphatic or nutritive system, which culminates in the cellular tissue and lymphatic glands, is also receptive of the vascular and nervous systems. The sanguine temperament which ultimates in the chemical activities of the blood, derived through the nervous system, has its seat in the lower, frontal and middle lobes, and is distinct from the cerebellum, only acting upon it by induction. These both unite in the middle lobe, which governs the active forces of the lungs, muscles and cellular tissue. The seat of animal life is manifested in the base of the brain, namely, the cerebellum, and anterior and middle lobes from which the bodily formation takes its development. As the base of the brain approximates a circle, the middle lobes predominate. The chest is large and full, the shoulders square, the limbs tapering to their extremities ; the complexion florid, and the hair red, giving the general characteristics of the sanguine temperament; as the base of the brain becomes acutely elliptical, the cerebellum and anterior lobes prevail over the middle. The head being thin and long, if the front and posterior portions of the skull terminate sharply over the eyes, projecting in the occipital region, the temperament is bilious; the figure tall in proportion, muscular and long. The eyes are brown, the hair black and the complexion dark. If the base of the brain is oval, regular and smooth, the perceptive faculties and cerebellum neither sharp nor prominent, the temperament is lymphatic, the skin of a milky white, the eyes of an indistinct blue, the shoulders small and drooping, and the abdomen and lower limbs large and full.

The full development of the continuous degrees of the temperaments, which have their locality in the middle and superior hemispheres of the brain, exercise a controlling and modifying influence upon the temperaments, and indicate the size and height of the man, together with his intellectual and moral powers; as a well developed and harmonious brain can only exist in connection with a similar body.

We shall now take up the temperaments and treat them in their separate and combined form with their marks and mental characters.

No. 9. There are several distinctive marks of the bilious temperament found in the head. Sharp and projecting perceptive faculties, thin head in the region of the temples, and protuberance of the occipital bone, are the basular marks. The spiritual region or middle belt of the head recedes; the forehead slopes backward, and the sides, in the region of the semi-intellectual faculties, incline inward; sympathy is low, and self-esteem high. The base of the head is large and rises high in a sugar loaf form in the region of dignity. When all of these marks are found in the head, the subject is of a full bilious temperament. The man is about six feet high, with long and bony limbs, with well developed muscles; the movements are slow and sauntering; the heart has about sixty beats to the minute. The complexion is dark, the eyes are brown and hair black, the nose Roman, and lips firm. The character of the mind is cool and determined, weighing every question well before acting;

the scholastic and religious instructions of youth are adhered to with great tenacity. Persons of this temperament are firm friends and untiring enemies, and either sceptics or fanatics in religion, and opposed to any change or progress. In proportion, as any of these marks ·are found interblended with the other temperaments, the character and form partake of the bilious. The spiritual or intellectual degree of this temperament is called the nervo-bilious, and is known by the fulness of the central belt of the head, in part or in the whole. The eyes are black, the hair fine. The intellect is quick and active, with refinement of person and tissues of the body.

No. 10. The lymphatic temperament arises from the lymph of the blood, which is a vehicle of nutrition. The stomach, bowels, lymphatics and cellular tissue prevail in the body ; all of which are referrable to the vegetable kingdom of the blood. The distinctive features of the temperament, in the base of the brain, are its oval and smooth form. The posterior frontal, and sides of the head rise perpendicularly in the central or spiritual belt of the head. The superior frontal lobe of sympathy, and the posterior lobe of dignity, and the organs of conscientiousness are well and broadly developed.

The devotional faculties, in the region of the organ of reverence, are deficient, leaving a hollow in that portion of the head. All the corners and angles are well rounded. If the corporeal or base of the brain predominates, the man is about five feet eight inches high, with small well formed drooping shoulders and rounded limbs. The abdomen and hips are large, and limbs full; the flesh soft and placid to the touch. The countenance is smooth, the lips thick, the nose on its bridge curved inwardly, and pugged at the end. If the spiritual or central belt of the head is well developed, the man is about five feet ten or eleven inches high, and of symmetrical form; and when the head is large and high, combining the sanguine temperament, the body is frequently of gigantic form. The corporeal man, of this temperament, has a free, easy and unsolicitous character, coarse and practical in his intellect. When the spiritual degree of the temperament is well developed, it forms the basis of the great scientific mind, by giving patience, endurance of investigation; and when combined with the sanguine, it gives the grace, ease, dignity and quiet, requisite for the orator. The habit of this temperament is sedentary, its combination

with all the other temperaments is highly important for health and mental equilibrium. The religious character is liberal and progressive. The
personal marks of the temperament are a large
abdomen, rounded form, light complexion, brown
hair the ends tinged with red, blue eyes, curved
nose, thick lips and placid countenance. The
character is friendly and sympathetic. Murder is
unknown to this temperament. Its perversion is
the love of the world, and its perfection  charity.

No. 11. The discrete temperaments rise above
each other like a majestic column with its base,
shaft and capital. The bilious supports, the
lymphatic sustains, and the sanguine crowns, vi-
vifies and enlivens the whole. The sanguine,
without the lower temperaments, is like the animal kingdom without the earth or vegetation. It
rests upon the bilious for stability, and feeds upon the lymphatic, which gives it animal spirit and
support. It wanders to and fro, like the animal,
upon the surface of the earth. It loves to bask
in the sunshine of intellect by the crystal stream,
and behold its own image in the still waters, or
ascend the mountain peak, and gaze upon the
lovely scene below. It delights to hold its lodge
in the highest mountains and lowest valleys. It

loves to stand upon the beach, and view the mighty ocean as it rushes upon the shore. It contemplates with reverence and awe the raging storm and heaving billow; it reclines in the moon-light dell, and surveys the heavens with wonder and delight. It is the rhapsody of poetry, and the zeal of argument. It is the heart of friendship, the warmth of love, and the life of society. The sanguine temperament, like the oxygen of the atmosphere, induces the chemical changes of the blood, which warms and vitalizes the system. This temperament is known by full and rounded perceptives, a sloping and broad forehead, by full moral organs, by sometimes a flattening in the region of concentrativeness, a perpendicular posterior of the head, large and full sustaining faculties, a circular and uneven base of the brain, and sometimes an unevenness of the head. These marks are seldomly all found in the same character.

This temperament is decomposed into its corporeal, intellectual and moral degrees, which may all, or in part, be beautifully and harmoniously blended with the degrees of the other temperaments, in their nine respective portions of the head. When the corporeal degree of the temperament is well developed in the base, the man is about five feet eight inches high, with square shoulders, large chest, muscular and tapering limbs, and small hands and feet. The hips are small, and the entire body tapers from the shoulders downward. The cheek-bones are high, the nose broad upon the bridge and straight, the chin double, the hair red, the eyes blue, and the skin florid. The man is active and restless, always preferring an out-door life. If the intellectual and moral degrees are well developed, the mind is restless, scientific, searching, sympathetic and affectionate. It is a law of the temperaments that the corporeal and moral degrees react against each other, concentrating their common and combined force in the intellectual. Hence, no man can be truly great without a well developed base and coronal region. Each temperament is liable to different diseases, and should never be treated alike by the physician.

No. 12. Each temperament has its corporeal, spiritual and celestial degrees, which we shall term the corporeal, intellectual and moral. The corporeal degrees reside in the base of the brain, the intellectual in the central belt, and the moral in the sympathetic, dignifying and devotional

faculties.   The discrete temperaments are three,
namely, the bilious, the lymphatic and the sanguine. These arise from the quality of the blood,
and reside in every part of the brain.   They are
distinct, yet blending with every part; they
have each three continuous degrees; the corporeal degree residing in the base of the brain,
the intellectual in the middle, and the moral in
the superior brain.   The bilious resides more in
the base of the brain than it does in any other
part of the head.   The lymphatic resides more
in the middle portion, and the sanguine more in
the superior.   Yet they are decomposed, and,
like the nine numeral digits, recombine, forming,
like the nine colors of the positive and negative
spectrums, an infinite variety of light and shade
in the human character.   It is the office of this
work to treat only of the normal conditions of
the temperaments, and to leave their endless dis-
tortions, arising from diseased and weakened parents, from their habits of mind and confirmed
evils, which they transmit from their blood to
their children, precociously developed by forcing
an early education, or neglect of their moral,
spiritual and bodily training, developing an unna-
tural, sensual and corporeal state of the body,

and mind, or precocious conditions of the nerves, with top shaped heads, or bell-crowns and small base, subject to ill health in life, and premature death. Physiologists have dignified this condition with the name of the nervous temperament; the distorted corporeal states, as the lymphatic, and the depraved conditions of the passions, and the violation and profanation of every holy condition, as the sanguine; but we must leave these states for correction to the physician and theologian, and proceed to develope the normal conditions of the temperaments in their harmonious and beautiful blendings of the human character.

Each individual has a different arrangement of the temperaments in the head. The sanguine may be found developed in prominent, oval and full perceptives, with a broad and receding forehead governing the entire countenance, or it may be found indicated in the large sustaining faculties, a perpendicular posterior brain, or a flattening of self-esteem and concentration, or indicated by a general unevenness of the head. The bilious and lymphatic temperaments may be indicated in either of the nine groups by their marks as before described.

# THE ORDERS IN MAN.

No. 13. The corporeal temperaments should not be confounded with the discrete degrees of the mind, which reside in the perceptive, domestic and devotional faculties; two of these, namely, the perceptive and the domestic, are located in the base of the brain, and constitute the natural degree or order which is common to man with the brute creation. The devotional faculties are located in the coronal region of the head, and flow into the sympathetic and dignifying faculties, constituting the celestial order of the mind. The celestial and natural orders react against each other, and combine in the central belt of the head, in the rational, semi-intellectual and social faculties, constituting the spiritual or intellectual order.

Thus, there are three orders of men which are separate in their character, and which may be compared to the Doric, Ionic and Corinthian orders in architecture. The natural or Doric order takes its character from the base of the brain. The spiritual or Ionic order from the central belt, and the celestial from the coronal regions. These orders arise from the perfection and perfect blending of the discrete degrees in their continuous degrees of altitude and longitude, see No. 80. A compound degree intervenes between the natural and spiritual degrees, indicated by the fulness of the belt of the head just above the perceptive faculties, and the top of the ear, which gives a different style of body and character, which may be compared to the Tuscan order. The spiritual and celestial orders compound in an intermediate order which may be compared to the Composite, and are indicated by the fulness of the upper portion of the head, on the line separating the semi-intellectual and devotional faculties. These orders constitute five classes of men, in each of which, if examined, the temperaments will be found equally blended, and yet each individual class will be decidedly different in the form of the body and character of the mind.

The natural or Doric order represents the perfection of strength and stability of character. The head, features, body and limbs all partake of the square and oblong forms, and the mind is geometrical and practical.

The Ionic or spiritual order of men, are oval and round in the form of the face, head, body and limbs. Their manners are graceful, polite and polished. The character is mild, gentle and firm, with great activity and breadth of thought.

The celestial or Corinthian order are characterized by the more oval forms of the head, features, body and limbs. The figure is tall, erect and gracefully formed. The mind is luxuriant in thought and perceptive in character.

The natural spiritual man or Tuscan order, are lower in stature, blending the round and square forms of body, limbs, and head. The memory is quick and tenacious, and the mind strictly literal and practical, the habits inclining to the sensual.

The spiritual celestial or Composite order is denoted by the length of fibre, the slender and delicate form of countenance, body and limbs, with less stability of constitution and purpose, than the Corinthian. The mind is rich and profuse in thought, with great diversity of talent and exactness of expression. This class of men are the natural teachers, both in science and religion; but lack originality and fortitude in striking out a new course.

These five orders are not arbitrary divisions of

the head, but correspond to like divisions of the body and limbs, which are the foot, the leg, the femur, the abdomen and thorax, which have their common origin in the head. These orders are also manifest in the articulations of the hands and feet, into the toes and fingers, and hence these parts of the body correspond to like parts of the mind. The upper limbs also have their five fold order, the hand, the fore-arm, the arm, the shoulder, and the thorax.

There is also a sevenfold order arising from the spiritual-natural and spiritual-celestial degrees, which are only a slight variation of the natural spiritual and the natural celestial degrees, constituting seven in the series, and which are manifested in the natural division of the limbs, and also in the height of the entire person, each limb in itself having a sevenfold division in its length, namely, that of the fingers, palm of the hand, wrist, arm and forearm; and that of the toes, foot, ankle, leg and femur. There is also a sevenfold division in the general height of the person, namely, the foot, leg, femur, abdomen, thorax, neck and head; the whole man being divisible into a ninefold order, consisting of threes, namely; the head, chest, abdomen and the three general parts of each limb,

5*

which arise from the degrees in man, which are so
many principles, manifesting themselves in the outward appearance and inward qualities of the three,
five and seven orders of man, together with innumerable styles of human form and character, which
all refer to the three, five and seven orders.  The
two orders constituting the seven are but slight
changes of the Tuscan and Composite.  The temperaments which signify qualities correspondent to
the animal, vegetable and mineral kingdoms of nature, arise from the natural, celestial and spiritual
degrees in man.  In the bodily textures they are
manifested as the temperaments ; but, in the mind,
which arises altogether from spritual qualities, they
are called the natural, celestial and spiritual degrees, there being a parallelism between them and
the kingdoms of nature.  Where one is found, the
other exists, there being no manifestation of spiritual qualities except through corresponding developments in matter ; therefore there is no mental
power that is not manifested either in the size or
quality of the brain.  Between the brain and body,
there exists an agreement of parts and qualities, so
that, if we understand the brain, we may infer the
form and quality of the body ; for there is a universality of forms in all the parts.  If we carefully

consider the forms and properties of the head, we may rest assured that they are confirmed in the forms of the body.

The orders constitute the full and complete development of the three degrees in three, five and sevenfold order ; but the styles are but partial developments.

# OF THE FACULTIES.

————————◄─●─►◄─────────

No. 14. Plate 1, Fig. 1. represents the nine groups of the faculties contained in the human head, divided longitudinally by horizontal lines, into the natural, spiritual and celestial degrees. The horizontal lines, indicate the position of the intermediate degrees. The head is again divided, by perpendicular lines, into the anterior, middle and posterior colums of the brain; thus dividing the brain into nine groups of organs or faculties. These groups or faculties are separately colored by the nine colors derived from the positive and negative solar spectrums, illustrated in Figs. 2 and 3. The three primitive colors, red, yellow and blue, are so arranged in the head, that they are separated, by their natural combinations, in the secondary and tertiary colors.

As colors represent the states of light and heat to the eye, we have made use of them in coloring

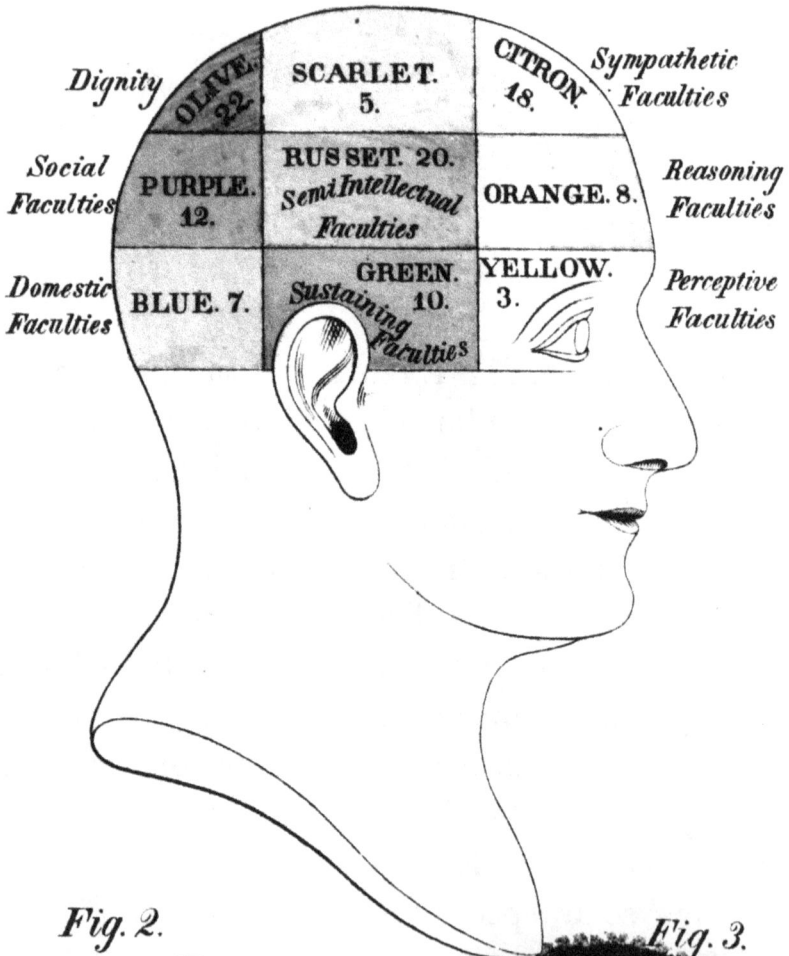

# FORCES OF THE BRAIN

*Plate 1.*

*Devotional Faculties*

*Fig. 1.*

*Dignity*

OLIVE. 22.

SCARLET. 5.

CITRON 18.

*Sympathetic Faculties*

*Social Faculties*

PURPLE. 12.

RUSSET. 20. *Semi Intellectual Faculties*

ORANGE. 8.

*Reasoning Faculties*

*Domestic Faculties*

BLUE. 7.

GREEN. 10. *Sustaining Faculties*

YELLOW. 3.

*Perceptive Faculties*

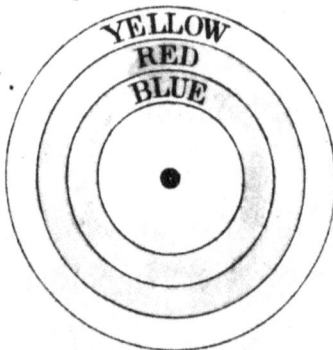

*Fig. 2.*

YELLOW
RED
BLUE

*Fig. 3.*

BLUE
YELLOW
RED

the plate of the head to represent the states of spiritual light and heat, with. their electric forces that flow in through the medium of the blood, the organs of sensation, and surrounding world, by which the natural light, heat and electricity of the mind and body receive their vital power of action, and by which there is intelligence and love. The three primitive colors are numbered three, five and seven, which are the great representative numbers in Masonry, and the exact combining powers of the most perfect colors, when combined by either weight or surface. Three of yellow, and seven of blue, and five of red, balance and harmonize with each other, when laid upon the canvas side by side, or combine by weight in producing the secondary colors of orange, purple and green. The secondary colors again combine in equal parts, producing the tertiary colors of citron, russet and olive. The combining numbers of the first three discrete colors of red, yellow and blue, are added together and multiplied in the secondary and tertiary colors agreeably to the combining powers of the primitive colors as they enter their compounds, and their numbers placed upon the group of the faculties. The combining numbers of three, five and seven are not merely incidental, but are illustrative of the series and degrees that run through all created things ; and hence, they are found representing the leading and prominent principles in every art and science. They represent the three links of creation by which there is design and unity in the whole.

By means of these colors in the head, we are unabled to present, to the eye, the most abstruse, difficult and subtle operations of the human mind, and their direct connection with the great interior forces, of the natural and spiritual world, and also their relations to the divine attributes and the Masonic degrees ; thus giving a demonstration, to the eye, of what we present through description to the ear, enabling the reader to demonstrate its truth by obervation.

We shall now proceed to give a demonstration of the foregoing principles by instructing the reader how to apply them in the examination and observation of the orders, temperaments and forms of the human body, and their agreement with the spiritual degrees and powers of the mind.

# DEMONSTRATION.

No. 15. The first thing in examining the head is
to ascertain to which of the general forms it belongs. If the head is square, oblong or round,
these forms prevail in the body, and if the head
is high and well developed, the temperaments being equally blended throughout; the base of the
brain full and rather predominating, the man belongs to the natural order, corresponding to the
Doric in architecture, being of the same general
form large or small, as the head is developed in
size.

The round head, which is well and smoothly
developed in the base central belt and coronal regions, indicates the same form and style of body
which corresponds to the Ionic before described.

The head being high and oval, and well developed in the natural, spiritual and celestial regions,
the body, also, partakes of the same forms heretofore described as the Corinthian.

The Tuscan order is indicated by the fulness of the head on the line separating the perceptive and reasoning faculties, the sustaining and semi-intellectual faculties, also, the domestic and social ; if otherwise, the head is well and smoothly developed,with a general absence of the temperamental marks, the body also partakes of the round and angular forms, and the mind is strictly literal.

The composite orders of mind and body are indicated by the fulness of the head along the line, separating the higher and middle faculties, the head, in all other respects being well and smoothly developed in the three belts.

Each of the orders have their higher, lower and middle developments, which give the various colors to the skin, hair and eyes, ranging through every shade, from the light to the dark. The eyes are universally gray, and of every variety from the light blue gray to the green-gray, citron green gray, olive gray, purple gray, the light neutral gray, in all of its gradations from the light to the dark, terminating in the black. If either of the temperaments decidedly prevails, the character of the order is lost in the temperaments, and the eyes may be blue or brown, and the hair may be

decidedly red or black.　See the temperamental
marks, Nos. 8, 9, 10, 11.

The unequal blending of the temperaments determines the various styles of men who constitute
the great mass of the human family, in their more
elevated and depraved conditions, which have been
heretofore described together with the temperamental marks of the head and body, with the form
of their features, color of the hair and eyes, the
size of the person, and contour of their forms.

We shall notice several of the peculiarities
arising from the combinations of the temperaments.
When the social and perceptive faculties are largely
developed, and the head thin and high; the body
is slim and rather over the medium height, the eyes
blue, and the hair brown.　When the habits are
perceptive, active and social, the dignifying faculties are large, the head thin, the man tall, the hair
and eyes black, and the thought intense but not
expansive.

Length of head gives intensity of thought;
breadth of head gives activity and expansion, and
a great variety of application.

After considering what has been said upon the
temperaments and orders, let the reader be blind-
folded and a subject placed at his right, letting

the left hand rest firmly upon the perceptive faculties and the forehead, place the right hand firmly
on the domestic group, raising it successively and
placing it on the social, dignifying, moral and
sympathetic faculties; recollecting their forms and
comparative size; then shifting his position to the
back of the subject, let him place the hands upon
the sustaining faculties, and raising them successively, rest them on the semi-intellectual and moral
groups, and the operator will be able to take the
exact form of the head, the relative proportions
and size of the groups into his mind, and reflecting
upon the general form and development of parts,
he will at once be able to decide whether or not
the subject.belongs to one of the orders before described, and, if not, let him consider the temperamental marks and their combinations, and which
has the ascendancy in the character and body, ob-
serving, at the same time, the relative size and influence of the other temperaments, and the effect
that they are likely to have, on the character, features and form, and make his combinations from
what has been said upon the subject of the various
orders and temperaments, and then let him describe
minutely the color of the hair and eyes, the peculiarities of the skin, features, limbs and form of

body, drawing his conclusion of the general size from the relative development of the head, and it will be found that the operator has described the personal appearance with more minuteness than one who has not examined the subject, and made a study of the forms and features, can do, by the most minute examination and comparison by sight.

Let the operator continue the practice of examination, according to the foregoing rules, blindfolded, and he will be able, after he has made the examination of any individual, to recognize him by sight, whenever he may see him ; and if he takes particular notice of the sound of the voice, the form of the hand or foot, he will recognize the subject from each, after having made the examination of the head ; but this requires long experience and close observation of the orders, temperaments and their combinations in human form. Should the reader fail, it will be from the want of a proper attention to the foregoing outlines of the human system, and not the fault of the science.

# DEGREES IN LIGHT.

————————◆◀●▶◆————————

No. 16. If a ray of light passes from a rarer to a denser medium, it is refracted and decomposed into its discrete degrees of red, yellow and blue light. Let the experiment be tried by a common triangular prism, by receiving the ray in a dark room, through a small aperture in the wall or shutter, passing it through the prism, and throwing it upon the opposite wall or a screen, and we have the well known prismatic colors, consisting of red, orange, yellow, green and blue, with the indigo and violet rays. Let the thermometer be placed in each and they will be found to be of different degrees of heat. It will also be found that their attendant heat rays have been refracted and decomposed, and occupy different positions upon the screen. If the red, yellow and blue rays be again passed through another prism, they will not be decomposed, but remain the same. But if the orange and green rays be submitted to the test of the prism, they will be divided into their component colors, thus showing conclusively that they are compounds of the red, yellow and blue. The reader will remark, that in this order of colors, the purple is absent, and that all the rays are joined by continuous degrees; the red passing through and adjoining to the continuous degrees of the yellow and blue appear in the indigo and violet rays at the extreme of the solar spectrum; the indigo ray consisting of the deeper portion of the discrete blue ray, which is adjoined to the red ray in passing through the blue, portions of the yellow ray, also passing through the three, combining and compounding to produce the violet ray at the extreme of the spectrum. The indigo and violet can readily be produced by the artist from the three discrete colors of red, yellow and blue. It is further observed, from close inspection of the primitive rays, that each consists of a deeper, middle, and lighter tint as they approach each other, thus showing conclusively that each discrete ray contains all the other rays within itself, it being impossible to entirely decompose them. Hence each discrete ray consists in greater or less degree of the combined powers of the other degrees, passing, as it were, from dark to light by three distinct powers, the middle tone being the average power of the ray,

which is represented by a number called its combining power. This may be illustrated by the
white light itself, which, in passing from light to
shade, manifests three distinct powers, light, half
light and dark, or tint, middle tint and shade, and
must always appear in their distinct forms in every
picture.

It is the theory of writers on symbolic colors,
that there are but two primitive rays, male and
female, or the red and the yellow, the yellow being
a different state of the white. The blue they hold
to be the first offspring or active sphere. Hence it
represents the Holy Spirit in regeneration, and the
fecundating principle in nature; and this principle
seems to be carried out in all the great architectural
works of the middle ages. The Holy Spirit and
also the Virgin are attired in blue. It is the peculiar symbol of ancient craft masonry, and signifies the conjunction of the truths of the Word with
the will wherein there is a life of truth from love,
which is charity, arising from the third day of
regeneration, or the Master's degree. Abstractly
speaking, it signifies the celestial good of truth.
There are three gradations of the blue which have
different significations, which will be hereafter
explained in No. 22.

No. 17. A spot of any shade or color, on a ground or medium lighter or darker than itself, being viewed by a lensic prism, will be deflected by the ordinary refraction of light and shade into an orb of three colors. See figs. 2 and 3, pl. 1.

The prism decomposes the white light into its three discrete or compound rays, which are the well known colors of red, yellow and blue, which interblend, giving the secondary colors of orange, green and purple. In the deflection of the light spot upon the dark ground, all the light of the spot is deflected in its primitive and active state, as it came from the sun in which the red ray occupies the centre. The next ray being the yellow, and the outer ray of all being the blue. These rays interblend, giving the secondary colors of orange and green. The more refractive portions of the red, yellow and blue are thrown outward, blending into indigo and violet. These orbs of light and color form the positive order of colors, well known as the prismatic, which are beautifully illustrated in the rainbow, the drops of water decomposing the white light, throwing its concentric belts of prismatic light upon the dark ground formed by the clouds. The reader will observe that in the foregoing order of positive light the secondary color of purple is missing.

The dark spot upon a light ground being deflected is called the negative order of light, which agrees with the ordinary reflected light, in which a part of the rays are absorbed and the discrete rays of red, yellow and blue change positions with each other. The blue takes the inner circle, the red ocupies the middle, and the yellow the outermost orb, blending from the centre outward with the blue, purple, red, orange and yellow. The indigo and violet, being the most active chemical rays of red, yellow and blue are drawn to the centre. The more subtle portions of the rays, contain the greatest chemical powers, and are more freely absorbed in nature from the light. The reader will observe that in the negative order of light, decomposed by the lensic prism, the purple makes its appearance ; thus establishing, in the combined results of the positive and negative orders, three discrete rays of red, yellow and blue, and three continuous colors derived from their compounds, namely, orange, purple and green, which are called secondary colors. If these again be compounded, we have the tertiary colors of citron, russet and olive.

From the foregoing it will be perceived that the colors are derived from the decomposition of white light. The crystaline lens of the eye decomposes the light still further, bringing out the various colors of objects agreeably to their chemical qualities and powers of absorption. Cases now and then are met with where the lens of the eye recombines the light, destroying the power and pleasure derived from colors, the eye only perceiving the light and shade which are derived from the white light; such persons are said to be colorblind.

When lenses are used to assist the eye, the light is greatly excited by decomposition, which will be readily understood by letting the light of a lamp pass through a pair of glasses, and fall upon the wall some distance beyond their focus, which will produce·a spot of white light even much larger than the lenses themselves, showing that the light has been much excited and its color improved by the partial decomposition. The positive and negative orders of light represent the positive and negative orders of regeneration. The negative order of regeneration represented by the blue, ascends until man has come into a state of divine order; thence it descends in divine order from the Lord, in which the celestial spiritual corresponds to the scarlet, occupies the centre.

# THE ZONES.

No. 18. The atmosphere and subtle fluids act as a lens, decomposing and refracting the light; long before it reaches the surface of the earth, throwing its rays with full force along the equator. The red or heat rays being more of a subtle nature, pierce the atmosphere in nearly direct lines, passing entirely through the upper regions of the air, north and south of the poles. Thus, owing to the spherical form of the earth, the heat decreases rapidly as we approach the poles. The yellow light, being more refractive, is thrown directly to the surface of the earth, along the temperate zones, while the blue rays, being still more refractive, are collected by the atmosphere, north and south of the poles, and concentrated in the arctic and antarctic regions. Thus forming three degrees upon the surface of the earth of light, heat and color, known as the torrid, temperate and frigid zones.

As the earth is constantly varying its position

in relation to the Sun in passing around its orbit, giving the four seasons, the heat and light are constantly distributed, giving the blue ray in the winter, the red in the summer, and the yellow in the spring or fall, in the temperate zones. The decomposed light constantly sets at liberty its electric fluids, in its three discrete and continuous degrees, which become absorbed, and identified with the substances of the earth. It floats with a mighty current over the surface of the earth, from the equator to the poles, constantly ·pervading and magnetising every substance, sustaining and vivifying the mineral, vegetable, and animal kingdoms, in the four seasons, which are produced by the decomposition of the light. Thus light, heat and electricity have again blended in the work of a constant creation. The torrid zone becomes the great reservoir of heat; the arctic region of cold; they continually flow back upon each other, recombining, neutralizing and tempering the atmosphere for vegetation.

The polar regions are the workshops of elemental creation. The blue ray of light, being the offspring from the marriage of the red and the yellow, contains the most active chemical principles and these when separately brought together being thrown upon the icy surface of the poles, are again reflected, condensed, cooled, and, being deprived of their heat, their expansive and repulsive powers are destroyed. The law of their existence is changed from the expansive to the contractive, forming the gases of the atmosphere. They flow back through the great currents of the atmosphere to the equator. Thereby the atmosphere is constantly supplied with new and living elements for the vegetable kingdom. While no less has been the new elemental creation for the mineral kingdom, in the currents of electricity.

No. 19. The intelligent traveller will observe, with wonder and delight, the harmony and beauty displayed in the three zones. As he ascends the lofty mountain, in the tropical regions, and gains the summit, let him behold the wonders of the setting Sun. The red rays are mirrored along the horizon, ascending in their prismatic beauty to the orange, the yellow, the light gray, instead of the green, it being neutralized by the continuous degree of the red; and blending into the azure of the vault of the heavens, thus wonderfully illustrating the prismatic powers of the atmosphere, and demonstrating to the eye the great truths heretofore explained.

Let him now turn his face to the east, and he will see an illustration of reflective light, shown in figure 2, plate 1. The colors have now changed their position; the blue mountains rise in the distance, blending upwards with the grayish purple to a subdued red and yellow light, terminating with the bluish gray light in the vault, turning to the right and left, let hm follow the gentle gradation of the negative order of colors, until they again assume their prismatic position in the West. These are principles that should be embodied in every landscape painting, but, as yet, have been imperfectly understood and practised. The facts have been known, but the reasons hid. Let the traveller again descend and stand upon the ocean beach, and turn his face to the East, and he will behold the whole heavens streaming with the light of the red and yellow rays of the negative order of light, as it is reflected back from the clouds in every conceivable fantastical form The Western sky is illuminated with the decomposed positive rays, piercing the clouds in direct lines to the earth.

These are but a few of the glories that adorn the tropical landscape. Here we behold the orange, the lemon, the cocoanut and palm; the banana, the plantain and the pomegranate, with an inexhaustible variety of tropical fruits. In its forest are found the elephant, the lion and the tiger; the monkey, the ape and the gorilla. Its birds are of the richest plumage; and its reptiles are of the largest kind.

As the traveller passes north, to the temperate regions, the light of the zone changes to the yellow, with a subdued, mild and springlike appearance; the whole face of the country is changed. The sky and the clouds are gilt with the yellow; the landscape is decked with the lofty oak, the elm and the maple. Its animals are the buffalo, the deer, and the bear. Its cultivated grounds produce the sereal grains. Its fruits are the plum, the apple and the pear.

As the traveller passes on to the frigid zone, the sky has become blue and cold; the stately pine, the spruce and the hemlock appear. The wild animals are the bear, the elk, and the furry tribes. No less is the marked difference in man. In the tropical regions, he is impulsive, perceptive and devotional. All the prominent religions of the earth have originated in or near the tropics. In the temperate regions man is cool, temperate, thoughtful. This is the field of science and invention.

As we pass northward, man becomes the great worker. The light, heat and electricity, with their red, yellow and blue rays, have had their marked effect upon him, as well as the animal, mineral and vegetable creation. They constitute the three distinct spheres, or orders of creation in man, adapted to the zones in which he lives, so distinct that he requires an acclimation, usually followed by sickness when he changes his residence from one to the other, the dread of which, in a great measure, prevents his emigration north and south, preferring to continue in his native zone ; thus, he emigrates East and West.

The governing principles of characters, in the different latitudes, are not less striking. Man, in the tropice, is immotional and governed by his will ; in the temperate zone he is thoughtful and governed by his intellect. In the North, he is practical, and governed by uses. These three classes of men, mentally, morally and religiously are different, although connected and blended together by continuous degrees, so that a certain likeness of these three discrete classes of men, appear in each zone, constituting a trinity, which is again repeated in each, giving a series of nine, three in the Torrid, three in the Temperate, and three in the Frigid.

A certain likeness and type of the three zones exist in each, but in different degree, so that there is a complete likeness of the nine degrees of Ancient Masonry.

Man passes through a certain likeness of these degrees, as he advances, step by step, in his regeneration, coming into different influxes of spiritual light and heat, and the nine different groups of the faculties are successively opened. In the beginning, the negative order of light prevails, the blue ray forming the centre and verging outward with the red and the yellow, until all the faculties have been opened and brought into divine order. When the entire order of the man is changed, the red and scarlet rays hold a central position, proceeding outward from the red to the yellow, and the blue. The red signifies celestial love, the yellow celestial intelligence, and the blue charity. With the Master Mason, the blue or charity holds the first position in his mind, the red, or the love of the Lord, the second place, and lastly, the yellow or faith constitutes the outermost of the man. With the celestial or Royal Arch Mason, the red or love of the Lord is innermost, the yellow or faith hold a second position, and charity clothes the whole.

# DEGREES OF THE BRAIN.

No. 20. The brain, in its unity, is one organ, in its duality, it has a right and left lobe ; in its trinity it consists of the anterior and middle lobes, and the cerebellum. In unity, the mind consists of the intellectual faculties, in duality of the will and understanding ; in trinity, it has the will, understanding and action. In the ninefold order of the brain, it is divided into nine particular groups ; each of which is duplicated in the right and left lobes of the brain ; they again are articulated or subdivided into organs, in their two, three, five and seven fold order, like the multiplication of the prime numbers. Three of the nine groups of the brain are fundamental, like the three, five and seven of the nine digits, which agree with the three fundamental colors, red, yellow and blue.

These colors also have their combining powers of three, five and seven. In their unity, they consist of the white light. In their duality, as male and female, of the red and yellow rays. In

7*

their offspring or action, they add to themselves the blue ray, constituting their trinity. In their combination they constitute nine distinct colors, in perfect harmony with mathematics and the tones of the human voice, which will be hereafter explained. And in particular they agree with the nine affections of the mind.

In the first column are the affections to know or perceive, to understand and enter into the feelings of others. They occupy the frontal portion of the brain, and are colored, yellow, orange, and citron. See diagram of the head, plate 1, fig. 1. These constitute the reflective degrees of the brain, and are called the intellectual faculties, which rise in a threefold order, above each other like the base, shaft and capital of the column.

The next great column of the brain, which is one of the principal supports of the Temple, is the love of family, the love of friends, and of use. They occupy the posterior region of the brain, are colored blue, purple and olive ; and are called the domestic, social and dignifying faculties.

The third and last order is the great sustaining column of the central portion of the brain. It has its foundation in the earth, and its capital in the heavens. The base is composed of the collec-

tive loves of man, its shaft is life and its capital
devotion ; its base is receptive of the animal spirit,
which supports the reasoning faculties, and its
capital is the divine influxes. It is colored on the
chart scarlet, russet and green, which are called
the sustaining semi-intellectual, and devotional
faculties. These three columns are the principal
support of Masonry, Wisdom, Strength and Beauty,
as it is necessray to have wisdom to contrive,
strength to support, and beauty to adorn all of
our undertakings. Thus it is that the Brain is in
the likeness of the Lodge, the Chapter and the
Council.

21. There is no heat without light, neither is
there thought without affection. The affection
opens into thought, and thought is the light of
love. Light flows in through the medium of the
eye, and produces its chemical effect upon the perceptive fluids ; but it is received or rejected as it
is in harmony with the affections. If the form
received is agreeable, it is at once elevated into the
understanding, and there elaborated and worked
as food for the spirit. And when the curtain of
sleep is drawn over the cerebral brain, all the
thought fluids that have been elaborated during the
day, retire into the chambers of the will, and are

blended with the corporeal fluids of the body, where they come directly in contact with every cell and fibre of the bodily tissues. Thus, what man does from the will during the day, is incorporated into his affections at night, coming forth into the understanding in the morning, confirmed as a component part of the human understanding, never again to be eradicated except by temptation, it may be put one side and locked up by repentance, but never destroyed. Truths thus received are colored according to their combining affections, and are psychologically seen in all their forms and beauty of color, and constitute the clothing of the spirit. This is what we mean by coloring the different groups of organs. There are three fundamental groups of affections, that rule and govern all the others, namely, the domestic, the devotional and the perceptive, which we will now proceed to consider.

These three groups of organs receive their spiritual light and heat from the three zones of the heavens, which, like the light of the zones of the earth, are of different colors and qualities ; and, when they flow into the brain, are received into different groups of organs which correspond with the zones of the earth. The three discrete rays of spiritual light and heat give three distinct powers of affection and thought. From the affections of each there comes forth a perception in the mind which adjoins with the light of the spiritual world, giving the power to understand and comprehend spiritual things. These spiritual thoughts and affections are in likeness of the animal, vegetable and mineral kingdoms of the heavens in their different zones. As the light and heat of the natural world, in their decomposed conditions, flow into the brain, through the medium of the blood and the five senses, giving animal perception and life, there is formed in the mind the likeness of the spiritual world, by which there is a perception of spiritual things when the faculties of the human mind have been opened by regeneration. Regeneration, in its normal condition, is a natural progression from state to state, whereby man comes into the power and ability to understand and enjoy heavenly things. But evils and falses restrain and destroy the order of regeneration. When man restrains the evils within him through a faith in the divine Word, the progression of regeneration commences. First, by the light and power of the blue ray which represents the celestial good of truth. The mind however must first be restored and brought into a natural rational state, by which the truths of the Word can be received. We shall now describe, in general, these three groups of the human faculties in their regenerate condition, commencing with the blue, which has its seat in the cerebellum.

## Of the Blue.

No. 22. Grave, indeed, is the conjugal relation of life; its responsibilities and rewards are great; it receives the soul germ from the hand of the Creator, and stamps upon it its own virtues or evils. It provides for the support of the infant. With tender caresses and affections, it dandles the innocent child; it insinuates the germs of remains, that, in after years are to come forth in justice and judgment, and lays the foundation of friendship and usefulness, which constitute the man and the Mason. It deals directly with the first principles of life. It is the fecundating power of celestial love with the truth, implanting in the first ends of creation, all the orderly relations of life.

The conjugal affections descend through the angels of heaven, and instamp the male and female ·rinciples upon all things in nature. They descend in the blue ray of light, to the creative spheres of earth. The blue ray contains the active, chemical principles of light, and gives substance to the elemental formation. It enters equally with yellow into the life principle of the vegetable kingdom, as is manifest from the color. It softens and adapts the light to the eye, and aids the chemical effect of the outer world, upon the thoughtfluids of the brain. It is to the creative sphere of the world what Masonry is to the spiritual man. Hence, it becomes the peculiar emblem and symbolic color of Ancient Craft Masonry.

To the domestic faculties, belong the issues of life and death ; for these are fought the great demoniac battle. If they be made the receptacle of scortatary love, the whole brain is lashed with serpents of fire, which terminates in an opposite cold, both of body and mind. The skin has an eating and burning sensation, followed by alternating chills ; friendship dies ; the mind becomes cold, suspicious and cruel. But, if conjugal affections prevail, the bodily heat is gentle and warm, the physical system active and strong, and friendship and peace prevail in all the relations of life. They gather around the family circle all the emblems of beauty and use, the mansion, the tree, and the flower. The mind is practical in all the business of life, and adorns itself with every beauty and grace, and, when warmed by the devotional faculties, becomes the true seat of happiness and eternal life. Deep blue, when tinged with scarlet, is its peculiar emblem.

The domestic faculties, when illumined by faith, give intelligence and wisdom ; and light blue is their correspondential color, and when lighted by the understanding of the Word, are like the blue vault of heaven. Hence, azure blue is their true representative color, and signifies child-like belief or true faith, when there is no envy nor mistrust. Blue, in general, signifies celestial love of truth ; its combining powers will be treated of more fully when we come to explain the secondary and tertiary colors. Its combining powers being seven, signify that which is holy, relating directly to the male and female principles of all things in nature, and is directly connected with the fecundating principle in man ; which is enshrined in the *sanctum sanctorum*, or holy of holies. It also signifies secrecy in a lesser sense.

The family relations have their seat in the cerebellum, and from them spring all the laws of society and civil order. Charity forms the innermost principle and life of the man, from which all the objects and motives of life are drawn.   The love of the Lord holds a subordinate relation, and faith is the ultimate end.   And hence, to teach the goods and truths of the Word, is the highest and noblest object of the Master Mason, for which he is peculiarly qualified by state and condition of mind.

There is a co-ordinate pulsatory motion of the cerebellum with the respiratory motion of the middle lobes of the brain, their influxes adjoined sending a current forward by the fornix and floors of the lateral ventricles which are collected and pass backward by the corpus callosum, by which the current of the animal life is complete.   A rational plane of thought is formed by the inflowing of the celestial faculties of the cerebral brain by which the spiritual degree is opened in the cerebellum ; this is not the case with the animal creation, which receive only the spiritual from the natural degree of the heavens.   Thus the animal mind cannot partake of eternal life, which is derived from the Lord through the three discrete degrees, No. 23.   With the Master Mason who is regenerated, the cerebellum is open as to its discrete degree which is a life of charity from the spiritual heavens.

## Of the Scarlet.

No. 23. The scarlet or devotional faculties next claim our attention. As the letters of an alphabet enter into all the words of a language, and yet refer themselves to a few vowel sounds, so thought ranges the fields of the heavens and earth; yet it relates to a very few and simple loves. There can be no thought without a motive or end to be accomplished. Without it, thought would be indeterminate, and there would be no plane of understanding. The will is the store-house of motive or first ends, which are called loves. It has been shown in No. 5, that every element is stamped with the vegetable, mineral and animal kingdoms, and arranged in distinct affinities. So it is with the mind of man. The spiritual substances have been arranged in their will and intellectual forms, in a simultaneous order, susceptible of being opened or brought forth under favorable circumstances.

The will principle is ever pressing to come forth, like the seed in the ground, and when excited under favorable light from the understanding, it leaps forth with joy and gladness. This delight, we call affection, and, in ordinary language, not unfrequently it is substituted for the love itself. The scarlet, or devotional faculties, are the receptacles of the divine will, when not perverted ; and hence are the fountain of all divine order in man. The peculiar delight which we feel in the acknowledgment of the divine will, is what we call devotion. It is a speaking with Deity. To be real and unfeigned, all the laws of divine order must be brought forth into the understanding, and performed through the active principle of the man, in the keeping of the ten commandments. The delight we feel in so doing, is the only true adoration of the heart, and alone acceptable unto the Lord. But humility, connected with repentance and acknowledgment, is always due unto Him. The ends and motives implanted in the will, by the divine influxes, should enter into every thought and affection of the human understanding. They are the heat and active principle of the human mind, constituting in man what the red rays does in nature, and are the peculiar chracteristics of Royal

Arch Masonry, and hence the scarlet is the symbolic color of that degree.

This color has also its continuous degrees proceeding from deep to light. The deep golden scarlet signifies the divine love, or love of the Lord; scarlet signifies celestial good, and light scarlet spiritual good. When the devotional faculties are large, they become intuitive ; and if the life of the man be in accordance with divine truth, they impress the rational and perceptive faculties with a perception and understanding of divine ends.

When the divine motives fall into the perceptive faculties, and, thus, into words, the state is called *inspiration*; such was the case with the prophets of old. When the divine falls in order into the rational faculties, so that, the reason and application are understood, it is called *illumination*; and is the highest state of the human intellect. For that which is most rational is also most divine with man. When there is a mighty influx of the divine sphere into the top of the head, it appears as a flame of fire. Such was the case with the apostles on the day of Pentecost. See acts of the apostles, 2. 3. This influx is frequently felt on the top of the head, as a rushing or breathing of the air.

These faculties are the receptacles of divine good with man; but, when perverted by a bad life, they lead to all hypocricy and fanaticism. They give a peculiar persistency, order and zeal to all the operations of life. When they combine with the perceptive faculties, they give great power of ratiocination and confirmation. These faculties combine readily with all the others, as will be seen when we come to treat of the secondary and tertiary colors. When the frontal portion is large, falsely known as the organ of marvelousness, they sometimes become intuitive, giving second sight and vision, and when properly balanced by other organs of the mind, and the affection and life are pure, the divine ends or motives of life are seen in an objective form, with more clearness than the natural forms of the world are with the eye. Such were the visions of the prophets of old. These organs, in their natural state, are the promptings to prayers and faith, and commune with Deity. But, when perverted, they lead to all foolishness and fantasy. The combining power of red is five, and signifies man, or the law of divine order proper to him. It also signifies, in a lesser sense, the five senses, the five fingers, and the five orders of architecture, three of which are held in high estimation among Masons. The articulation of the limbs of the body into three and five, is a conclusive proof of the representative meaning of this number, and the combining power of red being five, identifies it with this order in man.

The vital forces of the cerebellum and the base of the brain are complete in their cardiac and respiratory motions, being collected and passing backward by the *corpus callosum*, as has been shown in Articles 6, 7, 22. Thus the animal mind is complete in all its functions and powers, the influxes of the cerebellum being derived from the spiritual heavens in man. The influxes of the perceptive faculties are derived from the natural degree. These react and adjoin with the cerebellum in the great current of the animal life that passes the corpus callosum. The influxes of the devotional faculties are derived from the celestial heavens, and are complete in their pulmonary and cardiac motions.

## *of the Yellow.*

No. 24. The next in order is the yellow ray representing the perceptive faculties. These are the lowest and stand directly connected with the five senses; and are to the intellect what the foundation is to the building. They supply the mind with sensuous facts, without which there is no reason nor understanding. They are to man, what the yellow ray or light principle is to nature. The yellow is the first affection of truth upon the white light. The white light being decomposed by the senses, and the eye in particular, the yellow ray appears. When facts are confirmed by an affection of knowledge, they are stored up in the memory or upper portion of the perceptive faculties. When elevated into the scientific faculties, and there adjoined to motives and ends of life, they are arranged into principles, being conjoined with their appropriate loves, derived from the blue and the red, thus giving

the power of reasoning, or arriving at a just conclusion, which is truth. When conclusions are
elevated into the sympathetic faculties, they give
the peculiar power of discerning the motives of
others, and entering into their thoughts and
feelings. These faculties are sometimes used by
psychologists to read character, which is true or
false, just in proportion as the operator is in the
truth himself. What is more singular and not
the less true, is, that the divine order of facts,
principles and truths, as arranged in the great
column of the intellectual faculties, decides the
color of the man. The .man is white just in
proportion as this column is perfect; and black
in proportion as the order, harmony and beauty
are destroyed; and the power lost to comprehend
divine ends. This statement must not be confounded with the power of ratiocination or
talking of truth, which exists equally with the
bad as well as the good. But just in proportion
to the power of the intellectual faculties to see
and grasp a great practical truth of nature, so is
the color, varying agreeably to the law of temperaments. There are no black angels; yet
many black men may make white angels by regeneration, and the divine operation of the spiri-

tual world.   The normal color of man is white, tinged with the color of the various affections. Hence, it is necessary for man to be free born ; that is, he must be able to control his passions, through the intellect, to become a Mason.   The intellectual faculties from the affections, give color to the sphere of the man in the spiritual world.   And his quality is there known by his garments and light.   Hence, the prophets and the saints have always been represented in garments and haloes to signify their state and condition.   The yellow has its continuous degree, like the other colors.   The deep golden yellow signifies celestial love, or the highest light that the celestial angels attain to.   Hence it is represented by gold, in the temple, and garments of the priesthood.   If the intellectual faculties prevail over the affections, the man is of the spiritual order. With such, the yellow ray becomes silvery, which is the highest light of the spiritual angel.

With the natural angel, or spirit, the light is common yellow, and signifies the first dawning of hope.   Every confirmation of truth through a life, agreeably to the Word, gives a metallic appearance to the sphere.   Hence, the white and yellow metals, signify goods and truths of the understanding. Therefore, in Masonry, the uninitiated are said to possess nothing of the metallic kind; poor indeed is his representative condition. The order of the reasoning faculties and governing power, exists in man alone. Woman does not arrive at truth by reason, she possesses a higher order of intellect. The affection with her comes forward into the intellectual principle. Hence, she feels and perceives the truth of her interior principle and at once adopts whatever pleases her. She is governed by her affections, and not her understanding. She deals not with stone and building materials, but the tender emotions of the heart. She is the form of love, and man of truth. Hence, she cannot be made a Mason. The affections are her field and sphere, which she and her form represent. She imparts the affections, and implants the emotional in the tender mind of the child. She resides in the mansion of truth, securely erected by the Mason. His is the field of science, her's of love.

The combining power of yellow is three, and signifies the fulness of light and faith. It is through the perceptive faculties that we receive all the knowledges of faith. When these knowledges are carried into life, the acts performed are the goods of faith, and the experience we receive, is the light of faith.    Thus the perceptive faculties stand as the foundation and reflecting point like a diamond, for all the external lights of the human understanding.    " The light of the body is the eye, if therefore thine eye be single, thy whole body shall be full of light.    But if thine eye be evil, thy whole body shall be full of darkness.    If therefore the light that is in thee be darkness, how great is that darkness ? Mat.  6—22 and 23.    Luke 11. 34, 35 and 36.  If thine eye be single, signifies without passion or lust ; but if thine eye be evil, signifies to have  passion or lust. From this we may perceive, that evil  affections destroy the entire order of the  human understanding, and turn all of our reasonings into darkness, and the most direful perversions ; in which we see error as truth and *vice versa*, using the reasoning faculties with great force and  plausibility, to confirm the false.    The yellow or white is the peculiar representative of the Entered Apprentice Degree.

The yellow, the blue and the red are the discrete degrees of the mind.    They occupy a triangular position in the head and react against each other, when opened and completed in the Royal Arch degree of regeneration ; therefore the triangle is the true emblem of this degree, the angles of which represent the three discrete degrees of the Entered Apprentice, Master and Royal Arch. When all the faculties of the head are opened in the nine degrees, they are represented by the triple triangle, the angles of which are the nine degrees of Ancient Masonry. These all act and react against each other, and co-ordinate in every act of the will and understanding. The opening and conferring of the degrees of regeneration, commence with the Entered Apprentice and terminate with the Royal and select Master's degrees. The sensual and corporeal alone are open in the natural man, but the degrees of the mind are successively opened into states of intelligence and love, as regeneration takes place.

No. 25. There is a unity and agreement between all the parts of nature, if it were not so, there could be no harmony. To understand what we feel, see, hear, taste and smell, constitutes the perfect intellectual man. If this were the case, nature would be an open book. To discover the law of correspondence between mind and matter, in the symbols of masonry, is one of the objects of the present work. As it is well known, at the

present day, that light, heat and electricity constitute the warp and woof of elemental nature, we
have, therefore, more particularly chosen them for
the sake of illustration. The colors represent the
state of the light and admit of an occular demonstration, and being the last link or transition state
between mind and matter, afford a striking example of their parallelism and correspondence.
We shall thence carry out their symbolic relations
in all of their combinations, using light as synoni-
mous with the understanding in general, and color
with the state of the affections ; showing that all
things exist in a discrete order of degrees, combining by agreement of uses, and not by infusion
of the degrees. Yet, each degree has its continuous degrees proceeding from coarse to fine ; if
this were not so, the order of nature would be like
an arterial system without valves, in which the
blood would flow back upon the heart, and destroy
the circulation. If there were no discrete degrees,
progressive order would be destroyed, and there
would be no difference between nature and God.
But when we view things in their discrete degrees
of elemental formation, we find no difficulty in
discovering their order, either in ascending by the
analytical mode of reasoning to the heavens, and

beholding the throne of Deity, or descending syn-
thetically to the lowest ultimates of earth.

Without a knowledge of the laws of *discretion*
and degrees, we are unable to proceed in our investigations of the laws of mind and matter, con-
founding the spirit with the body, and God with
the nature. Losing all knowledge and reverence
for the Deity, the mind becomes cold, and the
normal growth is checked and destroyed. If we
would reason upon these subjects, we must keep
distinctly in view the discrete degrees of the faculties, in all their combinations and powers, as well
in the human mind as in the lodge. The degrees
of Masonry being but the out-birth of the divine
mind, through the revelation to Moses, in arranging the tabernacle agreeably to the order of
heaven; and afterwards to David and Solomon.
See Exodus from the 25 to 32 inclusive, and first
Chronicles, 11 to the 19 inclusive. These things
being given by divine revelation, when rightly understood, explain all the mysteries of creation.

The numeral 1, being the foundation and starting
point of all things, this number has two qualities,
namely: multiplication and addition, which signifies marriage and offspring, as twice one are two,
which signifies inseparable union, and the addition

of one makes three, which signifies progression, action, or offspring. Thus the number one, has only completed the family relation; which is, trinity and unity; or the Father, Son and Holy Spirit; which is the marriage of divine Good with divine Wisdom, the offspring being action, procedure, or creation. See 97. From the foregoing, it will be seen that the prime number three, is only one in its completeness; that is by multiplication and addition. And in this order, follow all the prime numbers, as twice two are four and one is five; and twice three are six, and one is seven; twice five are ten, and one is 'eleven, and so on. Prime numbers always consisting of the multiplication of a prime number, and addition. Hence, all the even numbers singnify conjunction, marriage, or multiplication. The prime numbers signify fulness or completion of the state; and these two principles run through all creative substances; dividing all things into series and degrees, as end, cause and effect.

By numbers, in physics, we arrive to the knowledge of quantities; by numbers in the mental creation, we arrive to the knowledge of states of affection and truth; showing always (when we have the representative number of the thing,) its

exact series and the degree in which it is removed
from its first great cause. And this is the true
signification of all numbers that appear in the
divine Word. The combining power of these
numbers is attached to the colors, and is made use
of, to unfold the representative meaning and states
of love and truth of the perfectly regenerated man,
which is illustrated in fig. 1, pl. 1.

It will at once be perceived, that Masonry does
not deal with the perversions of things, but is only
illustrative of the regenerate man. We therefore
must leave his depraved state and condition to the
physician.

In the combinations of affections and truths,
a love is always adjoined to its wisdom or understanding. Its combinations and works are perceived and. understood by the light, while-the
simple love remains concealed. The loves are two:
the domestic and devotional faculties. They work
at low twelve at night, when every prying eye of
intellect is asleep, through the involuntary nerves.
They are located in the cerebellum,and great central
column of the brain. The combination of these
loves, forms a single exception to the general rule.
See what is said of the purple, No. 29.

9*

# COMBINATION

## DISCRETE DEGREES OF THE BRAIN.

No. 26. The combining power of yellow is three, both in weight and surface. The combining power of red is five. The combining power of blue is seven. Hence, five of red and three of yellow, give an orange if combined ; and when spread upon canvas, in point of surface have equal power. Three of yellow and seven of blue, in their combining powers give a green. And are contrasted by their opposite power of red ; the contrasting or opposite power of orange being the blue, and *vice versa*, orange is the opposite power of blue. Five of red and seven of blue give the true purple, and balance its opposite power of yellow. Yellow representing the perceptive faculties, and purple the social, they balance and harmonize with each other. Green being composed of three of yellow and seven of blue, holds the just medium between the yellow and the blue, and signifies life or hope. These in man constitute the true executive or kingly mind. In painting they give the perfect yellow tone picture, when combined according to their powers, the yellow constituting the foreground, green the middle, and purple the distance. This view is adapted to a close and minute inspection of objects in the foreground, contrasted by the purple in the distance. This pictue corresponds to the well balanced perceptive mind. As the power of inspection becomes frivolous without association, so minutiæ are tiresome without the good of wisdom represented by the purple or social powers. From this it will be seen that every picture, as well as the world itself, is a transcript in part or in whole, of the human mind. The opposing colors hold an opposite position in the head as well as in nature, forming a circle round the brain, the green holding the middle portion in the base of the brain contrasting the red, as it is the seat of vegetative life. It will be observed that the colors as arranged in fig. 1, plate 1, represent the regenerate man or true Mason; therefore green holds the central position between the Entered Apprentice and Master Mason. There are three grades of the blue, its combining power is seven, which represents the medium; six represents the deep indigo ray, which is modified by a little red.  The yellow or perceptive faculties being the window of the mind, open into the other faculties, distributing light to the orange, citron, green, olive and russet, holding its full force and power in each according to its combining power.  There are but three simple groups of faculties that are discrete in themselves ; the blue, scarlet and yellow. These readily combine agreeably to their powers, giving the secondary and tertiary colors, which we now proceed to illustrate.

The continuous degrees are sometimes called degrees of longitude, when referring to those in the same plane ; and when they ascend by the same column, they are called degrees of altitude.

## Of the Orange.

No. 27. The orange being composed of three of yellow, and five of red is represented by light, which signifies the marriage of good and truth ; representing in the head the combination of the perceptive and devotional faculties, which signifies also conjunction. These two faculties conjoining with every principle, without which there can be no progression of thought, they are the second step in Masonry, and belong to the second section of the Fellow Craft degree ; and they constitute the mere scientific principle of the mind, in which facts are conjoined with motives, as faith in the understanding. These make the base and the shaft of the great frontal column of facts and science. And as the column is incomplete without its cap, so are the perceptive and scientific faculties without sympathy, which crowns the whole structure of the intellect, and is represented by the citron, which is a tertiary color composed of a due mixture of green and orange, its constituent parts being six of yellow, five of red and seven of blue. Its great power being a perception of divine ends and the conjugal relations of life, is represented by the No. 18, which is a multiplication of nine by two; which signifies a conjunction in the understanding of all things of the degrees, and is the seventh step in Masonry. The first step being faith in memory, the second step faith in the understanding, and thirdly the implantation of faith in the will, which constitutes true wisdom and understanding, thus completing the Master's Lodge, which is the natural wisdom principle of all the degrees in Masonry, as carried out in the great practical relations of life. Its prevailing quality being science, it equally combines the devotional and domestic relations, orange being composed of a due mixture of golden yellow and deep golden scarlet, it signifies the perception of divine ends, or love of science; and is contrasted by its opposite color of blue, which represents the domestic faculties; its combining power being seven, which numbers signifies that which is holy. Orange constitutes the light and tone of the great style in painting. The light of the foregrounds being orange, the middle ground of the deep red, green and olive ; and the distance of the clear blues and the light and delicate shade, being adapted to vast and expansive views which are the peculiar characteristics of the senator and statesman, or the law giving principle. The foreground of the picture being strongly marked by the cutting shades of the russet or brown, gives point and clearness of argument. The middle ground gives a full and rich devotional feeling, and the back ground, all tender emotions of life. The orange is the emblem of the second section of the Fellow Craft No. 34.

## Of the Green.

**No. 28.** The next in order of the secondary color is green, which being composed of a due mixture of yellow and blue, is the peculiar symbol of the first section of the Fellow Craft or the sustaining faculties, and signifies hope; being composed of three of yellow and seven of blue, its power is ten, which signifies remains, or all those tender emotions of affectional truth which are implanted in the will, by the caresses and instructions of parents and friends, during childhood and youth, from the time of birth until the age of ten ; from that until twelve, is a transition state; from the age of twelve until eighteen, the hereditary principles of the parents come forth, modified by the scholastic education, during which time the remains of childhood seem to be lost , being concealed by the delights and exuberance of the animal spirits. From the age of eighteen to twenty-one is a transition state from the perceptive to the rational mind, the law establishing the age of twenty-one as the period of rationality. When man becomes free, all liberty being predicated of the rational principle, the rational man is said to be free born, of lawful age, and under the tongue of a good report. It is the exercise of the rational faculties alone that constitutes liberty, although it is derived from love, for man is only at liberty to do that which is right, and not the wrong. And all men who are not rational are either slaves to their own passions or to others, and we restrain them by locking them up, and placing them under keepers, that they may do no harm to society ; hence, all punishment should be of love and not of vengeance. The tender emotions of affectional truth, insinuated into the mind of childhood, are the grounds into which all the laws of divine order (which are received from the influxes of good), take root and grow into justice and judgment, in the rational mind. These are stored up in the sustaining faculties in the central position of the head and are designated by green, which is a peculiar emblem of vegetative life, and signifies hope ; or as the summer approaches, we look for the fall, with its rich harvest of plenty. The sustaining faculties give a love for the beauty, science

and philosophy of mechanics; and when combined with the reflective faculties, balanced by the
scarlet and russet, are the great foundation of the
scientific mind, which proceeds from the hereditary
principles of the parents and the affections implanted in youth. The child until ten years of age,
should imbibe all the emotional feelings of the
mother. From twelve to eighteen the instruction
of the father. Hence, the great mistake that is
frequently made in placing the tender child under
severe scholastic education. Let all of his instruction before the age of ten, be from his mother,
sister, or female friends. From the age of twelve,
let the son be placed under the care of his father,
and subjected to the discipline of the male teacher.
The mother corresponds to the church, and the
father to the lodge. As the discipline of the
scholastic education directs and modifies the hereditary principle, so the lectures of Masonry, modify
and direct the formation of the tender rational
faculties by implanting the truths of faith in the
memory, next in the understanding, and lastly in
the will, which constitute the Master Mason ; and
are the first three days of spiritual creation of man.
Then he is required to perform three distinct days
of the labor of charity, in the several degrees

which embrace six days of Masonic creation. After this, all labor becomes a matter of delight, and hence of rest; which is called the Sabbath of repose, in which God rested from all his labors. The ten principles of remains, in their most interior celestial principles, ascend inwardly and are adjoined to the celestial degree in the dignifying faculties. See No. 23.

*Of the Purple.*

No. 29. The purple or the social faculties, are the last of the secondary powers of the mind, and are representative of the kingly office. The purple is only produced by the negative system of light. See No. 17. It is composed of seven of blue, and five of red. Therefore its combined power is twelve; which signifies, the conjunction of every principle of faith with its appropriate love. Hence it signifies the fulness of faith. It is a representative of divine favor, and he, that is dressed in purple, mentally and spiritually, has favor at the hands of the Lord. It has, threfore, in all ages of the world, been a representative of royalty. And among most of the ancient nations of the world, the royal purple could be worn only by those connected with the throne. It was the color of one of the veils of the tabernacle, erected by our ancient brethren, and is the peculiar emblem of cryptic Masonry, and the intermediate degrees; and also signifies union; it is the bond of all the principles in Masonry from the entered apprentice to the most sublime degree of Royal Arch. Hence, it includes all things of use and devotion, representing the domestic. and devotional faculties conjoined. Every affection of the purple relates to use and devotion. Therefore, it gives the good of wisdom and its power of thought; all the affections are opened, and brought forth into usefulness, by the light of the understanding. As well might a man work in the dark, as for the affections to do any thing without the light of the understanding, and yet the affections themselves are prepared in the cryptic foundations. Although the affections are first in creation, they are last to assume control in the orderly regeneration of the man. Hence, there are six states of ascending regeneration of the intellectual or spiritual man; and six states of descending regeneration of the celestial man; in which are brought forth all the perceptions of divine order implanted in the will principle of man. For these reasons, there are two accounts given of the creation in Genesis. One representing the spiritual, the other, celestial regeneration. The first six days of creation in

Masonry, terminate with the Most Excellent Master's degree, extending through the subordinate lodges. The second state or celestial regeneration, culminates with the most sublime degree of Royal Arch Masonry, in which man is admitted into the presence of his Creator ; having passed the white veil, all his perceptions descend from the divine mind. The new temple being erected as emblematical of celestial regeneration.

Thus, the spiritual and celestial, constitute twelve distinct states of regeneration, represented by the number twelve, which represents the combining power of the purple and signifies the twelve states of progression, which we will now enumerate. The three first degrees of Masonry, represent first, the implantation of truth, in the memory ; secondly, in the understanding or scientific principle, and lastly it is implanted in the affections, when faith comes into the will and a life of charity. These states are also represented by the three first sons of Jacob, Reuben, Simeon and Levi. Then follow three days of labor in the three several degrees of the intermediate lodges; which are the works of charity, confirmatory of the truths inculcated in the Master's Lodge. The **fourth state represents the external doctrine of the**

Word. · The fifth state the conjunction of works with doctrine. The sixth state represents the divine marriage of the affections with truths, which is represented by the blue in the purple, which signifies the fecundating principle of the Lord, or the conjugial principle in man from which arise all the relations of friendship and charity.

The three preceding states are represented by Judah, Issachar and Zebulon, which are all the sons of Leah. The descending states of celestial regeneration, are those by which these principles come forth into tangible· perceptions and life, which is the love of the Lord working in man. His first work derived from divine love, is a holy faith, which constitutes the seventh state or day. The eighth state, is a day of temptation and trial, in which man overcomes, and is admitted into the presence of the Grand Council, and assigned a place for the reward of his labor. The next or ninth state, is a state of increase or faith by works, signified by Gad or multitude. The tenth state, is a state of mutual love, in which a man, loves his neighbor better than himself, and becomes the servant of all; which must take place in man, before the divine can be manifested, which is represented by Joseph and Benjamin. The eleventh state is represented by Benjamin, which is the intellectual or spiritual opening of celestial love, represented by the scarlet in the understanding. The twelth state is represented by Joseph, which, in a supreme sense, represent the Lord as to his divine spiritual nature, also the divine good of faith. Externally, salvation is signified, and multiplication as the stars of Heaven.

These last are the sons of Rachel and the hand maids. These things are also signified by the twelve precious stones set in the breast plate of Aaron; by which the high priest, when he had progressed in an orderly manner of regeneration, to the state of high priesthood, had communication, by Urim and Thumim, with the divine mind, which was by the opening of the scarlet or devotional faculties. See devotional faculties No. 23. The twelve state of regeneration and principles of faith and love, are represented also by the twelve apostles.

It will here be observed, that the coloring of the head fig. 1, pl. 1, represents the orderly or full states of regeneration, as well as the separate degrees of Masonry. These colors and faculties of the human mind have been perverted in man, so that his passions must first be subdued. The old man must die, as the new man is created. This is re-presented by the wars of the Holy Land, in driving out the Canaanites, the Perrizites and the Jebusites. The perverted state of the faculties will be treated of when we come to speak of temptation. The lecturers upon the science of the mind are under the necessity of taking man as they find him, in his depraved or unregenerate condition, which is represented in Masonry as a state of darkness, which will not be treated of.

We have simply in the foregoing illustrations of the intellectual and corporeal formations of the man, given such physiological facts and statements as serve to show and illustrate that man, as to his physical and mental condition, is an exact form and receptacle of Masonry.

Thus Masonry is the key stone of the Royal Arch that completes the *sanctum sanctorum*, or holy of holies in man, in which he is dedicated unto the Lord; as the divine work of the temple, not made with hands, but eternal in the heavens, standing before the Lord an angel of light and love. The purple is the emblem of the Royal Master's as well as the Most Excellent degree, No. 34.

No. 30. It has been shown in Nos. 22, 32, 24,

that there are three orders of intellect, that in which the yellow prevails, is called the natural, that in which the scarlet, is called the celestial, that in which the celestial love of truth prevails and which is represented by the blue, is called the spiritual. Hence, the blue represents the first light of creation as well as the other significations. See Nos. 22, 18. The secondary colors that have been treated of, are all compound colors which will be readily understood; if we consider that each color maintains its full force and power in the combination, and that the combination itself acts with the full force of each, which is represented by its compound number. The tertiary colors which we are now to treat of, have all the combined force of the secondary powers of which they are composed. They are a third formation which will require explanation. A truth when it is combined with its appropriate love, produces actions or works. These actions or works from their relation to use, are sometimes called uses and goods, therefore, frequently we say, the good of love and the good of faith; which simply means that it is the work or fruit of faith or love. From these works arise experience and confirmation, from this experience and confirmation again arise a third order of intelligence, wisdom and works, which prepare the man for greater and higher uses, or rather a broader field of thought and affection, or in other words, the man extends his life to a greater variety of uses on the natural and spiritual planes.

## Of the Russet.

No. 31. The next in order is the russet, which represents the semi-intellectual faculties, which are located in the centre of the head, holding the medium between the rational and social faculties; and as the orange and the purple combine to produce the russet, so these faculties conjoin in the semi-intellectual, giving a rational power from the social condition of man. Hence, the semi-intellectual faculties are the source of all true judgment derived from conscience. The powers of the devotional, perceptive and conjugial states of the red, yellow and blue combine giving the power of justice and judgment. These faculties are receptive of the devotional, perceptive, rational, sustaining, sympathetic, dignifying and social faculties. Hence, they combine the widest range of feeling and thought, it is here that the active powers of conscience or the spiritual man resides; as the inferior central lobes of the brain are the seat of physicial actions, so the semi intellectual organs are the active seat of mental motion. Here is built the great metropolitan city of the spiritual man, with its workshops, storehouses and temples, which are all illuminated by the great central sun of the divine mind, through the domestic, devotional and perceptive faculties of the man. It is here that the great circuit of animal forces spoken of in No. 5, 6, 7, 8, receives its vitalizing influence from the spiritual powers. The combining powers of the russet are twenty, which is a multiple of ten by two, which signifies the conjunction of all things of faith with remains, which gives conclusion and power of judgment.

11                                    F

## Of the Citron.

No. 32. The tertiary color of the citron or sympathetic faculties, represents the wisdom principle of the celestial man. Its great office is the adaptation of means to ends; it enables man to discover at once the correct starting point, to ask the proper question and to proceed logically step by step, in the unfolding of truth. It is contrasted by the olive, in the back ground, with the cutting shade of the russet, in the drawing and painting of the human head, with its delicate tint of gray softening and blending the whole. Being composed of a due mixture of orange and green, its combining power is eighteen; this being a multiple of nine by two, signifies a marriage or conjunction of all things of the nine degrees. The citron represents the Select Master's degree No. 34, it gives that peculiar perception and intuitive knowledge of character, which belong to the celestial degree of the mind, enabling the celestial man at once to arrive at a just conclusion without seeming to use the lower faculties of external perception and rationality; and as the green and orange unite to form the citron, so the experience of man derived from action and life, unite with the rational powers to form the sympathetic mind. Here, all the affections of use derived from the feeling of true dignity, the laws of divine order, from devotion and the sustaining faculties, combine with the rational, and unite in a crowning perception of use.

## *Of the Olive.*

No. 33. The last of the tertiary orders is the olive, being composed of a due mixture of green and purple. It signifies good will, brotherly love, charity and kindness. It covers as a cloak, the faults of all; and no spirit or man is permitted to see the faults of one who is clothed mentally and spiritually in olive. It harmonizes and contrasts with all other colors. Attracting nothing to itself, like true humanity, it shows to the best advantage the virtues of others. Its combined power is twenty-two, or the addition of ten and twelve, which signifies that it is the offspring of the twelve principles of faith, and the ten principles of charity, upon which are the ten blessings. See Nos. 134 to 144. Blessed are the poor in spirit: for theirs is the kingdom of heaven.

Blessed are they that mourn : for they shall be comforted.

Blessed are the meek: for they shall inherit the earth.

Blessed are they which do hunger and thirst after righteousness: for they shall be filled.

Blessed are the merciful: for they shall obtain mercy.

Blessed are the pure in heart: for they shall see God.

Blessed are the peace- makers: for they shall be called the children of God.

Blessed are they which are persecuted for righteousness sake: for theirs is the kingdom of heaven.

Blessed are ye, when man shall revile you, and persecute you, and shall say all manner of evil against you falsely for my sake.

Rejoice and be exceeding glad: for great is your reward in heaven: for so persecuted they the prophets which were before you. Mat. 5th, 2d, to the 12th inclusive.

The olive represents the character of the Royal Master's degree. The purple and the olive will be further treated when we come to speak of cryptic Masonry. The ten principles of charity will be gradually unfolded as we proceed in the various degrees until we arrive at their fulness of development in cryptic Masonry. They are all that adorn the human character and give true dignity to man. The dignifying faculties of the unregenerate man are perverted and selfish, and lead to all that is false and corrupt, but as they are restored by regeneration, they become the receptacles of a celestial life. As the three primary colors rise and culminate in the olive, so virtue and intelligence become the ruling principles of the celestial life, from which arises all true dignity. The Lord never permits virtue and intelligence to go unrewarded. There is a dignity for every one that fills his station well, from the lowest Entered Apprentice, in the North-east corner of the Lodge, to the Arch Angel of a sun sphere who intermediately from the Lord holds the destinies of unnumbered millions of human beings in his own person, and presides over worlds through his court. Although his intelligence is so great that he personally knows and comprehends the exact state of every individual under his charge, yet he has but a faint idea of the grandeur and dignity that are contained in the divine idea of the ten principles of charity, as they exist in the divine mind.

True dignity arises from great purposes of life,

which are brought forth in uses. They dignify the man according to the quality and quantity of the uses performed. When the feeling of greatness rises above the uses, it is called self-esteem which has all the air and style of true dignity without its purposes and uses. This becomes offensive in the business relations of life, the great ends and purposes of life having dwindled into the dignity of small things and general faultfinding with the minutiæ of operations.

# DISCRETE DEGREES OF MASONRY.

No. 34. There are three fundamental degrees in Masonry, to which all the others refer. These are the Entered Apprentice, Master's and Royal Arch Degrees. The Entered Apprentice Degree is altogether instructive, initiating the candidate into the motives of Masonry, and the nature of the Lodge. The Fellow-Craft's Degree is a continuation and elevation of the Entered-Apprentice Degree, into the middle chamber of the understanding, where the seven liberal arts and sciences are unfolded, the five orders of architecture, the support of the Fellow-Craft, and the knowledge of Deity. The Master's Degree introduces these knowledges and sciences into the *sanctum sanctorum*, or holy of holies, which is that divine order of use stamped upon the fecundating principle represented by the cerebellum or blue. These knowledges and sciences adjoin themselves to the heavenly order of the will, which governs the body in its

development and growth. Coming forth again
into the chambers of the' understanding and perception, they give the intellect that peculiar power
of adaptation of means to ends, known as heavenly
wisdom, of which our most ancient Grand Master,
King Solomon, stands as a living monument and
type, pre-eminent in the world, as declared by God
unto Solomon, in the Second Book of Chronicles,
Chap. 1, Verse 12th. Wherein the Lord declares,
that "Wisdom and knowledge *is* granted unto
thee; and I will give thee riches and wealth, and
honor. such as none of the kings have had that
have been before thee, neither shall there any after
thee have the like." This wisdom is the peculiar
governing power of the Master Mason. It sinks
its roots deep in the earth, and lays hold of every
principle of knowledge and science, and, like the
mighty oak, withstands the frosts of adversity and
the storm of passion. It supports the feeble, and
shelters the needy. It attends the bed side of the
sick and dying. It visits the widow and orphan in
their affliction, clothes the naked and feeds the
hungry. It presides in the halls of legislation, and
executes the laws with justice and judgment. It
is in this degree that natural truth, or the widow's
son, true to the affection of good, is elevated into

the divine light of heavenly charity, and life and immortality are brought to light in fellowship and love.

The Royal Arch Degree, or the scarlet, represents celestial love of use, or that peculiar order of heavenly motives or ends which are stamped upon the devotional faculties of man. The truths of the Word, in a heavenly life of charity, inculcated in the Master's Lodge, can only be elevated, or introduced into the *sanctum sanctorum*, to the presence of the Grand Council, through a state of humiliation, trial and temptation, known to those alone who seek to pass the white veil of the sanctuary with the signet of truth, and which none can do unless they are Most Excellent Masters indeed.

The Royal Arch Degree opens the seventh state of regeneration in man. See the twelve states spoken of, in No. 29. It represents the top round of the ladder which Jacob, in his vision, saw extending from earth to heaven, whereon the angels ascended and descended to the earth; the order of regeneration being first ascending and then descending; man being first instructed by the truths of the Word, which he conjoins with divine order, or the loves and affections implanted in his will by the Lord, through the remains of good and truth in infancy.

He thus becomes a divine spiritual man or Master Mason.

All the laws of divine order, proper to man, being confirmed, man becomes a receptacle of the divine life, in the likeness and image of God. He then dispenses good will, brotherly love and affection, directly from the Lord as a Royal Arch Mason. He is a messenger of truth, and harbinger of peace. There always shines in the chambers of his understanding the divine sun of illumination, which is no less than the Divine Mind flowing forth from the shekina of the will, in which the Lord has quickened every principle of divine order proper to man. The arch of the covenant is now opened, and the Word of God shines forth, enlightening the whole man. The pot of manna feeds him with the bread of eternal life; and the rod of Aaron, which budded and blossomed in a single day, becomes his power of thought and perception. Thus it is, that the degree of Entered Apprentice, the sublime degree of Master Mason, and the most sublime degree of Royal Arch, form the three primary degrees, represented by the yellow, the blue and the red; to which all the other degrees refer, and which are represented by the secondary and tertiary colors. These signify further ultimations of affections and truths, and represent the Mark Master, Past Masters Most Excellent Master, Royal and Select Master Degrees, which are ultimations and degrees of wisdom, referring to the three primitive degrees. See the combining colors. Nos. 26, 27, 28, 29, 30, 31, 32, 33. To the Royal and Select Masters is committed the great work of laying the foundation of the temple. These are, in Masonry, what Abraham and Isaac where to the Jewish nation. They are the fathers of their race. They prepare, in a secret vault, a spiritual and rational principle, which comes forth in the opening of the degrees by regeneration. The understanding of these degrees unlocks the casket of Masonry. They will be treated of, after some explanation has been given of the formation of man, and his growth from interior love. They are first, and yet last.

# DEGREES OF ANCIENT MASONRY.

No. 35. The fulness of all things appertaining to the human and divine affections, is represented by the number ten. Therefore, there are ten degrees in Ancient Masonry, nine of which are conferred in the Lodge, Chapter and Council. The degree of High Priesthood, which constitutes the tenth, is the fulness of Ancient Masonry, and can only be conferred upon those who have been regularly elected and have presided over subordinate Chapters.

The ten degrees, namely, the Entered Apprentice, Fellow Craft, Master Mason, Mark Master, Past Master, Most Excellent Master, Royal Arch, the Royal and Select Master, and the degrees of High Priesthood, have existed from the time of the building of the second Temple until the present day, unchanged and unaltered in spirit, although the Fellow Craft's degree has been separated and made into two degrees, namely, the Fellow Craft's and Mark Master's. The Past Master and Most

Excellent Master's degrees have at times in the history of Masonry, been conferred as side degrees or Honorary degrees, upon persons of distinguished merit, and at other times and places, have been entirely neglected, and the Royal and Select Master's degree have at times been conferred as Side degrees to the Royal Arch. Notwithstanding, these degrees in spirit, have had their existence and acknowledgment from the most ancient times of Masonry, although the jurisdiction of Masonry has been altered and changed in various countries, and other degrees have been added to these jurisdictions, of a spurious character, and at other times, only the four degrees of Entered Apprentice, Fellow Craft, Master and Royal Arch have been included in others ; but in the United States of America, the nine degrees of Ancient Masonry have been arranged in three distinct jurisdictions, the Grand Lodge retaining the jurisdiction over the first three degrees of Masonry, the Grand Chapter exercising authority over the Mark Master, Past Master, Most Excellent Master, and the most sublime degrees of the Royal Arch and the Grand Council, controlling the Royal and Select degrees.

An endeavor has been made, within the last few years, to introduce a new and spurious degree,

called the Super-Excellent Master, into the jurisdiction of the Grand Council.

There is a natural distinction existing in the very
nature of Masonry, in the order in which the degrees are divided in the United States; but the
separate and distinct jurisdictions are inconsistent
with the representative spirit and genious of the
institution. The laws of divine order require that
the nine degrees of Ancient Masonry should be
brought under one combined jurisdiction as to their
presiding officers, but with different Legislative
bodies. As well might we think of dividing the
faculties of the human mind and giving each a
separate and distinct control of its own affairs as to
discretely divide the jurisdiction of Masonry in its
officers. Heaven is one in general, but divided
into three distinct degrees or kingdoms, namely,
the natural, spiritual and celestial, each of which is
again divided into an innermost, a middle and exterior degrees, which make three, and three times
three. But, there is but one Lord over all, one
Grand Master who holds the jurisdiction over all,
the divine order requiring that the heavenly influxes should descend from the Lord through the
celestial to the spiritual, and from the spiritual to
the natural. It would be just as reasonable to

divide the jurisdiction of the heavens, giving one
to the Father, another to the Son, and lastly one to
the Holy Spirit, (these attributes being distinctly
one God), as it would be to divide the jurisdiction
of Masonry, giving one to the Royal Arch, one to
the Grand Council and another to the Grand Lodge,
with different presiding officers, although these are
natural divisions in themselves, yet they should be
presided over by one Grand Master, for Masonry
is representive of the heavens and the divine attributes. We cannot therefore speak of the parallelism that exists between Masonry and the heavens,
understandingly without bringing back the mind
to the primitive order of Masonry.

# Cryptic Masonry.

## Plate 2.

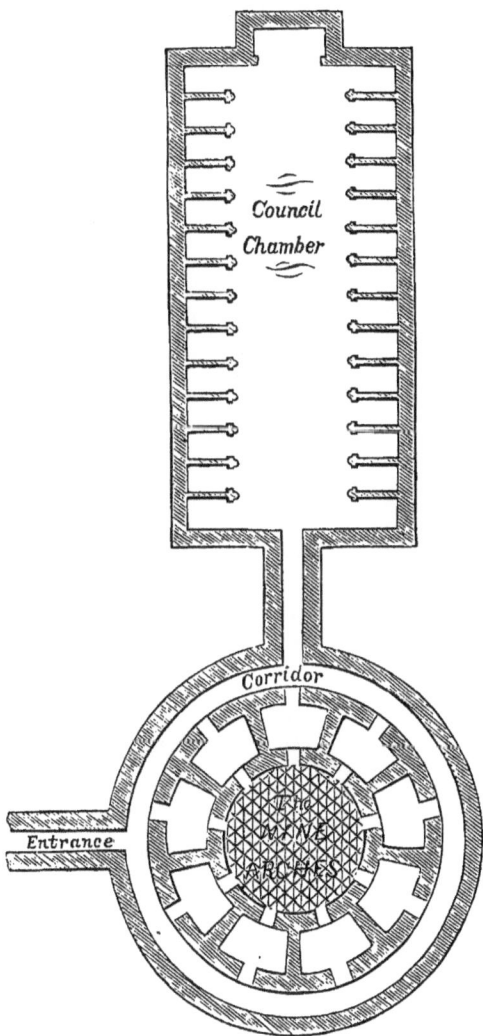

Fig. 2.

Fig. 1.

# CRYPTIC DEGREES.

No. 36. "The last shall be first, and the first last," is a principle taught in Masonry, yet it is but little understood. If the degrees of Masonry are representative of the regenerate condition of the nine groups of the human faculties, and the opening of those degrees representative of the work of regeneration, it must be evident to every reflecting mind that the Lord descends, by some mysterious way, into the interior of man, and prepares the rational principle for the reception of the truths of the Word. The mind is also prompted to these considerations by all the natural operations of life. If we wish to erect a building, we first prepare the plans, examine the ground, dig deep, and lay the foundations. Or if we wish to raise a crop, we first prepare the ground and sow the seed. These are operations important to the great end which like a germ in the matrix, lay concealed until brought forth and made manifest, by the erection of the building or the growth of the grain. So it is with the regenerate spirit of man. It is first procreated of the Lord, and is concealed in the womb, until brought forth by the new birth. This operation is represented in Cryptic Masonry, which is first in reality but last in manifestation.

No. 37. God is called Light and also Love. 1, John, 1. 5, 4, 8. Both are relatively true. For if we take a rational view of the operations of the divine mind, as we find it manifested in the works of nature, we shall see that all things of the earth proceed from the sun through light and heat, which correspond to mental light and love. We therefore conclude, that the Divine Mind, in its creative sphere shines forth as a mighty central sun, pervading the universe with its thought-rays of wisdom and love, which combine in a universal sphere of Divine Procedure, corresponding to the red, yellow and blue of our natural light. In surveying nature, the mind is also forced to the conclusion that the light and heat of the Divine Mind is the only life principle of the universe, not by continuity but by discrete degrees, as end, cause and effect.

In nature, the atmospheres decompose the light, setting at liberty its heat and electricity, which chemically combine with every change of the elements. It is reasonable therefore to suppose that a similar combination takes place between the divine light and the spiritual elements of mind. We cannot resist the idea that natural light, heat, and electricity are organized substances, subject to fixed laws. We therefore can see no reason why they should not enter into the elemental formations of natural substances, and become subject to to the laws of gravitation. Such being the case, we have no difficulty in conceiving that, at one time, all the solid substances of the earth were in the states of light and heat, and proceeding from the sun as such. If so, the reverse of the proposition is equally true that all substances of the earth are but changes of states induced on light and heat. Continuing the parallel between the natural and spiritual worlds, we are forced to conclude that the thought substances of the Divine Mind, by decomposition and *discretions*, may become the mental substances of the human mind. This being the case, those unacquainted with the laws of discrete degrees, will jump to the conclusion that men are gods. Such cannot be the case, for all progression of creation proceeds in an onward course, through discrete degrees, and, therefore, man can

never return to the state of the thought-subtances
of the Divine Mind.   But the Divine Mind must
be ever present, working and producing the changes
of state in all created things.   Thus all the substances of the spiritual world and every molecule
of our natural world must be in direct contact with
the thought substances of the Divine Mind.  Hence,
the omnipresence of the Divine and its Providen-
tial care over all things.   In this manner, the
Lord is ever present in the nine chambers of the
will, preparing them for their final opening into
the light of wisdom ; so that the decomposed substances of the degrees of the mind may again be
recombined in a new creation, in his likeness and
image.   These operations are entirely unperceived
by man, and remain so until the final opening of
the degrees by the Grand Master.

The law of man's creation is first through the
natural and afterwards through the spiritual, and
hence the nine chambers of the will must be prepared as natural receptacles of wordly loves.  The
death of these loves, one by one, must take place
before they can be supplied by spiritual loves, and
*vice versa.*   The natural loves of the world cannot
take the place of the spiritual, except by the death
of the former.   These are beautifully represented in

Cryptic Masonry. When love is found sleeping, it is sure to be supplanted by an intruder. The Lord provides for the introduction of heavenly love during sleep. The natural love is first laid asleep and made inactive, frequently by sickness and adversity; so long as the natural love remains active and watchful, no heavenly love can find admittance into the nine arches. Hence, adversity, sickness, the loss of friends and of property, are frequently the means of our salvation and even drunkenness is made use of to destroy the spiritual pride that prevents all usefulness in the spiritual world. The Lord is ever watchful, leading the blind by a way that they know not, making the crooked straight, and darkness light  By the nine arches of the brain, we mean the nine groups of faculties represented in plate 1, fig. 1, and treated of in the combining powers of the colors. See No. 20 to 33 inclusive. These are duplicated on the right and left sides of the head around a common centre.

The council chamber represents the commissures of the brain where each degree or arch on either side of the head meet by three fibres from each, making twenty-seven. These are the channels of the will by which the affections flow together and freely communicate with each other. This chamber when representatively seen by the Prophets would appear as represented in pl. 2. fig. 2, it was therefore constructed under the temple by King Solomon.

No. 38. The nine degrees of the brain are each receptive of the will principle; but the discrete powers of the will are three, residing in the cerebellum, the perceptive and the devotional faculties. These are distributed and blend in the continuous degrees, there are therefore nine chambers of the will in both hemispheres of the brain, in which, each of the powers of the discrete degrees reside. These are represented in Cryptic Masonry by nine arches, in each of which there are three workmen. In each discrete degree of the brain, there are three distinct fibres or tubules by which the forces and powers of the affectional fluids are collected and concentrated in the general commissures, which are represented in Cryptic Masonry by the council chamber, wherein there are twenty-seven departments. There descend into the three discrete degrees, in the right and left hemispheres of the brain, three rays of spiritual light and heat, represented by the red, yellow and blue. These again recombine in the continuous degrees represented by the

nine colors of the positive and negative spectrums.
The blue ray contains the fecundating principle
and the laws of natural order.   The red ray contains the devotional principle and the laws of divine
order.   The yellow ray contains the power of perception and individuality.   These are concentrated
in the twenty-seven commissures of the brain, and
descend in sleep to the three, six, nine and twenty-
seven tissues of the body.   Whence they return
to the chambers of the brain, having taken upon
themselves the spiritual form of the body.   They
descend to the nine lobules of the testus where
they are combined with the seminal fluids which
are abstracted from every part of the human form.
The spiritual forces and powers now take upon
themselves the form of the human brain ; nine
globules of spiritual substance are formed around
a central globule.   These are duplicated in the
right and left hemispheres of the brain, and now
descend to the mother, and are absorbed by the
ovum, which contains a supply of all the natural
substances, requisite for the putting forth of the
human form, serving as a matrix for the spiritual
principle of the father and the form principle of
the seminal fluids. These take form and commence
their growth in the womb, being constantly sup-

plied by the blood of the mother, and nurtured and cherished by her spirit, and supplied with an exterior intellectual principle, which comes forth in childhood ; but is put off in regeneration. Sinking inward, it remains inactive until the final opening of the intellectual principle of the father, when it is brought forth as the capstone, with shouting and praise. The intellectual principle of the mother, in Masonic language, is called the Widow's Son.

Thus it is, that the spirit of every one is from the father, derived from the Lord, through the substance of the spiritual world. The body being derived from the mother, through the natural substances of the blood.

The three discrete and six continuous degrees of the mind, descend into all the uses of the human form. Therefore the form of the body in all of its groupings, consists of series of three, six, nine and twenty-seven, as illustrated in Arts. 5, 6, 7, 8. Thus it is that Cryptic Masonry represents, in particular, the formation of the new birth.

No. 39. If the divine light were to flow into the disordered state of the mind of man, he would be immediately destroyed. Hence, the divine light is graduated by the heavens and the world of spirits, and even by surrounding minds of earth. Thus the divine influxes of light and heat are decomposed, recombined and graduated as food for the infant. Therefore the tender child is surrounded by the Celestial Angels. " I say unto you, that their angels in heaven do always behold the face of my Father which is in Heaven." Mat. 18th 10th. The child not only being surrounded by angels, but by tender friends who constantly caress, nurture and cherish it, the tender affections of the heavens and earth, both flow in, and are arranged in the interiors, while the infant is in a state of innocence and ignorance. See No. 48. These affections are interior and external, the external are by the perceptive faculties and are called remains ; they are constantly being stored up in the nine arches of the will, prepared and arranged for future use, and from the perceptive planes of the degrees of Masonry.

In the central or interior arch of the brain, there stands a pedestal, supporting the Arch of the covenant, which is the law of divine order, deposited there by the Lord, sealed up and overlaid with gold. Upon the top and sides, are mysterious hieroglyphics that can only be interpreted by the Grand Council, when brought forth after trial and temptation, by the Most Excellent Masters.

The divine influxes, working in the chambers of the will, first establish there the law of divine order, by the marriage of divine goods with the affections of divine truth, which beget an interior rational principle, the good of which is conjoined to the affection of interior truth, the offspring of which is natural good and truth. These are brethren, and reside in the right and left lobes of the brain, and are spoken of in the 133d Psalm, where it is said, "how good and how pleasant it is for brethren to dwell together in unity."

Natural truth resides in the left lobe of the brain, and natural good in the right, which is the power of the will. Without these two principles there can be no reflective thought. The will throws forth the thought fluids from the posterior portion of the brain into the left frontal lobe, which acts as a reflector, bringing forth the order which the fluids have received in the will principles. These thought forms being reflected into the right lobe of the brain, are absorbed, felt and sensed, which is the peculiar perception of reflective thought. Thus is constituted the rational mind, represented by the Council Chamber. See pl. 2, fig. 2. Fig. 1st representing the nine arches of the will heretofore described. The tenth or central arch being the combined power of the nine, the outer corridor representing their continuous degree. See No. 78.

Thus the Royal and Select Master's Degrees, represent the divine operations of the Lord, brought forth into natural good and truth, which are the foundation of the natural mind, and the receptive planes of the natural and spiritual degrees, represented by the blue Lodge, and the Chapter Degrees, the celestial being represented by the Royal and Select Masters, which are the first in reality, working in the nine arches or the crypts of the human mind. Unperceived, they continue their work at the dead hour of night, when the intellect is asleep. Thus all the thought material of the day is conjoined with the affections at night, and built into the chambers of the will and understanding, which form the receptacles of natural good and truth, which are again to be opened and built into the beautiful structure of Ancient Craft Masonry and the Chapter Degrees, when the interior principles of celestial love and truth, which are first manifest in natural good and truth, sink inward and are lastly and finally opened and brought to light in the beautiful degrees of the Royal and Select Masters, represented by the citron and the olive.

These, in reality, are first, laying the foundations of Masonry, forming the receptive planes of true wisdom and rationality for all the degrees, in the character of modesty and virtue. They are last to come forth into life. They form the complete circle of Masonry, represented by the nine arches, without which, no mason is perfect. The natural loves and truths within the nine arches, are gradually dying; and as one is found sleeping, or in an unwatchful condition, arising from repentance, sickness or misfortune, a spiritual love or truth is substituted in its place; until, finally, the Royal Master's work in the arches is performed by the loves and truths of the celestial spiritual, and the Select Master's by the spiritual celestial.

The combined symbol of the Royal and Select Master is the purple, which is a continuous degree derived from the discrete loves of the Blue and Scarlet.

The entire circle being complete, all the lower degrees having being brought forth in states of regeneration, the degrees of Royal and Select Masters are finally brought forth, they being the alpha and omega, the beginning and the end. So the first has been last, and the last first.

Thus we have traced the natural foundation of

man in his body and mind, and have shown, as we think, conclusively, that man is a trinity of three discrete degrees, each of which has three continuous degrees, and, hence, they consist of three, and three times three. We have also shown that nature itself is a trinity, consisting of three discrete degrees with their continuous degrees, and lastly, we have shown that the light of the sun, from which all the substances of the earth are created, also, consists of nine degrees; three of which are primary; and that these degrees of light, in the human mind, form the receptive principle of the spirit of man, which is a growth and out-birth of the divine light and heat of the spiritual sun, i. e. the divine love and wisdom of the Lord himself, forming the only real life and substance of the spiritual world; that these life-substances are built into a spiritual temple not made with hands, eternal in the heavens; that this spiritual temple is built, while man is in the body, and that, hence, the degrees of Masonry are representative of the nine states of the erection of that building, of which the temple of Solomon is an exact representative and type, and so designed to be, by the Lord himself, who gave the plan of the building, with full and complete instruction for its erection through

13*

the prophet David in writing. See First Chronicles 28. 11, to the 19. This was completely understood by Solomon in the erection of the temple, and also by his counsellors, connected with him. We therefore, contend that Masonry is a divine institution, representing the regeneration of man, and that all the symbols of Masonry are also divine repsesentatives of things in regeneration. We think that we have most fully sustained these views by the known facts of science, through an analytical course of reasoning. We shall, therefore, in full confidence, assume the sympathetical, and descend from the Creator himself, by a course of reasoning explanatory of the foregoing, showing how creation descends, by series and degrees from the Divine Mind to the lowest ultimates of the regenerate mind.

# OF GOD.

No. 40. Rising as a bubble, and glittering in the sun for a moment on the mighty ocean of time, we ask " What is God ? " The answer returns: "The invisible things of him from the creation of the world are clearly seen, being understood by the things that are made, even his eternal power and Godhead ; so that they are without excuse." Romans 1, 20. In nature we not only behold the form, but the quality of Deity. All things exist as a unit, yet unfolding in a progressive order, in which there are thing highers and lower. And proceeding from the lowest ultimates of earth ; we rise in our contemplation to man, who is crowned by the highest principles in nature, namely, a Will and Understanding. These cannot be God, for they are limited in their power. We again arise above ourselves, and see with the clearness of the mind, an infinite will, and an infinite understanding, and that these are distinctly one being, in whom there reside all the laws of creation in a simultaneous and progressive order. And we ask ourselves, "is that being a principle, or is he a person?" We pause for a moment to consider the definitions of words, and then answer unhesitatingly; that He is a person, for He has no law common to any other being. If there be any solemn conclusion of the human mind that is entitled to respect, it is this, and without it, none others are valuable, for it would be an evidence of insanity of the mind, or incapability of reasoning. Therefore, no atheist can be made a Mason.

Assuming as an undisputed point, acknowledged in all ages of the world, and by every enlightened nation, that God is infinite in will and understanding, we use all the synonymous terms as expressive of these attributes. We say, that He is love, and that He is light. We say that He is omniscient, omnipresent and omnipotent. We say that He is infinite in goodness and wisdom. As Masons to express these attributes we use the symbol of the sun, which in a natural sense, is a representative, but in the spiritual, it is real. In the former, it is apparent, and in the latter actual. One is the sun of the natural world, the other is the sun of the mind. One is matter,

and the other spirit and life. By the natural
sun, all things of nature subsist, as to its dead
forms; but, by the spiritual sun of the divine
mind, all things live and move. It is this sun
that rises in the east to open and illuminate the
Lodge. Taking these principles for granted, we
have no difficulty in reasoning on the subject, by
supposing ourselves to have passed the outer veil
of this world, and to have entered the Grand
Lodge above, where the Grand Master presides
in all of our thoughts and affections.

# OF THE DIVINE ATTRIBUTES.

No. 41. In the divine creative mind, there are three discrete separate and distinct, uncreated, self-subsisting and self-existing degrees of will, understanding and action or existence. Each of these degrees are continuous, having a most interior, a middle and exterior continuous degrees. Thus, in Him, there are three and three times three. All things of the will, are called celestial, those of the understanding, spiritual. The things of action, or of exterior existence, are called natural. These correspond to the body, soul and spirit. The body is called natural; the understanding, spiritual, and the will or soul, celestial. Name signifies quality or attribute, and hence, when we name a person or thing, understandingly, we mean to express its quality or attributes. Hence, God, in the Holy Scriptures, is always called by a name expressive of one, or all of his attributes. He is called "I am," to express his self existence or action in the heavens. He is called "I am that I am," to express that He is both the life of all things in heaven and in earth. He is called God to signify spiritual or creative wisdom and power. He is called Jehovah to signify all his attributes, and in particular his celestial princi-ple. This term is holy, because it represents his holy principle of love. This name is never pro-nounced by the profane, nor mentioned in con-nection with any profanity. The interior of man revolts at the idea, until he is entirely lost to shame. It is never pronounced by those of the true faith, except in a low breath, as it comes from the interior arches of the soul.

The degrees of Masonry correspond to the three discrete or primary degrees of the divine mind, with the continuous degrees. Hence, there are nine degrees in Ancient Masonry. The Entered Apprentice, Fellow Craft, and first section of the Master's degree represent the Natural degree of the divine mind. The will, understanding and ac-tion being present in each primary degree, it con-sists of three continous parts. The Entered Ap-prentice represents the divine Natural, the Fellow Craft's represents the divine spiritual natural, and the first section of the Master's degree represents the divine, celestial natural, principle, these are contained in the first or natural degree of the Divine Mind. The second section of the Master's, Mark Master, Past and Most Excellent Master, represent the continuous degrees contained in a primary degree of the divine spiritual. The Royal Arch and Royal Select Master's degrees represent the divine celestial principle. No man can be initiated into the quality or attributes of Diety by the spiritual or natural principles alone. Hence, the name of Jehovah cannot be conferred on the celestial of the natural principle, nor the natural of the spiritual which are represented by the Master Mason ; but a substitute is given that represents that there is good in the divine truth. Hence, the Master's Word is said to be lost, until future generations shall bring it forth. It appears to man as though he was being regenerated by truth ; yet, it is not truth that regenerates him, but love or the celestial principle does it. And hence, the name of Jehovah cannot be conferred on the natural or spiritual man. It can only be received by the celestial or love principle of the celestial degree. The name of God is conferred upon the Fellow Craft, because it represents his spiritual, natural principle, and can be received by all nations and people.

Christian Masons worship God under three names:
The Father, the Son and the Holy Spirit. These
are expressive of his attributes, representing his
manifestation in the work of regeneration, the
Father as the divine good, the Son as the divine
wisdom, the Holy Spirit as the divine and holy
procedure from the Father and the Son. These
are called one Lord. Lord signifying all the attributes, the same as Jehovah, that are manifested in
regeneration both in the heavens and earth. Hence,
the name Lord, is never used by man in connection with any profanity. Men swear by the name
of God, by Jesus Christ, but never by the name of
the Lord, until they are confirmed in evil, and
mean from the will to profane all that is holy. Our
ancient christian brethren received the name of
Father, Son and Holy Spirit as expressive of the
Godhead, which they held as being complete in
the person of Jesus Christ. "For in Him dwelleth
all the fulness of the Godhead bodily," Col. 2, 9.
Our Ancient Grand Master, St. John the Evangelist,
says, in speaking of the Son, that "In the beginning was the Word (or wisdom) and the Word was
with God, and the Word was God. The same was
in the beginning with God. All thing were made
by Him ; and without Him was not any thing made

14

that was made. In Him was life ; and the life was the light of men." John. 1. 2, 3, 4. "Philip saith unto Him, Lord show us the Father, and it sufficeth us. Jesus saith unto Him, have I been so long time with you, and yet hast thou not known me, Philip ? He that hath seen me, hath seen the Father ; and how sayest thou then, show us the Father ? Believest thou not that I am in the Father and the Father in me ?" John, 8. 9, 10. From these and many passages, it is certain that our Ancient Grand Master St. John, taught these doctrines in the Lodge and that they were received by our ancient brethren. The name of the attributes, Father, Son and Holy Spirit, are no where called persons in the Scriptures, and as such were never received by the apostles and early Christians. The term persons being first introduced into the Athnanasian creed which takes its name from Athansius, who lived three hundred and twenty-five years after the Christian era, but the creed was introduced about the 6th century, and then only as explanatory of the divine attributes. As the subject of the divine attributes, cannot be fully comprehended and understood by the unregenerate mind, the term person has given rise to much confusion in the church, relating to the doctrine of the trinity.

These subjects can never be fully understood until the celestial degree in man is opened, and the knowledge of the divine attributes of the Deity conferred over the triangular pavement, and under the living arch. Previous to this, the doctrine of the trinity is received by the mind as the mystery of mysteries. The love principle or the divine sensual order, will next claim our attention, (For all sensation is of love.)

No. 42. Order implies arrangement and progression of parts, as end, cause and effect. There is a kind of trinity in all things, as head, body and limbs, length, breadth and thickness. In all the works of art, where beauty is required, three distinct parts must appear in subordination, harmoniously blended and joined, so as to preserve the unity of the whole. Divine creative order requires that love should clothe itself with wisdom as a garment of light, acting through it as a creative sun of mind and also of matter, through three discrete and separate degrees. The first proceeding effect of the infinite will and understanding, is the outflowing of the divine love of use, or the divine creative good, which, with the angels of the celestial heavens, is perceived as the love of use, sometimes called the celestial love of good. This is the deep golden scarlet, treated of in No. 23. It contains all the laws of the divine will. The second proceeding of the Divine Mind, is from the wisdom principle clothing the first procedure with the celestial love of truth, which is the blue creative ray which appears by the decomposition of the divine light spoken of in No. 22. These constitute the will and understanding principle of the third and innermost heavens, where the angels dwell in the ineffable light of the divine countenance, always beholding the face of our Father who is in heaven as a divine sun. From its light and heat are all the laws of divine order, which are implanted in their nature equally to their several uses, as individuals. These constitute the Royal Select Master's, as far as they relate to the secret working of Providence through the celestial angels in preparing the human mind for the work of regeneration. See Nos. 36, 37, 38, 39.

From the foregoing, it will be perceived that, divine order proceeds from love, through truth. Therefore, the terms love and order have been used as synonymous in the preceding articles. These two loves, namely, the celestial love of use, and the celestial love of wisdom, represented by the blue and scarlet rays, combine in the purple, as representative of the Most Excellent Master's degree. See Nos. 22, 23, 32, 33. The deep golden scarlet is representative of the Royal Arch degree, which is the unfolding and opening of the celestial order of use. Thus these degrees, in their trinity, are significative, and symbolically represent the celestial heavens in their threefold order of uses, they being continuous, proceeding from the most interior, through the middle degree, to the ultimate power of the whole.

No. 43. As the light and heat of the divine mind descend through the celestial heaven, extending to the lowest ultimate bounds of the celestial degree, the red ray which has formed the interior, and has been set at liberty, (for the uses of the celestial heaven), with all of its expansive and repulsive powers, becomes diffused and localized, forming the magnetic aromal, and electric fluids of that world, which become condensed into the gaseous, liquid and solid forms of the celestial heavens. The red ray becomes cooled and locked within the blue and yellow, the expansive power being charged to the contractive. All the substances of that world, in this condition, undergo a kind of death, in which they descend below the controlling sphere of the celestial degree, and the white or yellow ray assumes the sway of empire, establishing its laws and order of wisdom. See what is said of the inhabitants of the Temperate and Torrid Zones, Nos. 18, 19.

The entire order of light, heat and color, is now changed. The proceeding of the divine mind has taken another step in its onward progression towards the ultimate creation of man. The deep golden scarlet has changed to the light. The pure white ray of the celestial heavens has assumed the silvery tones. The deep blue has changed to the azure. The rational principle has taken hold of the reins of thought, and guides the whole being by the power of reasoning derived from the loves of the celestial kingdom. The two kingdoms or degrees, thus formed, namely, the celestial and spiritual, act and react against each other, the celestial kingdom acting upon the spiritual, by a constant influx of affectional thought substances, and the spiritual kingdom reacting against the celestial, like the arterial blood against its valves. The substances of the celestial degree, having passed the bounds of its own kingdom become, changed, never more to return. The proceeding of the divine mind is now represented by the silver and azure rays of light. See correspondence, Nos.

22, 23, 24. The light scarlet represents the spiritual love of good, and the light blue, the spiritual love of truth. The marriage of the white and deep golden scarlet rays in the celestial degree, producing its offspring of deep blue. The marriage of the silver ray with the light scarlet of the spiritual degree, produces the azure. These three rays of light, in their decomposed condition, descend by their continuous degrees of three and three times three, in likeness of the divine rays of the spiritual sun into the magnetic and aromal fluids of the spiritual degree; becoming cool, localized in all the substances of the spiritual world, in their gaseous liquid and solid thought forms.

Thus, there have been two mental worlds, created in their full and complete series of degrees of affectional and rational substances, in likeness of the mineral, vegetable and animal kingdoms with infinite change and variety, the celestial kingdom, being the will or affectional degree, which corresponds to the Royal Arch, Royal and Select Master's degrees. The rational or spiritual degrees where reason or the intellect predominates, correspond to the last section of the Master and the Mark Master, Past Master, and Most Excellent

Master's degrees, which are governed and controlled by the celestial kingdom, or the will principle
of the mental world. Hence, they are made
subordinate to the Royal Arch. These two mental worlds or spheres, which have been thus created
from the infinite love and wisdom of the Creator,
constitute distinct mental worlds in themselves, and
are lighted by the divine mind, as a sun with different degrees of light and heat. These two worlds,
joined by marriage, descend by the blue into the
third or natural degree, with all their force, power
and energy. So that the last or ultimate degree
represented by the Entered Apprentice, Fellow
Craft, and first section of the Master's, becomes
the complex energy and power of the whole ; which
corresponds to the natural, rational and scientific
mind. The reader will bear in mind, that these
three mental worlds before the creation of the
world had no inhabitants, but were the direct offspring of the divine mind ; and that hence, all
their substances were life and vitality, and are just
as much organized thought substances, tangible to
the spirit, when created, as the natural substances
of this world are to the body. So that whatever
is perceived, as thought, in this natural world, is
sensibly felt, seen and handled by the spirit, so that

man, when he has departed from this life, if he becomes an angel, dwells in either one or the other of these three worlds, where all the substances are just as tangible to him as natural substances are in this life.

But these worlds, namely, the celestial, the spiritual and the natural, are utterly and totally incompetent to the creation or production of man ; and therefore would be entirely useless without the creation of our natural sun, and the natural earth upon which we live and are created. The creation of man first taking place in this world, the body being created from natural substances, wherein a spirit grows from spiritual substances as a germ in its matrix ; when the spirit is complete, it drops its mortal body and ascends to one or the other of the three worlds of mind, according to the various degrees received in this. The Master Mason ascends to the highest sphere of the third degree of the natural spiritual world and the first degree of the spiritual, holding a middle position between the two. He, in whom the Most Excellent Master's degree has been opened in this life, holds the upper degree of the middle or spiritual world in the next life. He, in whom the Royal and Select Master's degree have been opened in this world, dwells in the highest or the celestial heavens.

The next subject that claims our attention is the formation and creation of the natural world in which we live. The reader will bear in mind that the substances of the spirit are from the spheres just described ; but which cannot be formed into a living being without the aid of our natural creation, there being no bodily form into which they can be moulded, localized and personified without the aid of our natural creation. But when the spirit is once created by the aid of the natural world, it put off, in death, the natural, and assumes the spiritual.

The spiritual spheres descending from the Lord, through the divine sun, into the celestial, spiritual and natural heavens, in the form of the animal, vegetable and mineral kingdoms, are in themselves only archetype substances, but when they descend into the earth and are localized and ultimated in the growth and formation of the spirit, they become, through the spirit interwoven with the actual substances of the spirit world ; so that all spirits are their own world of substance, adjoining in spiritual societies and perfecting themselves in the most beautiful scenery of the heavens. And such is the case to a certain extent with all of the spiritual substances that have been employed in the growth of animal, vegetable, and mineral kingdoms of nature. They receive a further ultimation when in the natural sphere of the world so as to prepare them as receptacles for the life and thought principles of the spiritual world. Thus in all of the electric, magnetic and aromal spheres occupied by man in the spiritual, there is a further ultimation of these spheres derived from their office in the natural world ; but they do not take the absolute form of the natural, but are dissipated in the general spiritual spheres. Thus it is that the rose in the garden has had its use, and the blade of grass on the mountain side.

No. 44. The divine mind in its three degrees of wisdom, love and use, streams forth in effulgent beauty of divine light and heat, as the universal sun of mind, mirroring upon the atmospheres of the celestial world, in endless variety, the love substances of the human will in likeness of the animal creation. As these descend through all the substances of the celestial degree, and fall upon the atmospheres of the spiritual or middle heavens, they are seen by the spiritual angels as a living, moving and vitalized panorama of rational thought substances, in which is written, in hieroglyphic or correspondential language, the order of the divine mind. These again descend through the substances of the spiritual degree, falling upon the atmospheres of the lowest or natural degree, as living representatives in the forms of the mineral, vegetable and animal kingdoms, and are perceived in the minds of ·the natural angels, as the forms of natural science and use.

These spheres are what our Ancient Patron St. John saw and described in his revelations concerning the church. Such spheres are faintly mirrored upon the sleeping mind in dreams. In the waking condition they fall into the external, literal education of the mind ; and, are perceived as affections, and rational scientific thoughts. They constitute the order and vision principle mentioned in treating of the devotional faculties. See Nos. 23, 31, 32. This procedure of the divine mind is the creative sphere. The divine light being decomposed, prepared, electrified, localized and locked up ; the red ray of the light being enclosed in the yellow, and both surrounded by blue, the law of their existence is changed from the expansive to the contractive, by the recombination and marriage of the white and red rays of spiritual light. The affinity or love, that exists between these rays, in their combination and marriage, forms the first end of attraction or gravitation, producing the first molecule of natural substances. See No. 68. These are thrust and cast out, and forced by reaction beyond the laws of the spirit world. Each molecule being accompanied by particles of the spiritual atmospheres in three degrees, is directly under the control of divine Providence, and these molecules from the first end or substance of the natural creation, being brought together in innumerable sun spheres. These again, by the action of the divine mind, produce earth spheres, in which are implanted the mineral, aromal and electric spheres of the mineral, vegetable and animal creation. These world souls or spheres are surrounded with archetypal or electric atmospheres, which operate upon the light and heat of the natural sun, decomposing and separating it into its original molecules of three degrees, unlocking its internal fires, separating and cooling the blue ray, opening the continuous or ciectric degrees for the formation of our natural atmosphere, giving birth to the gaseous fluids, in their three and ninefold forms ; three of which are primary, the remainder, secondary and tertiary. These descending and combining again in an alitropical or ultimate condition, produce all the elements of the natural earth, stamped with the animal, vegetable and mineral affinities, and recombine in their gaseous, liquid and solid forms.

15                              H

Of about fifty-four elements, as far as yet been discovered by chemical science, about five or six are well-known; fifteen are very partially understood; the remainder of the fifty-four are but little known further than their simple existence and name, with a few of their qualities. A few of their combinations will serve to illustrate the connection of the gaseous, liquid and solid substances. The diffusion of oxygen and nitrogen produces the common atmosphere. Oxygen and hydrogen produce water. Nitrogen and hydrogen produce a volatile alkali. Carbon and hydrogen produce oil. The tertiary combination of these with mineral elements, enter largely into all the solid compounds of the earth. Many of the solid substances of the earth itself are liquid and gaseous, under different pressure and states of free caloric, and the various solid metals may be thrown into liquid and gaseous states by a sufficient elevation of temperature, or in the act of combining with other elements. When silver is decomposed with nitric acid, and precipitated with alcohol, and submitted to a slight elevation of temperature by friction, or otherwise, a combination of the elements takes place in which they rush into a gaseous state with the untold pressure of many hundreds of atmospheres.

Such is the case with many compositions, such as gun-powder and nitro-glycerine. These gases in their turn, under different compositions and pressures, again recombine, return to other solid and liquid forms. Thus we perceive that the base of the solid and liquid is the gaseous ; and that the base of the gaseous is the light, heat and electricity of the natural sun. And that the natural sun, with its ultimate forms and combinations, is an increment derived from the spiritual substances of the heavens, that the spiritual atmospheres attend every particle of natural light, so that the divine Providence is ever present through the great spiritual sun of the heavens, with every molecule of natural matter. The thought substances of the spiritual world, are woven into the spiritual body of man, while the natural substances of the body are derived from the earth, and can never flow backward through the discrete degree of the sun into spiritual substances ; the body is of the earth, earthy while the spirit is derived from mental substances, which are above our natural sun, derived from the great spiritual sun which surrounds the glory of the divine Being. Every thought and action of His, proceeds into the light, heat and electricity of love and wisdom, which form the first ends of spiritual creation, proceeding by three and three times three, in three successive orders, terminating in twenty-seven, and so on.

The natural creation proceeding from the light, heat and electricity consists of like series and degrees. These are positive and negative, acting and reacting against each other, combining and recombining, according to their affinities, which are expressed by colors. The natural elements in their molecules, proceed in the same order. Oxygen, Nitrogen, Hydrogen, and Carbon, are represented by the yellow, red, blue and purple colors. These four elements constitute the great bulk of the earth, and the animal, vegetable and mineral creations.

These, when decomposed by analysis, are the foundations of the kingdoms of nature. Further ultimations of these elements, in an alotropical condition, produce all the elements, like the further combinations of the three elementary colors in an endless variety of tints, hues, lights and shades.

# OF MAN.

No. 45. Man is not life in himself. The Lord is life and substance alone. Hence, man lives spiritually from the flesh and blood of the Lord, correspondentially, the natural body also lives from his flesh and blood. This is what is signified by the bread and wine in the Holy Communion. See what is taught by our Grand Master. St. John, the Evangelist, 6th chapter inclusive.

All substances of life proceed from the divine mind, which has been shown in Nos. 37, 38, 36. Man lives by the decomposition of these substances by which their life principles are set at liberty, and interwoven, fabricated and elaborated into the spirit of man, through the process of regeneration. The spirit is made into the likeness and form of the Lord, there being a corporeal likeness of uses in the forms and tissues of the body. Therefore its parts are arranged in a three, six and ninefold order. See No. 20. The brain is arranged into a series of nine arches. See No. 13, plate 1, fig. 1.

15*

The nine groups of organs contained in the brain, decompose the spiritual light, heat and electricity, that flow in through the spiritual world, from the divine attributes. Nos. 22, 23, 43, 44.

The nine groups of internal organs and viscera of the body, decompose the natural elements, and set at liberty their light, heat and electricity which have become subsidized and organized in the likeness of the three kingdoms of nature. The nine parts of the body are duplicated in the right and left sides, which are in likeness of the male and female principle in man, and as either of these principles prevails over the other, the person is male or female. These nine parts of the body, are groups of organs in themselves, arranged in the most complete harmony, agreeing with the organs of the brain, so that every force of the brain is conveyed to its corresponding organ in the body. Hence, arise all their peculiar motions, which are first established in the head. The whole body being connected, bound together and vivified by three systems, namely, the cellular, vascular and nervous systems, each seems to perfectly fill the entire man, so that if they could be separated, they would each present the complete form of the person. The lungs decompose the gaseous substances of the atmosphere. The heart, arterial system and blood decompose the magnetic pulsations, and set at liberty their vitality. The stomach and bowels decompose the food elements of the three kingdoms of nature ; setting at liberty their finer particles, their magnetic, aromal and electric fluids. These are all prepared and elaborated in the blood, the finer portions of which pass into the nervous system through the small capillaries of the brain and spinal cord. Being prepared for the finer portions of the human body or substances of the animal spirit, they are conveyed to the central portion of the brain, just above the ear, on each side of the head. The upper organs of the brain in their entire surface being glandular, act as the receptacles of the substances of the spiritual world, the right side receiving the will substances, the left side receiving the intellectual. The upper and lower portions of the brain are inverted to each other, being positive and negative, like the poles of a battery. The lower portion of the brain being a receptacle of the decomposed substances of the elemental world, through the medium of the body, and forming the substances of the animal spirit, is negative. The upper portion being positive by scintillation, like the pulses of the heart at intervals, the spiritual substances, from the upper portion of the brain, flow into the animal spirits, upon the right and left sides. The heart and the lungs are positive and negative to each other. The fluids thus united in the head, circulate in each side of the brain, and descending by induction to the heart and the lungs, cause their motion through their corresponding groups in the brain. The vital fluids of these organs returning to the cerebellum in the same manner, and pass forward by the fornix and floors of the lateral ventricles, and rising, pass backward by the corpus calosum, towards the posterior, being vitalized by the combined action of the right and left lobes of the brain, which are positive and negative to each other.

Thus, there is the likeness of three electric batteries in the brain; one on either side, between the upper and lower organs, and one at the centre, between the right and left lobes of the brain, and a third in the cerebellum. The central battery between the right and left lobes, must always be timed exactly with the motion of the heart or cerebellum. Should any disagreement arise, the whole arterial system would be thrown into confusion. In the excitement, the blood would be concentrated on various organs, if upon the brain, appoplexy would immediately follow. If the blood is concentrated upon other organs, they will be conjested; the arterial system possessing the power by contraction and expansion of parts, of focalising the blood, and throwing it rapidly on the various organs of the body. The right and left lobes of the brain, acting as a battery a̓d timing with the heart, throw their vitalized fluids by induction down the great central column and other nerves, leading directly to the head, the lungs, the stomach, the liver and other internal organs, from which the blood is saturated, magnetised and vitalized by part of the nervous fluid taken up by the blood.

By this means the coatings of the red globules are vitalized, bringing forth the forms of the three kingdoms of nature, illustrated in No. 5. There is a pulsation received through the cerebellum, magnetising the heart and the blood with its diastolic and systolic motions. The spriritual atmospheres are received in the upper portion of the brain, as a breath descending by inductive powers through the lungs to the red globules of the blood, so that every globule lives and breathes spiritually from it, in the regenerate man. For a more particular account of the vital forces of the animal spirit and their induced currents. See Nos. 6, 7.

The nervous system, in general appearance, connects every part of the system, with the brain, yet the nerve fibres do not extend singly from the brain to the ultimate parts, but each organic portion of the body has its own nerves and peculiar action, absorbing from the blood and the surrounding elements, vital forces peculiar to themselves. Thus all the groups of organs act and react upon one another, being separated by the ganglia which decompose the vital forces, giving off inductive currents to their appropriate departments. Thus it is that the human system is a likeness of the nine degrees of Masonry in their three, five and seven orders.

In the foregoing pages, we have given a brief outline of the degrees and orders existing in nature. To enter into arguments, quotations and experiments to sustain our views, would vastly exceed the limits of this work. We shall therefore, content ourselves with the simple statement of facts which have been the result of long observation, experience and study, and pass to the consideration of the Ritual in Masonry, in which we must rely on the foregoing principles of symbolism developed in the degrees for the unfolding of the progressive states of the spirit in regeneration.

# ENTERED APPRENTICE DEGREE.

No. 46. The parents procreate their own proprium, or likeness, in a combined form. The father imparts the will principle to the child, and the mother the first intellectual. If mutual love exists between married partners, the temperaments are equally combined in their offspring. See temperaments, Nos. 8, 9, 10, 11. Also the combination of the temperaments, Nos. 12, 13, 14.

If the temperaments of the two married partners are unequal, that is, if the temperaments of one be not the counter-part of the other, the offspring will be erratic, frequently not bearing resemblance to either of the parents. For instance, if the father be sanguine, and the mother bilious, the intellect of the son will partake of the bilious character, yet his will, will be like the father. And if mutual love prevail between the two, the son will be sanguine bilious, bearing resemblance to each of the parents. But if there be no mutual love, the son may vary considerably in his personal appearance and character. But if both of the parents be of the same temperaments, or of equal blendings of the same, but little physical and mental harmony will exist between the two, and the children will not partake of the mental power and energy of either. Some of the family may look like the father, others like the mother, and some like the grand-parents. But if the two married partners be in temperaments the exact counter-part of each other, embracing in full the temperaments, that is, the lacking temperaments in the father being counterbalanced by the opposite temperaments in the mother, mutual love and harmony are apt to prevail, and the children will be an equal blending of the full temperaments in the style of one of the orders, possessing great beauty of form and harmony of mind, although the parents may be uncomely in personal appearance, and possessed of few mental endowments or virtues.

It is a law of the temperaments, that each loves and respects its opposite, this tending to the perfection of the whole ; whereas, those of the same temperaments seldom agree in married life, the orders blend happily with each other.

The will principle or proprium of the father, can never be put off or laid aside. It constitutes the life principle of the man, and will come forth with great variety from generation to generation.

There is something that identifies the offspring with the fore-fathers, however, much the first in-tellectual principle, derived from the mother, may be changed by education or circumstances. In the regeneration of man, the will principle of the father always remains, growing and progressing to eternity ; the evil of the will being put one side, and the goods of love and truth implanted in their stead, until the evil of the will, is made entirely inactive, and the heavenly order of love is substi-tuted in the place of the evils of the will.

The goods of the will always seek truth ; and hence it appears as though man was regenerated by truth ; yet the will only attaches itself to the good contained in the truth, by which it governs and controls the truth, making the truth its own. It is the celestial love of truth spoken of in No. 22, which corresponds to the blue ray, which first is absorbed by the will principle of man ; putting one side the evils of the will, and attaching such truth as contained good to itself, putting forth the desire to be brought from darkness to light, and

16

to have and receive a part of the rights, lights and benefits of the heavens. Hence, it is said by the Lord, that "no man can come unto me, except the Father draw him." The proprium, self-hood, or intellectual likeness of the mother is entirely put away, rejected and cast off, during regeneration, and sink inward. It is the *widow's son*, or the natural rational principle, a spiritual rational or proprium being substituted in its place.

The desire of light is the first beginning of Masonry. Man, so long as this desire is restrained, is said to be wandering in darkness, of which it is said, seek and ye shall find, knock and it shall be opened unto you. Self-love and the love of the world, pervert and destroy the knowledge of truth, and prevent the affection of truth, from coming forth into the light of the Word or true faith. While the love of self and of the world are in full active force in the external understanding, no rational light from the Word of the Lord can be admitted, it being instantaneously expelled from the understanding, by the infatuated light of self-love. This state is called darkness. "For if the light that is in thee be darkness, how great is that darkness!" In this condition, the eyes of the man are blind to the most simple truths of faith. The affections of truth are unprotected, so that the man is neither naked nor clothed, barefoot nor shod, so that, if he was not especially protected and led by the Lord, he would inevitably perish for ever.

Every man is placed by the Lord in the care of guardian angels, who represent the man on every occasion, and conduct him safely through the various states of regeneration. Thus, when a man is prepared to become a Mason or to be regenerated, it is perceived by his guardian spirit, who leads him to the door of the Lodge. Hence, the states of man can never be forced, but his application and entrance upon the Masonic duty of life, must be of his own free will and accord. He must be free born, that is in a condition to be regenerated, must have attained to a lawful age, or rational state, and under the tongue of good report.

No. 47. There are intelligences and truths that relate to the natural world, and have for their object the cultivation of the soil and the mechanical trades. There are spiritual and celestial truths and intelligences, that have for their objects the cultivation of the spiritual mind and celestial affections. These knowledges can only be introduced, and brought forth in mature age. The natural knowledges and sciences, are receptive only of natural good, the spiritual of spiritual good, and the celestial of celestial good. The spiritual and celestial knowledges lie concealed and hidden in the natural, so that the natural must be first opened by education and science, without which the spiritual and celestial are like seeds that remain in the cold earth, until the fecundating principle is destroyed. See Nos. 3, 39. Truths, without good, only goad the conscience and do not prompt to action. Hence, there can be no regeneration by truth alone.

The good contained in natural truth, is received and stored up in the remains or affections implanted in childhood. See remains No. 28. These remains attract to themselves the love or good contained in natural truth. Thus, there is an intermediate plane between the understanding and the will. This plane is called conscience, and constitutes the rational plane as to good of the natural mind. The love or good of natural truth, thus stored up in the remains, inspires the mind with a tender regard for duty, and when reproached by truth, it shows wherein duty has been neglected, which is called compunction of conscience. The conscience thus formed by natural truth and education, is not real, for it only relates to the natural world. When the

spiritual principles of the mind are brought forth
and unfolded by the knowledges derived by the
Word of God, the natural conscience gives place to
a spiritual one, formed by the knowledge of faith.
The former conscience leads to salvation ; the latter
is salvation. Just in proportion as the natural or
spiritual conscience is active, it gives a perception
of either spiritual or natural truths, and power
of reasoning from them. So long as the conscience
remains active, man cannot reason against the
truth, but yields to its mandates. This is called
conviction. But if the conscience is perverted
and destroyed, man possesses equally the power
of ratiocination or talking plausibly about the
truth, with this difference, in the former case he is
led by the love of use, in the latter, by self-interest
or love. In this state, the man uses his reasoning
powers to combat the truth, and to confirm every
thing which he conceives to be for his own personal ends or pleasure. This is the state of darkness in which man is said to wander before he is
made a Mason. The perception of the darkness
and error of his own mind, from the affections of
truth derived from the Word of God, adjoined
with the influxes of the celestial truth, produces
the first desire of light, which prepares the mind

to receive the truth of the Lodge. The man in this condition, perceives for the first time, his own real state of poverty and nakedness, beholding himself as neither naked nor clothed, bare foot nor shod. He thus falls into a state of deep humility of mind, and almost despair of relief. No man can correct the errors of his ways until he utterly abhors the life that he has lived, and, through humility, receives the truth as a child. Such are said to be duly prepared, and desire to receive a part of the lights, rights and benefits of the Lodge.

No. 48. Regeneration is the work of works, without which all things would be created in vain. The earth was made for the reception of man, and man was created for the glory of the heavens, to which he attains by successive states of regeneration, represented by the degrees of the Lodge, the Chapter and the Council. The Entered Apprentice degree represents the reception of the truths of the Word, by the memory through the perceptive faculties, and hence, all knowledges of the heavens are taught in the Entered Apprentice degree. The same truths are elevated into the rational principles represented by the middle chamber, in the Fellow Craft degree, and are confirmed by the habits of life in the first section. Thus it is that the truths are elevated into science, and brought forth into acts of life, by the Fellow Craft. In the Master's degree, these sciences or doctrines are introduced into the will and brought forth into charity.

The blue Lodge represents the ultimate heavens, which receive their influxes from the spiritual heavens, which are represented by the intermediate degrees. The spiritual heavens again receive their influxes from the celestial heavens, which are represented by the Royal Arch, the Royal and Select Master's degrees. The heavens are not places into which man is let by any arbitrary power, but a state of the human mind attained by regeneration, by which the intellect and affections are prepared to understand and enjoy the knowledges and pleasures of the heavens. The evils and the falses of the mind, retard and prevent the growth of the spiritual man; but when these evils and falses are restrained by the truths of the Word, the spheres of the heavens put forth their vitalizing influence like the heat and light of the sun, causing all the remains of good and truth implanted in childhood, to spring forth and grow in the human mind, like seeds from the ground.

These spheres of regeneration, as they proceed from the heavens, are attended by the Holy Angels, who, like the officers and members of the Lodge, have their repective duties to perform in the great work of regeneration.

Each man that is about to be regenerated, is placed under the control of a guardian angel, who perceives and understands the states and conditions of the man, and when it is perceived that he is in a proper state of humility, spoken of in No. 47, he is led to the door of the Lodge, of which it is said, "seek and ye shall find, knock and it shall be opened unto you!" When the doors of the heavenly spheres of divine truth are opened to the humble mind, they are first felt in the left breast as a sharp instrument, which is contrition of heart, and is the first effect of repentance, manifested by a contrite and broken spirit. This state is also perceived by the guardian angel, whose business it is to conduct the man through the various states which follow. This state or condition of the man is also perceived by the natural, spiritual and celestial societies in the heavens, which are to assist in his regeneration. Hence, the man is inspected and examined in the state of humiliation to which he has been reduced, first by the intellectual angels in the south, next by the spiritual angels in the west, and lastly by the celestial angels in the east, for these several points of the compass correspond to the natural, spiritual and celestial states of the heavens, which are contained in each discrete degree or Lodge. See degrees, No. 44.

Hence, the candidate is made to pass through three several examinations in the heavens, at the south, west and east societies, where the same questions and like answers are returned, declaratory of his intentions and purposes of life, which represent that the man's whole nature, natural, spiritual and celestial, is capable of regeneration in the first degree. This being satisfactorily ascertained from his state of humiliation and repentance, the angels can safely proceed to instruct the candidate in the mysteries of the new life into which he is about to enter, after sufficient pledges given of his fidelity and sincerity in the great and important undertaking which he is about to commence.

Sincerity is necessary for the understanding of of any truth. No man can understand the principles of justice and judgment unless he is honest. The principles of truth, as quick as they are perceived by a dishonest mind, are turned aside and perverted, to subvert the ends of justice and judgment. An error is introduced and adjoined to the truths, by which the whole becomes falsified and perverted, subduing and destroying the dictates of conscience. Hence, the truth to a dishonest man, is a most profound secret in mystery. Therefore the principles of Masonry are kept entirely secret, and can never be conferred upon any one, except through a humble, innocent and contrite spirit, for, although a bad man may take the degrees of Masonry, and be received in full fellowship among the brethren, yet he remains in complete and total darkness, as to the great and vital principles of charity, so long as he remains insincere in heart. See No. 1. Satan may be well acquainted with all the doctrines of the church, and be able to falsify the whole; yet he can never attain to the truths of heaven. A state of contrition, and prayer is the first outbirth and emotion of the heart. Therefore, every candidate for Masonry should first kneel and offer up his devotions to Almighty God, declaring his belief in Deity, as a token of a sound mind. See No. 40. For he that trusts in himself, or any human being, is not in that state of innocence and humiliation which fits him to be made a Mason, and should at once be led out of the Lodge, without beholding the form and beauty thereof.

Prayer descends directly through the devotional organs, located in the top of the head, designated by the scarlet, pl. 1, fig. 1. These organs communicate their feelings in two distinct ways; one extending backward to the affections through the purple to the blue; the other descends forward through the orange to the yellow or perceptive faculties. The perceptive faculties and the domestic affections unite in the green, located in the centre of the base of the brain. Thus a complete triangle of the organs is effected in the head. The triangle must be complete in every prayer. If the triangle is broken by any one group of the faculties failing to perform its duty, the prayer amounts only to nonsense, and is simply an infatuation of the person praying; for he that prays without the spiritual affections, represented by the purple, or a rational perception, represented by the orange, joined by the conscience which has been introduced into life, represented by the green, is not heard by the Lord. If the intentions of a good life, represented by the green, is wanting, no prayer ascends.

"Not every one that saith unto me, Lord, Lord, shall enter into the kingdom of heaven; but he that ·doeth the will of my Father which is in Heaven."

No. 49. When the spheres of the heavens are first opened to man, (which is represented by his entrance into the Lodge), his affections are perceived by the angels; the natural affections are examined in the south, by the light of science, the spiritual affections are examined in the west, by the light of wisdom. and lastly, the celestial affections are examined by the Lord in the east. Every degree of the mind contains the natural, celestial and spiritual principles. The natural are examined by the natural, the spiritual by the spiritual, and the celestial by the celestial; for no man nor angel can be in these three states of affection at the same time. They are like the south, west and east of a state, in which its various officers reside. No man can be admitted into the light or knowledges of heaven, unless the natural, spiritual and celestial states of the degree of his natural mind, are capable of regeneration. This must first be ascertained. There are certain classes of men who cannot be regenerated; among whom are the atheist, the irreligious libertine, the mad man, and the fool. The states of regeneration are not arbitrary ; if they were so, these classes could be admitted into heaven by the mercy of the Lord. But regeneration consists in life states of the will and understanding, which can be only attained through life and charity. The affections are the groundwork of the intellect. The intellect is but a second state of the affections, in which truth and affection join, without which there is no power to conclude.

When it is perceived by the heavens that the continuous degrees of a natural mind are capable of regeneration, the man is placed under the care of spiritual angels, represented by the Senior Warden, who instruct him in the knowledges of truth. The first step of the understanding which is represented by the left foot, signifies the power to receive the divine truths of the Word, without which no man can make any progress in a divine life. The power of the will to progress in truth, is represented by the right foot. which must adjoin with every act of the perceptive faculties, which produces the power of memory. To receive and remember the divine commands from the intentions of the will, is the first step of an Entered Apprentice.

Truths, when they have been received in the memory, require confirmation, by which they are brought into habits of life, and become a part of the memory, never to be eradicated. A truth, before it is confirmed in the memory, may be dissipated and lost ; but, after confirmation, it remains to eternity; although it may be apparently forgotten for the time being, yet it remains in the chambers of the brain, and assists in every conclusion, although it may not be perceived by the man.

No truth can be confirmed except in a state of humiliation of the intellect, which is represented by kneeling upon the naked left knee. The left knee signifies the conjunction of the spiritual things of the natural degree with the celestial. Hence, to bend the left knee, signifies humiliation of the spiritual principles. To extend the right knee forming the angle of a square, signifies the consent of the will.

**The** first divine command to be confirmed is, Thou shalt have no other Gods before me. Thou shalt not make unto thee any graven image, or any likeness of any thing that is in heaven above, or that is in the earth beneath, or that is in the waters under the earth. Thou shalt not bow down thyself to them, nor serve them: for I, the Lord thy God, am a jealous God, visiting the iniquities of the fathers upon the children unto the third and fourth generation of them that hate me, and showing mercy unto thousands of them that love me, and keep my commandments."

The first commandment is the foundation of all faith and charity, which the Entered Apprentice solemnly affirms to receive, to ever hail, ever conceal and never reveal. No man is permitted to cast his pearls before his enemies, for they are sure to trample them under their feet, and turn again and tear him; for although the gospel is preached to the world at large, yet none receive it except those who have been brought into a proper state of the affections. This is represented by the secrecy of Masonry.

All the strength and power of a man's faith are pledged for the maintenance of the divine commands. This is symbolized by the left hand supporting the Holy Bible, Square and Compass, by which he is pledged to use every natural good and truth represented by the compass, and every virtue that is represented by the square, for the purpose of a divine life. To all of these, he pledges fidelity, which is represented by the right hand.

No. 50. The love of the Lord, and our neighbor is holy. The love of self and the world is profane. To prostitute a spiritual truth to a selfish end, is a profanation of holy truth, which is never permitted by the Lord. Hence, the mind cannot receive and understand a spiritual truth, until it is in a proper condition to receive it. Although the truth may be stated a thousand times in the hearing of the selfish mind, it only perceives the natural forms of the spiritual truth, which it will apply to its own ends, and the spiritual truth remains unseen. Hence, profanation can noly take place with those that have been initiated and intromitted into spiritual truths, by their falling away and final denial, which is followed by a complete and total death of the spiritual man. Neither can a spiritual truth be received by the mind, without displacing and putting away some falsity, arising from self-love or the love of the world. The old man must die before the new spiritual man can be brought forth into life. The substitution of one is the putting away of the other. This is what is represented by the penalty of the Masonic obligations. Every solemn act of the human mind is confirmed by some holy declaration, by which all the principles of truth in him are pledged for their maintenance. The decrees of the court are confirmed by its promulgation. The temple is dedicated, and the deed is completed by the signing of the act. Thus, every state of the human mind, in its orderly progression, must be completed and bounded by some definite declaration or act, before it can proceed to the next state in its orderly progression, as one step is completed before the other is commenced. A truth, thus confirmed, is received by the memory, and becomes a definite fact, or starting point . of the intellectual mind. It is "like a nail driven in a sure place, by the master of assemblies." Such a fact may apparently be forgotten for a short time, or the mind may be unable to call it forth, yet it is ever present with every conclusion. An affection or truth, thus confirmed, forms a part of the spiritual man, and goes with him to all eternity ; although it may be put one side, or thrown to the circumference and made inoperative by repentance, yet it remains as a part of the. human mind. This confirmation has been variously represented by the nations of the world ; but its true representation is an oath or obligation, resting upon the truths of a man's faith. Hence, the Christian swears upon the Holy Bible, the Jew by the law and the prophets, and the believer in a God affirms, by holding

17*

up his hand to heaven. To reveal a spiritual truth, and promulgate it in a disorderly manner, to those who are not justly entitled to receive it, is to profane the truth itself, in which case the truth dies the death of profanation, agreeably to the penalty of the obligation.

Hence, every man, receiving a spiritual truth, is bound by the nature of the truth itself, to ever receive the truth, never to reveal and ever conceal the same from all those who are not justly entitled to receive it ; and not to expose the same to the profane gaze by writing, printing, cutting, carving, etching or engraving the same. Thus, false deities, idols and painting are for ever excluded from the true worship. "For God is a spirit and seeketh such to worship Him, as worship Him in spirit and in truth."

Such is the representation and spiritual meaning of the obligation of an Entered Apprentice Mason. Spiritually, he solemnly swears to worship only the true God, and never to permit his likeness to be profaned by idolatry. This the angels of heaven understand by his obligation, and so did our Ancient Grand Masters. The obligation of an Entered Apprentice Mason, is but another form of the first commandment. See Exodus, 20th. 4th,

5th, 6th verses. This state constitutes the evening of the first day of regeneration, while the spirit of God is brooding or moving upon the waters; which are the truths of remains, and affections of good, received in childhood. The only visible effect perceived in the mind, is the consciousness and the desire of light, for, although the whole Lodge streams with the glory of heavenly light, like the sun rising in the east, to open and illumine the day, yet man, while he is in this state, is excluded from spiritual light, and appears like a man walking blind-folded among men. His ardent desire is to be brought into light, to see and understand the things of heavenly truth. Man, in this state, is entirely under the guidance of the angel, who leads him by a way that he knows not, while the affections and truths of remains are being confirmed as a ground receptive of heavenly truth and love.

No. 51. The first day of regeneration consists of the evening and the morning, or a state of darkness, by which man is led by the Lord, and the morning, or a state of light, in which heavenly and spiritual truths are received in earnest desire, and implanted in the memory. This state is beautifully described by the parable of the sower in the re-

ception of the seed. The preparation of the
ground is the work of the night, or state of darkness in man, and the reception of the seed is
the morning. See Mathew, 13. 4. The same is
also represented in Genesis, 1. 2, 3, 4. In the
beginning God created the heavens and the earth.
And the earth was without form and void; and
darkness was upon the face of the deep. And
the spirit of God moved upon the face of the waters.
And God said, Let there be light: and there was
light, and the evening and morning were the first
day.

Masonry is not the reprsentation of the creation
of the natural world alone, as some may suppose,
but, it is an actual creation by the regeneration of
the spiritual man, for which all other creations were
made ; without which the whole machinery of the
world would be useless ; for man is made for the
sake of a heaven, wherein the Lord may dwell, and
this heaven cannot be made without the regeneration of man ; for regeneration is the actual creation
of the angelic spirit, a temple not made with hands,
but eternal in the heavens, of which the literal
ceremonies of Masonry are representative. Hence,
a man in the insincerity of his heart, may deceive
the brethren, and pass through all the ceremonies

of the Lodge, without receiving any spiritual benefit, perverting and destroying the principles of
truth, thus becoming a profound hypocrite, using
Masonry for his own personal ends. But if the
heart is sincere, and immediately applies the truths
of Masonry to life, from sincere motives, and the
man lives the life of charity inculcated in the Lodge,
there is actually and spiritually a creation that
takes place at the time, not momentary, but gradual and progressive. To such, there is a spiritual
light in the Lodge as brilliant as the sun at noon-
day. And if he progresses in regeneration, until
the Royal Arch degree is spiritually conferred, he
then is able to survey the whole of the degrees
below, like a man that has gained some lofty
eminence and views, in clear day, the surrounding
landscape. He that has been spiritually obligated
as an Entered Apprentice Mason, is in proper condition to spiritually receive light. "And God said
Let there be light; and there was light." The
first things the candidate now beholds, are the three
great lights of Masonry, by the aid of the three
lesser lights. The three great lights of Masonry,
are the Holy Bible, Square and Compass.

The candidate is now in the receptive condition
in which he can be taught the great truths of

eternal life contained in the word of God. The
square teaches him that the affections, ends and
motives of good, make a part of every heavenly
truth. For truth without love and action, is
represented by the twenty-four inch guage. The
square is the addition of a perpendicular line,
by which every truth is squared, fitted and prepared for the builder's use, in which there is a
knowledge not only of truth but of the affections.
The work may be measured and comprehended by
the twenty-four inch guage. Yet the man cannot
proceed to perform the work of regeneration, by
the understanding alone. But when the ends and
motives of good, which are love, are joined to
wisdom, man is enabled to attain to virtue, by
which he squares every act of life. The compass
represents natural good and truth, which teaches
man the attributes of God, and also that every
affection and good should be circumscribed and
bounded by truth. Without truth, no affection is
safe. Virtue would be immediately destroyed and
prostituted by evil. Man resists evil by truth, as
the general does the enemy, by the implements
and arms of war. Hence, the sword corresponds
to truth. In the first stages of regeneration, until
man acts from a will of good, it becomes necessary

to curb and restrain his evil passions by truth. Hence, it is said that the compass teaches us to circumscribe our desires and keep them in due bounds with all mankind, but especially with a brother.

The Bible is the inestimable gift of God to man, as his rule of faith and practice. And hence, there can be no Lodge without the Bible. The square teaches us to square our actions by the rules of virtue contained in the Word. The compass to circumscribe our desires and restrain our passions. Hence, Masonry is a life of faith and practice ; for no man can be a Mason by theory. He must live the life inculcated by the tenets of Masonry, or he is not considered a Mason, among Masons. Therefore, it is said that Masonry is a life of charity, agreeably to a certain system of natural, moral and spiritual truth. See. No. 2. The great lights of Masonry are said to be seen by the aid of the three lesser lights, which are the Sun, Moon and Master of the Lodge ; which are represented by three burning tapers set in a triangular form. Many masons suppose, inasmuch as the Sun, Moon and Master of the Lodge, are represented by burning tapers, that they are the mere literal lights, through which Masons see and read the Word, and are instructed in the principles of Masonry by the Master. But, with such a mind as Solomon's, literals were made use of only to convey great truths. Hence, there is no such thing as mere literals in Masonry. All things are symbolic and representative of Deity, and his divine attributes. The triangle is a representative of the trinity of the divine attributes. Therefore, it is at once seen, that the lesser lights are representative of the doctrine of these attributes. They are called lesser, not that they are so, but because they are farther removed from man, and therefore they appear to be the lesser. The Sun is emblematical of the divine celestial good. The Moon is emblematical of the divine spiritual. These are received in man as the scarlet and blue rays, which are treated of in No. 22, 23.

The Master of the Lodge, represents the divine natural human of the Lord, hence, the doctrine of the personality of God, is clearly taught by the lesser lights. That God is a person, may be seen by his appearing to Moses in Mount Sinai in a personal form. This doctrine was well understood by Solomon, for God appeared and spoke to him in vision, Chronicles 3. 1. 7. This was also well understood by our Ancient Grand Masters St. John

the Baptist and St. John the Evangelist, as will
appear from the first chapter of John. "And the
Word was God." " In Him was life, and the life
was the light of men ; " " and the Word was made
flesh and dwelt among us." " And John bare wit-
ness of him." John 1. 1, 4, 14, 15. From these
quotations, it is clearly seen that God has a divine
human natural form, and that he took upon himself
flesh, and dwelt among men. This is no doubt the
true doctrine, taught by our Ancient Grand Master,
St. John, in all the early Christian Lodges, and as
such was received by every Christian Mason. From
the foregoing doctrine of the attributes of God
and the truths of the Sacred Scriptures [which is
one of the great lights of Masonry,] it is clearly seen
and understood. The sun represents the divine celestial or soul, which is called the Father. The Moon
representing the divine spiritual or Word or wisdom,
form the spiritual principle or Son. That these
dwell in a divine natural body, or proceeding principles, constituting one divine man ; in which
there is all the fulness of man in both male and
female principles. See the male and female principles, No. 123.

This being the case, the Christian Mason con-
tends that there is no inconsistency in the divine
18

body taking upon itself flesh in the womb of the
Virgin, and dwelling among men, as the soul and
spirit of every individual man is from the father ;
the mother giving it a body in the womb. • Whatever difference there may be, the Jew and the
Christian agree in this, that God has a divine natural
human body. Hence, the regenerated man is
created in his image and likeness.

By the lesser lights, we are instructed in Masonry
by three different ways. First, by the influx
of the divine celestial principle, flowing into the
top of the head. Secondly by the celestial love
of truth flowing into the back of the head.
Thirdly, by the divine spiritual principle, flowing
into the frontal region of the head. These are represented by the blue, red and yellow rays, treated
of in Nos. 22, 23, 24. It is the light of the three
divine attributes of the Deity, that stream through
the Holy Bible, Square and Compass, by which
we are taught all the precepts of faith and charity;
faith always referring to the intellectual principle
of Deity, and charity to the divine good or soul
principle manifest in one Jehovah or Lord. Their
image and likeness in man are faith and charity.
From the foregoing it will be seen, that the Worshipful Master represents the Lord in his divine

natural principle, in which dwells the fulness of the Godhead bodily.

No. 52. The Worshipful Master approaching the candidate from the east, represents the coming of the Messiah. This among our ancient brethren was held to be the great event of the world, and the fulfilment of time. The law and the prophets all pointed to his personal appearance. Our Jewish brethren look forward to that event, as, in its fulfilment, they are to be finally acknowledged as his chosen people, fully conscious that without his final appearance, the law and the prophets must ultimately be considered as a mere pretence, and themselves impostors. To them, therefore, his coming was looked for as the final consummation of the Jewish Scriptures and their acknowledgement as the chosen people. It is the subject of the first and the last prophecy, the beginning and the end, the Alpha and Omega of the Jewish nation. To them, his personal appearance was the fulness of all time. The final acknowlegement of the truth of the Holy Scriptures and the acceptance of his people. To them the law and the prophets prophesied until John. The Jew looked for the coming of the Messiah as the coming of a mighty and glorious king, to sit upon the throne of David, and reign over the nations; thus placing them pre-eminent in natural power and glory, over all the nations of the earth. The Christian acknowledged his coming upon the first step of an Entered Apprentice Mason, in humility, meekness and simplicity, as an example and pattern of life to the humble and lowly, thus supplying the deficiency and wants of a depraved and fallen human race, entering alike the cottage of the poor, and the mansion of the rich.

The due guard of an Entered Apprentice Mason is an acknowledgment of the Lord, and represents our acceptance of the life taught by the Holy Bible, Square and Compass. The penal sign signifies that spiritual death arises from their profanation. Thus to see the Worshipful Master approaching us, under the due guard and penal sign, teaches us that he is the Word and the life; that all things in the Holy Scriptures refer to his coming in the fulness of time, to impart life and salvation to all those that believe in him, that he is the life of all, is clearly taught by the Compass and Square. The doctrine that the Lord is the life of all good, has been received and acknowledged in every age of the world. No man can receive a single spiritual truth, until he is brought into a state of humility, in which he sees and acknowledges that there is no good in himself. For he that thinks that there is any good in him, is not in a condition to receive it from the Lord. The extending of the right hand of the Worshipful Master to the candidate in token of brotherly love and affection, teaches us that all who are confirmed in the affection of good, and have been brought to light, beholding and acknowledging the Lord in his divine human as the Messiah, and accept his coming, are received and acknowledged by Him; and that he alone teaches the way of life and salvation, which is represented by the Worshipful Master teaching the Word and grip of an Entered Apprentice Mason. The sign of the cross is conferred in Baptism, and the Catholic Christian gives the sign of the cross as the pledge of his faith. The Mason gives the due guard of an Entered Apprentice, as a pledge of his faith and life in the Holy Bible, Square and Compass. The penal sign is an acknowledgment that all life is from the Lord, through obedience to their tenets, and that any pronfanation of them is spiritual death.

There are three things that constitute the true Mason, namely, wisdom, love and obedience. Wisdom, love and action are the attributes of the Lord; and hence, we commonly use in reference

to man, the terms intelligence, truth and obedience. True wisdom is the power of discerning
between good and evil, arising from a life of love,
and hence, belongs only to man in a regenerate
state, and cannot be applied to the Entered Apprentice. It is his province to learn, acknowledge and obey. Learning is received through
the exercise of the perceptive faculties. Acknowledgement is the conscious conviction of the
understanding, from which arises obedience.
Obedience is of two kinds; that which   arises
from conviction, peculiarly belong to the Entered
Apprentice. The obedience which arises from
love, in which there are delights and pleasure, is
the orderly state of regeneration. Three of the
five senses have always been held in high estimation among Masons, namely, seeing, feeling and
hearing. The eye corresponds to intelligence,
feeling to the will; and hearing to obedience.
Through the medium of the eye, we see the sign by
which acknowledgement is made. Through the
feelings the token is implanted in the will. A
word or name signifies quality or state. Hence,
the giving of the word of an Entered Apprentice, signifies obedience to it. These collectively
are representative of the three qualities of an

Entered Apprentice, viz: intelligence, truth and obedience.

Truth arises from the power of the human mind to come to a conclusion. This power can hardly be said to be exercised by the Entered Apprentice. Yet as it arises from the combined action of the perceptive and will principles, there must be something of truth in every action of the human mind. Three things must combine to make the act complete. There must be intelligence to know, conviction of the understading to conclude, and obedience to obey. Obedience belongs to man, but action or procedure, to God. Hence, the ability to obey is implanted in the will by the Lord, which is represented by conferring the grip and word by the Worshipful Master. The natural, spiritual and celestial principles join in every act. The motives of the will are dissipated unless they descend into the appropriate wisdom, or power of discerning between good and evil. The motives and wisdom again are entirely dissipated, unless they are brought forth in act. Then they are confirmed and become a part of the spirit or mind, and remain with man to eternity. Hence, the celestial, spiritual and natural, must join in every degree. Yet the degree itself partakes more of one than it does of the other. It therefore takes the three first degrees of Masonry to complete the first discrete natural degree, the Master's degree being intermediate between the natural and spiritual, partaking of both.

The Entered Apprentice, Fellow Craft, and Masters' degrees are adjoined by their continuous degrees, and constitute the natural spiritual and celestial principles, which are contained in the first or natural discrete degree or Masters' Lodge. Hence, the coming of the Messiah is represented to the Entered Apprentice and conferred upon him, in the sign, grip and word. It is from the manifestation of this trinity of attributes, that there are three seats or gates representative of the divine influx, in the East, South and West, at which the Entered Apprentice must give an exhibition and proof that he has been made a Mason in each of these departments of his mind. Proving that he is not only intelligent, but willing and obedient.

No. 53. Truth can only be received and implanted in the will through a state of innocence, which is produced by repentance. There are three states of innocence, the innocence of ignorance, the innocence of intelligence, and the innocence of wisdom, which exist in youth, middle age and old age. The affections of childhood are implanted in the innocence of ignorance, the affections of truth or grace, in intelligence, and truth itself, in the innocence of wisdom. Hence, it is, that when man lives an affectionate and orderly life of regeneration, the intellectual powers constantly increase with age, until the face shines with the beams of light and love in old age. Such are beloved by all and are looked up to as models of virtue and counsellors of peace. But when the affections are distorted by error, through a disorderly life, the countenance in old age becomes rigid and sharp; the eye is piercing, and the features bespeak the hatred and suspicion that lurk within. Thus the confirmation of truth or error is the clothing of the human spirit. Our most ancient Grand Master, St. John, calls white garments of fine linen the righteousness of the saints. Rev. 19. 8. Man, previous to the confirmation of spiritual truth, is said to be neither naked nor clothed, barefoot nor shod. But when there is a confirmation of spiritual truth, in which there is love or good, the man is clothed by the Lord, with the innocence of the intelligence, which corresponds to the lambskin, the lamb representing the Lord. The lambskin is presented by the Worhipful Master to every Entered Apprentice, as the emblem of innocence and the badge of a Mason. This he should wear with honor to himself and credit to the fraternity. It is the gift of the Lord, and therefore more honorable than any order or gift of any king or potentate of the earth, and can only be received through an orderly and progressive state of regeneration. Man cannot work or correct the irregularities of life, until he is clothed with innocence or the badge of a Mason, which is the confirmation of spiritual truth after repentance by which there is the affection of truth or grace. The lambskin also signifies favor.

No. 54. The twenty-four inch guage and the common gavel compose the working tools of an Entered Apprentice Mason. The twenty-four inch guage is an instrument made use of by operative Masons to lay off and measure their work; but we, as Free and Accepted Masons, make use of it for a more noble and glorious purpose, that of dividing our time. The twenty-four inches being emblematical of the twenty-four hours of the day, are divided into three equal parts; giving eight hours for the common avocations of life, eight for devotion and the relief of a worthy, distressed brother, and eight for refreshment and sleep.

Ther are twelve days of regeneration; six ascending, and six descending. The six ascending states are represented by the Masters' Lodge and the intermediate degrees, three of which are natural and three spiritual.

In the seventh day of creation, the Lord is represented as finishing his work, and resting from all his labors. The term work implies resistance, and so long as there is any opposing principle in man to the operation of the divine will, there is disorder in the spirit, which must be overcome by work or force. But when ever divine order is established in the will of man, there is a full and complete rest, althongh every principle is a thousand times more active than it was before. All things being done from love, it appears as though the activity itself was only a state of rest, as it is with the young and vigorous, when they have been long confined and go forth to play. The action itself gives relief and rest. Thus it is when man loves the Lorfl and his neighbor as himself. It does not appear as work to perform the labor of love.

The Entered Apprentice degree is the first day or state of regeneration, which consists of the evening, as the state of darkness, and the morning as the state of light, in which there are three things, namely: love, wisdom and action, all things proceeding from love, through truth to action, as end, cause and effect. These three things are in full power in every degree or day. There are three celestial degrees corresponding to the Royal Arch, and the Royal and Select Masters. These degrees, each, descend through the intermediate degrees, and Masters' Lodges. So that into each degree the higher degrees descend in six states with their full force and power. Yet they are entirely concealed and hidden from view until they are finally opened and conferred upon the candidate. Thence they again descend.

The Entered Apprentice degree derives its virtue from the fact, that the power of the higher degrees are concealed in it. Hence, there are three distinct principles in the Entered Apprentice degree, derived from the attributes of the Lord, descending through the celestial, spiritual and natural degrees, each consisting of a higher, middle and lower principle, which are continuous in each degree. The Royal Arch and Council Degrees constitute the celestial degree. The second section of the Masters', Most Excellent, Past and Mark Masters' degrees constitute the spiritual degree.

The first section of Master, Fellow Craft and Entered Apprentice degrees, constitute the natural degree, with its continuous degrees, in which all the upper degrees are concealed in their full force and power; the Entered Apprentice, Master and Royal Arch Degrees are intermediate and discrete to which the others belong.

No upper or higher degree can be conferred upon a man, until he has received the lower; for although the upper degrees are first in power and virtue, yet they are the last opened and conferred in man. All the truths and affections of the Masters' Lodge, below the second section of the Master, are natural in three forms, first, the lowest natural of the Entered Apprentice, the middle or interior natural, and most interior natural principle, which may be called natural, spiritual and celestial principles. These ascend toward the spiritual. The Fellow Craft degree is spiritual, consisting first of the spiritual natural and the spiritual, and the spiritual celestial natural. The third or Masters' degree, is the celestial, consisting of the celestial natural, the celestial spiritual and the celestial of the natural, ascending to the spiritual.

These are the ascending orders of the natural. The same order continues to the Royal Arch. The descending orders are reversed, commencing with the celestial and decending through the spiritual, to the natural.

The existence of these three principles in the

19                     K

lowest degree or Entered Apprentice, is the reason
why the twenty-four inch gauge is divided into
three equal parts.   To measure signifies to know,
to comprehend and understand.   The twenty-four
inch guage spiritually represents the natural power
of knowing or learning.   This power is given of
the Lord in the Entered Apprentice degree to the.
candidate, and hence it becomes one of his working tools, which is divided into twenty-four parts,
which is the multiplication of twelve by two,
two signifying conjunction or marriage, when used
as a multiplier.   Hence, twenty-four signifies that
the affection of natural truth or grace is adjoined
equally with the twelve or entire natural principles
of faith.   See the twelve principles of faith, Art.
29, also combining numbers, Art. 25.

From the foregoing it will be seen, that the
twenty-four inch guage is representative of the
natural power given by the Lord to learn and understand the twelve principles and affections of
faith, in each of the three natural principles.
Hence, it is said to be divided into three equal
parts, each consisting of eight, which signifies the
truth of the natural, the truth of the spiritual and
the truth of the celestial, conjoined with their interior loves and affections, which are contained in
the natural degree; for each of the continuous degrees

has its natural, spiritual and celestial principles, there being three discrete degrees; each consisting of three continuous degrees; and each continuous degree, again, has within it the three principles of the three continuous celestial degrees. Thus, Masonry runs in series of three, nine and twenty-seven.

Regeneration or Masonry proceeds in progressive order of days or states heretofore described. Hence to measure the day with the twenty-four inch guage, signifies to learn and acquire a knowledge .of all the truths and affections contained in the degree, for no man can really acquire and retain any knowledge outside of his own state or degree. He may seem to acquire such knowledges, but they are forgotton and dissipated, only such knowledges remaining with him as the affections can receive and adjoin to themselves. These are confirmed and remain with the man to all eternity, and are always present, giving a perceptive power to the mind. These knowledges are adjoined in the tranquil or sleep state of the mind, to the affections. Hence, eight hours, or equal portions of time, are said to be given to refreshment and sleep. In the common avocations of life, all the principles of truth and affection that have been previously confirmed in the state of darkness or night, are brought

forth into active exercise. These again are all
laid upon the altar of our devotion to Almighty
God and the relief of a worthy, distressed brother.
To know and to learn these principles is to use the
twenty-four inch guage in measuring, and laying
off the work of an Entered Apprentice Mason.
See Ezekiel, 48. 3, Rev. 11. 1. Also 21. 15.

There are also three degrees of the faculties,
namely: the perceptive, domestic and the devotional. These furnish three sets of fibres in the
brain that govern during their respective portions
of the day in the regenerate man.

No. 55. The common gavel is an instrument
made use of by operative masons to break off the
rough corners of stones, the better to fit them for
the builder's use. But we, as free and accepted
Masons, make use of it for a more glorious purpose,
that of divesting our hearts and consciences of all
the superfluities of life ; the better to prepare us for
that building not made with hands ; eternal in
the heavens. · The good of the understanding,
and the evil of the will, constantly act and react
against each other. The will principle is received
from the father, with all of his peculiar hereditary
principles. These can never be put off, being
joined to the soul of man. The mother clothes the

soul with first an intellectual or spiritual body, also a natural body ; or rather she supplies the material out of which the spiritual and natural bodies are formed. The soul principle of the man, with its intellectual, comes forth as the prime moving cause and equally blends in the spiritual and bodily forms. The bodily form, given by the mother, is put off by natural death ; also, the hereditary spiritual principle of the mother, is put off by regeneration ; so that the soul principle received from the father, stands forth in the regenerate man, perfectly clothed with its own spiritual and intellectual principles. Hence, woman is only a helpmeet to man, having and retaining the hereditary principles of her father, as the form of her love ; whereas the man's form is of truth. The evils of the will principle, derived from the father hereditary, are checked, restrained and put aside, making them inoperative, while the hereditary principle of the mother, which forms the first natural rational principle of the man, is entirely put off in the process of regeneration. This process or principle is represented by one of our Ancient Grand Masters, Hiram Abiff, hence, he is called the *widow's son.* But the work of the natural principle adorns and beautifies the Temple, not made with hands, eternal in the heavens.

19*

Hence, arises that peculiar sweetness of his recollection in all our works. The truths of the natural
rational principle, constantly react against the
evils of the natural loves, putting them away and
purifying natural good, thus establishing good in the
natural rational mind, which is a kind of conscience
in the unregenerate man. But, as regeneration.
progresses, a true conscience and spiritual rational
principle are formed from the celestial love of truth,
which is the blue fecundating ray of light, treated
of in No. 22. This celestial love of truth comes
forth quickening all the remains or affections of
childhood. See remains, No. 28. This good of the
celestial principle of truth constantly acts against
the evils of the will principle of the father; curbing,
restraining and putting them aside, and preparing
them for that spiritual building, not made with
hands. These evils with their falsities, are ultimates in the will, and form a part of the very soul
and spiritual principles derived from the father;
and hence, cannot be destroyed. They give identity, peculiarity and self-hood to the man. They
are the rough stones of the builder, that must first
undergo a preparation which is the peculiar work
of the Entered Apprentice, whose quality is to
learn, to know, and to comprehend the natural
principles of faith, by which he receives the power

to break off the rough corners of these stones or ultimations of the hereditary will, and to restrain them, the better preparing them for the hand of the Fellow Craft. By the work of the Mason, good is insinuated in the evils of the will or proprium of the father, and the evils themselves, with their falsities, are so prepared and arranged as to give strength, protection and support to the building.

The common gavel represents the trúth of doctrine. The power to use the gavel is a gift from the Lord, in conferring the word of the Entered Apprentice, which signifies strength. Were it not for the foregoing male and female principles, there could be no Emanuel or God with us. The Lord, in his death, resurrection and glorification, put off the body and spiritual principle of the mother, retaining their life and works while in the body, which he glorified and made divine. The Father coming forth and manifesting himself more powerfully in his own divine natural bodily form, retaining the principles of life in the flesh, is enabled to approach more nearly the hells or evils of man, without destroying them ; thus, subduing and ultimately triumphing over all evil and accomplishing the redemption of man, by his divine mercy, through a life of regeneration, which is a likeness of the Lord's glorification. This may appear strange to those who do not realize that the Lord is the human form, and that every regenerate man is in likeness of that form.

There are some who have no other idea of God than as vastness and power ; others, that he is a kind of diffused principle ; and some conceive him to be the soul of nature, and hence, that all things are but parts of his body. Such persons can have no conception that God is truly a divine man, existing in infinite will, wisdom and action, and that these act and react upon a centre which is without regard to size, one divine person, whose goodness, wisdom and action shine forth as a universal sun of mind. To some, the salvation of the human race appears to be of no great importance. They ask the question, "Why did not God create man perfect at once?" not realizing that every change of state in the progression of the human will, is absolutely a spiritual creation, and that the divine power is ever acting through a progressive order ; and that the coming of the Emanuel is as much a part of that divine order, as any other link, and equally affects the universe.

No. 56. The tenets of Masonry are like good seed planted in the garden of the soul, that spring up and bear fruit, " some thirty, some sixty, and some a hundred-fold," for they are united with the remains of childhood, and, like the tender child, require the utmost care and watchfulness. Hence, a new name of caution is conferred upon the candidate, for no spiritual truth can thrive without watchfulness and care. Watchfulness is the duty of the candidate ; care is the. duty of the Lodge. The very moment that the door of the Lodge is found untiled, some evil affection, with its falsity of doctrine, is ever ready to step in. These are the cave-droppers and cowans of Masonry.

Within the nine arches of the brain, (See Nos. 37, 38,) and the twenty-seven seats of the Council Chamber, reside all the affections and truths of the mind. If the affections are evil, their truths are falsities. If the affections are good, they ever seek truths as their companions ; and, so long as the affections remain active and watchful, they admit only such things as favor them. In every spiritual truth, there resides celestial good or love of order. As long as evil affections are watchful, they reject the truth, and keep the door of the Lodge tiled ; but the watchful care of the Lord, being ever over the human mind, the evil affections by his divine care, are laid asleep, when truth finds admission through the portal to the soul. Therefore, the Lord is called "the door and the good

Shepherd." Truth having once gained admission commences the arrangement and preparation of the mind, for the reception of other truths and goods, until all the hereditary affections of the father, which have been ultimated in the world, are prepared as living stones, and set in their proper place in the Temple not made with hands, while the hereditary principle of the mother is put off by death through temptation, and buried beneath the *sanctum sanctorum* when its work is complete. No designs are left upon the trestle board, and the key stone, of the arch lies neglected among the rubbish until found by the Grand Master, and brought forth at the completion of the Temple with shouting and praise. The stone which the builders' rejected, has become the head stone of the corner.

Thus, it is that the principles of the mother, through the Lord in his humanity, glorified in his death and resurrection, become the cap stone of the regenerate life. These divine operations would be supplanted and destroyed by evil and falsity, were it not for constant watchfulness and care. "What I say unto you, I say unto all, watch." Watchfulness is that peculiar, wakeful and active state of the good affections of the heart, which is ever anxious and ready to receive truth. The care of the Lodge arises from sympathy and brotherly love. When these grow cold, the care and good feeling for the newly initiated languishes, and self-love and hatred take their place. "Truth and union," are the watch-words of an Entered Apprentice Mason. The affinity that exists between truth and love is the cause of all union in society.

The Lodge owes to the newly initiated member, the bounden duty of care and watchfulness. The world at large has but one cause of complaint, which is not the fault of Masonry, but arises from electing some negligent man to the Mastership of the Lodge, who delays the work of the Lodge until a late hour of the night, keeping the better portion of the community from their homes and families, depriving them ultimately of the privileges of Masonry, and the society of the Lodge, and throwing the care and keeping of the Lodge into the hands of those that have but little regard to order. Thus, Masonry is justly reproached for the acts of a careless and negligent Master. There are but few circumstances that prevent an active and diligent Master from closing his Lodge promptly at nine o'clock, as years of experience have satisfied the writer. With this single exception, the Masonic society stands unrivalled for good order in the history of the world.

No. 57. There are both natural and spiritual subtances. Natural substances exist and subsist from our natural Sun, that sends forth its light and heat in the natural order of creation, stamped with the three discrete degrees of the animal, vegetable and mineral kingdoms. The rays of light pass through the various elemental formations, until they finally reach their last or ultimate forms in one of the three kingdoms. In their elemental changes, they present the vast variety, harmony and beauty of nature. Every gas has its mineral, vegetable and animal form of use. It may to-day combine in the animal, to-morrow in the vegetable, and lastly with the mineral forms. Again, it may be decomposed by heat, and returned to a gaseous state, throwing off such portions of light and heat as have not yet been fully combined, and stamped with the law of gravitation. These again may enter into various combinations and return to ultimate conditions, the law of creation being constantly an onward progression from the light of the sun to the gaseous liquid and solid forms which flow like a mighty river. The decompositions of matter are only the little eddies arising from reaction. They are again caught by the stream and borne on to the great ocean of liquid substances, bounded by the shores of the minerals and solids.

The spiritual substances exist from the divine light of the great eternal mind, that flows forth into love, truth, affections and facts. Thus they supply an exact parallel to all the substances and ultimations of the natural creation, so that when we speak of any natural thing, we also speak of that which is spiritual or belongs to the world of mind. If the mind is in a state of darkness, not yet brought to light, nothing is seen or understood, but such things as relate to the natural world, and man's existence in it. Here the natural mind stops refusing to go farther, and says, "I do not beleive." After the mind is brought to light in the Entered Apprentice degree, it catches a glimpse of the great spiritual truths contained in the natural substances, as symbols of moral truths. As the mind still progreesses in its onward course of regeneration, through various degrees, until the Royal Arch is spiritually conferred, it ascends into a clearer light, and beholds the great spiritual truths in the full light of day, as clearly as the natural eye sees the objects of the world.

It is the grand object of Masonry to unfold spiritual objects and truths by a constant and continuous system of symbols, representatives and correspondences, thus teaching the candidate the laws, rules and regulations of heaven, which he makes his own. Just as he puts them into practice and lives the life of love and truth, he is prepared for that building not made with hands, eternal in the heavens; and in proportion as he lives the life of love or charity he receives these heavenly truths and makes them his own, in the degree of regeneration in which he is, and in no other. If the Mason does not understand the great spiritual truths of Masonry when stated, it is because he has not yet mentally been initiated into the degree to which they belong; and if he does not see their lowest symbolical meaning, and feel a delight therein, he is yet in a state of darkness and under the bonds of iniquity.

Minerals and metals signify the truths and goods, or spiritual riches, that a man has made his own by living a life agreeably to the truth. An Entered Apprentice is not yet in a life of good and truth, signified by minerals and metals, but in a state of spiritual poverty, in which he is unable to satisfy the demands of charity made on him. This teaches a great and important spiritual lesson of love.

Clothing is representative of the more external truths, which man has made his own, through a life agreeable to the precepts of Masonry. To be divested of garments, signifies an intromission into a state of humiliation and innocence, by which the mind is brought into a state receptive of higher truths. When the mind relapses after instruction, into its former state, it appears to be re-clothed. It is impossible to continue the exalted state to which the mind is raised during instruction, beyond a limited period, when the mind again returns to its former state, in which all the goods and truths of life are made subservient to the new condition of the man. He then reverts to the Lodge for farther instruction. Thus the former life becomes a part of the man, like the soil into which good seed is cast. Hence it is said, that the Entered Apprentice returns to the Lodge for farther instruction. Here close the first and second sections of the degree which have been conducted together, having given the reasons as the work of the first section progressed.

# ENTERED APPRENTICE DEGREE.

No. 58. The North-east corner of the Lodge cannot be fully explained until the nature of the Lodge is understood. The Lodge must first be conferred and then explained; for a man is not in a condition to understand any subject, until he is brought into a receptive state. This state is represented by the conferring of the various parts of the degrees. There is something connected with the responsibilities of an office, that enables a man to more fully understand his duties; and, therefore, the judge when he has taken the oath of office, is better prepared to discharge its functions. This is true even of every profession and trade. A man in a business takes a more practical view than an amateur. Hence, the Entered Apprentice Mason, is not in a condition to understand the nature of a Lodge, until he is assigned to some position in it. Every day is divided into four states. First, the state of darkness, followed by the morning. The light first appearing in the North-east, or the North of East. Then the progression of light until twelve o'clock, and the decline until evening or shade. This is a representative of the day's labor of each degree or state of regeneration. Each heaven is arranged into societies, corresponding to the various states that man passes through on earth, so that he is always under the care of some society in the heavens during his progressive state, in which he is being regenerated; so that, in whatever state he dies, he finds himself in a like state and society of angels in the next life. Man in his first commencement of regeneration, is in the societies of the North, or of darkness. His journeying is towards the East, and he first approaches the light at the rising of the sun from the North-East. Hence, the Entered Apprentice enters the first society of the Lodge, in the North-East corner, and progresses through all the states of light in his onward course of progressive instruction. He is now in a receptive state to understand the nature of a Lodge, or heaven which next follows.

No. 59. Sound reason requires that all things should be created for one object or end; and that these objects or ends should be subservient to

more interior purposes, until they rise and concentrate upon one great use, for which all things
were created. This use, is the universal heavens
existing in a three, six and ninefold order. All
things adhere in1 conjoin with each other by
uses or loves; from which arise all the laws of
order. Hence, the parallelism is by uses, and not
the forms of things, any farther than the forms
of things are subservient to the uses themselves.
The world of mind conjoins with the world of
matter, by states and uses, and not by geometrical forms of truth. A principle may be the life
of an object; and yet it is not seen by the natural
mind, as having any relation to the form of the
object itself, the appearances to the external
eye, being quite different from the perceptions of
the principle from which it lives. But if the
principle itself be seen by the spiritual eye,
which is the case when man has put off this
body, or sees in vision state, the principle itself appear in the form of a natural object,
although the object seen, is not the same as the
natural object by which it is represented in the
natural world. Hence, the constant influx of representatives into the mind, as seen in a sleep or
vision state, are not the mere geometrical truths
and forms of the external world, but are the

divine creative spheres which flows down through the heavens of mind, stamped with the forms of the mineral, vegetable and animal kingdoms. See Nos. 5, 23. Thus, these forms exist in spiritual light, or the light of the divine mind, which flows in with the light of our natural sun, into all created things. The forms of ultimate objects in the natural world, react upon the soul principle through the medium of the five senses; and assist in the ultimate formation of the human mind. Therefore, man is first created upon the natural earth; and puts off the principles and body derived from the mother, in regeneration and death, and comes forth an angel in the heavens. Masonry is representative of this operation, the symbols signifying spiritual things, or the operation of the mind. Hence, when we wish to understand a symbol or representative, we must first think of the uses it performs to the natural body, and then elevate the mind into regions of the spiritual world, and consider what principle performs a like use, or office to the regenerate mind. This will at once enable us to perceive the parallelism, or correspondence that exists between the two worlds. So complete and exact are the representatives, or correspondences of Masonry with the process of regeneration, that if an angel himself were to come down, and take the seat of the Worshipful Master, and proceed to confer the representatives of regeneration upon a candidate, they would not be more exact than the work of the Lodge now represents it. The divine care and influxes of the Lord, have preserved them in the world as a constant guide to the true principles of religion ; working silently and unseen in every Masonic community, without regard to any particular dogma of sectarianism, always presenting the Holy Scriptures, as the rule of faith and practice, and inculcating the precepts of a life of charity.  The most wonderful knowledges of heaven lie concealed and locked up in the representatives of its Rituals. Hence, a Lodge is representative of both the heavens and the earth.  It is permitted to teach by representatives, but not to worship by them. A Masonic Lodge is not a church ; but, partakes of the church so far as spiritual instruction is imparted by representatives, and the heart ascends to God in humble devotion.  The Jewish Church and Temple service, were altogether representative, for man, in that age of the world, was not susceptible of spiritual thought. But after the descent of the Lord in his divine human, there was a connection established by him between man and heaven; and Temple, or representative worship ceased, never to be revived.

No. 60. A Lodge in general signifies Heaven, or the dwelling place of the Lord ; and includes all on earth who are being regenerated, or prepared for heaven. In general, the heavens are divided into three. The first or lowest, the second or middle, and the third. These are discreted or separated from each other. Each discrete Lodge or heaven in particular, is again divided into three continuous Lodges or degrees. The first discrete heaven or Master's Lodge, is divided into the continuous degrees of Entered Apprentice, Fellow Craft, and Master's Lodges, the Master's degree being discrete or intermediate dividing the jurisdictions. But as the Master's Lodge has control or jurisdiction over these three several degrees, they have since the formation of Grand Lodges, been called one Lodge, consisting of three degrees ; but for the sake of preserving the representative sense, we shall describe the Entered Apprentice Lodge separately. The Entered Apprentice Lodge is discrete, or intermediate between the states of darkness and light, and consists of all the various progressive states of regenera-

tion, that man passes through during his first
instruction, or initiation into the knowledge of faith,
progressing from a state of darkness, through the
morning, to the light of the full meridian sun in
the south, which is represented by our Grand Master, Hiram Abiff, or the first natural rational power
derived from the mother. This power is limited
in its reception ; having three degrees or days in
itself, like youth, manhood, and old age. In the
first day of its existence its power is peculiarly
receptive, in which memory is matured at high
twelve, and begins to decline in the after part of
the day, as the desire to reason and understand
spiritual things of faith, comes forth in the mind.
After the lectures have been committed to memory
and laid up in the store-house of the intellect, the
desire of mere memorising, gives place to the
understanding ; and the day of memory declines
to the shades of evening ; and man, feels that he
is again in the dark, and yields to the desire to obtain more light, which he hopes to find in the
second degree. Knowledge is the common stock
of all mankind, derived from one universal sun of
mind, that rises in the east to open and adorn the
Lodge. No one has any peculiar patent for truth
any farther than he lives the life of truth, and
thereby makes it his own ; and then he is bound

by all the ties of humanity, to impart the riches of his faith as freely as he has received them. His life, or love, he cannot give to another. Hence, there can be no substitution of the righteousness of one man for the sins of others. Each man must stand or fall by the virtues of his own life. Freely has he received, and freely must he give of the truths he has acquired. They are the water of regeneration, and must not be withheld from any, that are in a state to receive.

The Entered Apprentice Lodge is composed of a due proportion of Masters, Fellow Crafts and Entered Apprentices, by which there is a constant state of progression, through instruction imparted by the Master, to the Fellow Crafts ; and from the Fellow Crafts to the Entered Apprentices ; by which there is consociation and desire of progression ; for all instruction must be imparted from a source higher than the receiver. Hence, the more degrees a Mason has taken, the greater is his obligation to others ; and this increases in regeneration, until his individual life is lost in mutual love. The spiritual angel loves his neighbor as himself, and the celestial angel better than himself. At the building of King Solomon's Temple, the Entered Apprentices assembled and held their Lodge on the ground floor. The Fellow Crafts held their Lodge on the ground floor of the right hand nether chamber, and also the middle chamber, and the Master Masons in the Sanctum Sanctorum. There were three separate and distinct places of meeting, contained in the Temple; which are representative of the three states of the natural or ultimate heaven. The kingdom of heaven cometh without observation; it is in you. Luke, 17, 20, 21. Heaven consists in the states of its individual members; and hence, the entire societies of each heaven, constitute not only a place, but places, through which there is progression from place to place, in the spiritual or world of mind.

Every truth and love of the human intellect is as completely an organised substance, as the products of the natural earth. These conjoin in the great world of mind, with all the harmony and beauty of the heavens themselves. So that the ultimates of divine truth and love in every regenerate man, add one feature to that world, or a stone, to the Grand Lodge above. The light proceeding from the great celestial sun of the divine mind being organized, prepared and stamped with the most interior principles of the animal, vegetable and mineral kingdoms; it follows that every ultimate individual mind is in a certain likeness of nature itself; but with endless and infinite variety. Hence, a Lodge may be held upon the highest mountains, and in the lowest valley; wherever the Holy Bible, Square and Compass are to be found. The Holy Bible is the chart, or warrant to work. There exists no correspondence in nature or heaven, of a separate charter or warrant. The true representative of authority, is the Bible itself; hence, the charter or warrant must be considered representative of the Word, in order to have any representative meaning at all. He who has the divine commandments, needs no other warrant to work. Our Ancient brethren held their Lodges, and proceeded to labor, wherever a sufficient number met together in any part of the world. But organized as society is at the present day, it is practicable and convenient to hold Lodges permanently in local places; and, for the sake of communication and consociation, Grand Lodges have been established, which are representative of higher authority. And, for the sake of order and subordination, they grant dispensations and charters, which, owing to evils that exist in society at the present day, appear to be necessary with a view to promote the general good. Hence, the charter has been introduced as one of the component parts of the Lodge. But in the early periods of the existence of Masonry, it was the principle repository of the Word itself; copies of which could only be produced at great expense, and hence, it was sufficient authority for the good motives and standing of those that maintained it. When the truths of the Word are committed to memory, understood and practised, they become the living and vital principles of a regenerate life. Hence, man, as to his interiors, becomes a Lodge in its least form; and when consociated with others in different and orderly states of regeneration, the Lodge or heavenly society, becomes properly constituted for the guardianship of others.

No. 61. Our Ancient Brethren held their Lodges, on the highest mountains and in the lowest valleys, the better to observe the ascent and descent of cowans. The natural man is a microcosm in an uncultivated condition. The regenerate man or Mason, represents the World in a civilized and cultivated state. Yet the principles of Masonry are as much the foundation of all that is good and true in the uncultivated states of man, as in his more refined life. Masonry, in all ages of the world, has represented, and promoted civilization; the regeneration of man and civilization have progressed hand in hand; although many are civilized, and but few regenerated, yet it is the regenerated man that gives life and vitality to the community. In the unregenerate and less cultivated conditions of man, Masonry was equally the foundation of all that was noble in his character. There are two fundamental loves, with the savage as well as with the enlightened. These are represented by the blue and the scarlet, or the domestic and devotional faculties, Nos. 22, 23. The one is situated at the crown of the head, and the other at the base of the brain. The scarlet gives the feeling of temperance and fortitude. The other, prudence or meekness, and justice or humility; for meekness and prudence are but other names for the same thing, and there is always a feeling of justice in humility. Yet justice implies judgment. These feelings and principles are only brought forth in the Mason, as he progresses in the degrees of regeneration.

The domestic and devotional faculties are the two great centers of vitality and life in man. They are receptive of the red and blue rays of light, which give feeling and sensation to the mind and body. The blue governs all the natural relations of life; and the scarlet the principles of faith. Over these, the Lord watches with the utmost care, flowing in through them by an interior way, so that they are preserved from the evils and falses, by the divine Providence, which reside in the internal mind. Otherwise the fountain of life would be corrupt. Evil flows in by an exterior way and re-acts against the vital principles, which flow in from the Lord. This is the tree of life and the tree of the knowledge of good and evil. The tree of life is at the East of the garden, which the Lord guards with cherubim and flaming sword; were it possible for evil to gain possession of these life principles, man could never be regenerated, and creation itself would be a blot upon Deity. These two groups of faculties, are the highest and lowest loves. They reach the two extremes without which there can be no perception ; for just in proportion as the mind reaches high and low, there is breadth of intellectual vision. The mind always draws its conclusions from the first, the last, or the highest and the lowest. Rising from the lowest principles of truth, or the more external forms to an interior perception, it endeavors to form its conclusions from all that is known of the subject. Hence the Lodge is said to be held upon the highest mountains, and in the lowest valleys, the better to observe the ascent and descent of cowans and eaves droppers. Cowans signify evils, and eaves droppers falsities. The operation of the human mind must be determined by the highest, and lowest principles, reacting upon each other, in order to concentrate upon a conclusion. The highest hills, signify the celestial loves, and the lowest valleys the natural. Hence, it is by the middle, or spiritual degree, that all the conclusions are arrived at. The intellectual holds the just mean between the two. The two fundamental loves, the blue and the scarlet, are the celestial of the highest and lowest discrete degrees of heaven. The scarlet is the love of the celestial good, that prevails in the highest heaven. The blue is the celestial love of truth, which is the first active agent in regeneration, and forms the celestial principle of the lowest or natural heaven. The intellectual principle prevails in the intermediate, or spiritual heavens. These three discrete degrees exist in every individual man, in a three, six, and nine fold order. The only difference between the natural and regenerate man, is, that, in the former, the degrees lie dormant, and, in the latter, they are opened and vivified with life. Hence, in the regenerate man, there exist all the forms of the natural, spiritual and celestial heavens; and therefore, the heavens are in the likeness of one man. A regenerate man on earth, is a Lodge or Heaven in its least form. All the principles of Heaven concentrating in their descent upon man, they flow into his natural form, correcting all the irregularities caused by evil, purifying the spirit, adorning and beautifying the physical and intellectual person, casting out all disease, giving health and strength to the man. Every evil however is uprooted with pain. The starry galaxy of our natural universe of stars, so far as the telescope has revealed it, approximates the form of a man. Hence, heaven, spiritually and naturally, is the man of men, through which we live, move and have our being from the divine Father; a certain likeness of the divine attributes and the universe, concentrate in each regenerate man.

No. 62. The Entered Apprentice degree was conferred in the outer Court of the Temple, and upon the ground floor of the left hand, nethermost chamber, the length of which greatly exceeded the breadth. Hence, the Lodge of an Entered Apprentice is said to be an oblong square. The first section of the Fellow Craft was conferred in the middle Court, and the second section in the middle Chamber on the right hand side of the Temple. The

Masters' degree was conferred in the Sanctum Sanctorum, or Holy of Holies, which was an exact square, the length being equal to the breadth. See description of the Temple, No. 87.

Length is predicated of the will, from which is derived the affection of truth, for no truth can be retained in the memory unless there is an affection to receive it. Breadth is predicated of truth, it being a second state of the affections, in which truth is conjoined with love, which is represented by the multiplication of one number with another, by which there is breadth: and hence length signifies love, and breadth truth.

The addition of a number or quantity gives depth or thickness. The multiplication of a line, or surface gives expansion. Addition is the third quality of a number, which represents thickness. These are the three principal qualities of matter; length, breadth and thickness. These are representative of the attributes of love, wisdom and use.

A Lodge is said to be situated due East and West, which refers to its length or the goodness of the Lord in regeneration. Its breadth is said to extend from the North to the South ; or, from perfect darkness to light, and is predicated of the divine wisdom of the Lord. Its height is said to be from the surface to the highest heavens, which includes all the degrees and states of regeneration; its covering being no less than the clouded canopy and starry decked heavens, where all good Masons hope to arrive by the aid of Jacob's theological ladder, which is predicated of the ascending and descending degrees in man. Three of the principal states or rounds of which are faith, hope and charity. The depth of the Lodge is from the surface to the center, which is predicated of all the truths and affections of earth or the natural man.

The square, which is the form of the Masters' Lodge, signifies perfection, the truth being equal to the love. These are perfected in works which extend from the surface to the center, and from the earth to the heavens.

No. 63.   The Temple of Masonry is said to be supported by three large columns, which are called wisdom, strength and beauty. Column is predicated of an order, and is representative of an order itself.   Every order throughout nature is the arrangement of three things, namely: end, cause and effect, or the motives, means and effects produced.   The effect may again become the cause or means to produce other effects, or last or ultimate ends. Thus, there may proceed from one cause , an endless variety in a series of three. The first effect may join with the second, producing a combination of the two; and this combination again becomes a cause or means. Thus, there may be first causes, secondary and tertiary; and so on, giving an infinite variety, in series and degrees. These all refer back to the first motive or love of the divine will. The first end, being motive or love, manifested in the cause which is wisdom; these two are manifested in the effect, which is the natural result or principle of the two former, which exist together as the soul, spirit and body. Therefore, there is will, wisdom and procedure in all things. The will or love principle is first manifested in wisdom, which is the very existence of love. In God, these two principles are distinctly one; manifesting themselves in the divine natural principle, in which they dwell and act in their full force and power, as one being. From him, proceed the divine attributes of love, wisdom and use, as a great sun of mind going forth throughout the universe in its creative principles. Hence, God is the life and light of all things, evil excepted. These life and light principles, are more or less decomposed and separated in their onward course of creation, decomposing and recombining in myriads of forms. They constitute creation itself. But as the great channel can never be turned back upon its fountain, no created thing can become God. All strength is derived from the life principle or love; all wisdom is derived from the divine love and the divine truth, which give the perception of good and evil; from which there is liberty of action. The choosing of the right, is called wisdom. The just and harmonious combination of love with wisdom, gives that particular delight and playfulness of thought and action which is called beauty. Beauty is the attractive form of wisdom. The delight of love, through wisdom, is beauty. The delight of truth with love is grace or dignity. The just combination of love, truth and usefulness, working in harmonious action, constitutes the wisdom, strength and beauty of Masonry; which are the three great columns that support the Temple.

No. 64. The covering of the Lodge is the clouded canopy and starry heavens, where it is said that all good Masons hope to arrive, by the aid of Jacob's ladder; three of the principal rounds of which are faith, hope and charity. The symbolism of the clouded canopy and the starry heavens, cannot be easily understood, without reflecting more fully upon their uses, for all parallelism between the mental and physical world, is not by forms of truth, but by uses. The clouded canopy of the natural world, is one of the effects produced in the atmospheres, usually supposed to be the condensation of vapor, which has arisen from the earth. But it is a well-known fact, that the lighter gases exist in the upper atmospheres, and more or less commingle with oxygen gas, which is both a component part of water and of the atmosphere ; and that, if a spark of electricity be passed through these two gases, namely, hydroden and oxygen, they are combined and form water ; from this we may readily conclude that there is a constant creation of water in the atmosphere, and a corresponding loss of its component gases, which would occasion a want of their constant supply.

We therefore infer, that there is a continual creation, going on at all times, it being nothing less than a condensation of light itself, that is decomposed by the atmospheres, which are constantly saturated with electricity, and form the great chemical work-shops of the elemental world. We may also conclude that the solid substances of the earth, through their exhalations, react upon the atmospheres, and assist in the great work, that the animal kingdom, also, exhales its animal, aromal and magnetic electricity, as prepared substances from light, for farther and lower forms of ultimate uses. We, therefore, perceive at once, that the clouds and mists of the atmospheres are manifestations of first, or gaseous forms of elemental creation. These misty forms in nature, are like the first literal forms of objects in the mind, for thought forms are created as well as other substances. Nothing can reach the sensorium of man, without the decomposition of light, heat and electricity. The light is decomposed and concentrated by the crystaline lens, and deprived of its heat by the humors of the eye. Thus, the eye itself acts as a kind of atmosphere upon the light in vision, being a chemical process by which changes are produced upon the thought substances of the mind. There is also a constant inhalation and exhalation through the skin, by which there is the sense of feeling, which contributes to the form substances of the mind. The case is similar with each of the five senses. The mere literal forms of the thought substances, appear before the eye of the mind in visions as clouds and mists.

Hence, clouds signify the mere literals of thought, or first forms; water signifying truth or falsity; for each symbol has its opposite meaning.— Every man, when spiritually seen, is surrounded with clouds; some are so dense as to exclude all the mental light of the divine sun. White clouds appear in the brilliant light and clear atmosphere of the spiritual rational mind. These are the clouds of the canopy, that cover the Masonic Lodge, which represent a state of mind, that all good Masons hope to arrive at. These are the clouds of heaven, and appear yet above the heavens or man of men. The stars are suns of other worlds within their own atmospheres and circles; they are creative powers through which the divine mind operates for the creation of other worlds. They hold the same position in the natural universe, as the vast and powerful societies of angels do in the spiritual world of mind. And, hence, stars represent spiritual knowledges; these are the knowledges of the good Mason. Jacob's theological ladder, as it is called, is representative of the states and degrees of man, which are opened in the course of his regeneration; commencing at the lowest or Entered Apprentice degree, and opening upwardly through the preparatory states of regeneration to the

22

Royal Arch, whence they commence to descend. Divine order, or love having obtained complete and perfect control over all passions and faculties of the man, as his work has been spiritual and natural, therefore, it now becomes celestial, as he clears away the old rubbish from the North East corner, and begins to lay the foundation of the new celestial temple.

For the foregoing reasons, Jacob, in his vision, saw the angels first ascending and then descending. The discrete and continuous degrees in man cannot be simultaneously opened, so that man can work in each at the same time, although the three continuous degrees of each discrete degree may be simultaneously opened; yet work is performed in each, separately. The difference between the Grand Master and the Craft, or the Lord, and man, is this: in the grand Master, all the degrees are simultaneously opened; so that he views all things in their simultaneous and progressive order, from the highest to the lowest of the discrete degrees. The Lord alone is able simultaneously to operate in each. When an angel descends from the Royal Arch to the Entered Apprentice, he must work in that degree only.

His views are partial and confined to the

discrete degree in which he is, although he holds his authority by the virtue of the Grand Master through the higher degrees. For the foregoing reasons, it is clear that no finite being can take a universal view farther than is contained in the discrete degree, in which he is. But the Grand Master, or the Lord himself, in whom exists simultaneous order can do it.· His intellect and affections are universal, containing every particular. Hence his power is ever present and operative, while man's power is limited. It is ever impossible for man to become God. Yet God is an infinite man or man over all, uncreated and eternal; for without the idea of God, as a man, there is no adoration or worship.

No. 65. The furniture of the Lodge consists of the Holy Bible, Square and Compass. Furniture, signifies such things as are necessary to carry on the work of regeneration. The three discrete degrees of the mind, are closed at birth. The sensual and corporeal mind is first opened with knowledges from without, and influxes from within, that flow through the discrete degrees. The evils and falses of an active life, are hereditary, transferred to the children. These evils and falses, destroy the transparency and clearness of the degrees; so that, ultimately, there is no interior light transmitted; and the man is born into complete ignorance. The transparency of the degrees, is somewhat restored by education and knowledges from without, which are received through the medium of the five senses; which exist and live by virtue of the degrees· from within. In the orderly state of man, where the degrees have not been darkened, the heavenly light shines through them as a clear atmosphere. In the passage of the light, the rays are decomposed, giving light and understanding to the natural mind; so that man, like the brute creation, would be born into all the natural knowledges and affection, requisite for the purposes of life and regeneration.

The mind continues to unfold to eternity; but this unfolding and progression has been arrested by evil and falsities; so that the divine forms of the animal, vegetable and mineral kingdoms, contained in the divine creative sphere, which flows down filling the heavens with its glory, teach the Angels the will of the divine Creator, and instruct them in all the laws of order, by which they understand and comprehend the natural creation itself. This divine descending sphere, is no less, than the Word of the living God. The Word was seen and perceived, in the first orderly state of man; natural objects serving as a resting point, giving the mind the power of reaction and reflection on the divine attributes. This perception and power was entirely destroyed by the fall of man ; so that, in order to preserve man in a state to be regenerated, it became necessary to guard the interior principle of the will, which is the tree of life, and also for the Lord to fill an angel with his presence, and cause the Angel to descend and occupy the bodies of the prophets of old, laying asleep, for the time being, their own personal identity; so that the prophets spake as the oracle of God, conveying, in the literal languages and historical ciscumstances of the man, the knowledges of the divine descending sphere of regenerative creation; and, in order to preserve these knowledges in the world, the Jewish nation was called and chosen ; so that, these knowledges might be identified with their history, and become a part of the world itself.

To make the identification complete, and to preserve it to all time, it was necessary that the divine Wisdom or Word, should descend into its lowest natural form,which is man, and take upon

22*                    L2

itself, a bodily form, from a virgin. The bodily substances of the mother, and spiritual form derived from her, were put off in regeneration and death, the life of the body being preserved, glorified and made a part of the divine.

Thus the divine wisdom of God stands identified with the human life in the body and flesh, by which there is communication of the divine with man. The form of the human body, in which our Lord was seen after death, was no less than the divine natural of God Himself, which is represented by the Master of the Lodge. The divine descending sphere of regenerative creation is different from the natural creation of substances in the world, being the divine Providence, or the descent of the divine will and understanding in the preservation and growth of all things.

When the three discrete degrees of man are fully opened, this descending sphere is perceived in the celestial degree as the divine life, motives and objects of the divine Providence. In the middle or spiritual degree, it is perceived in all the various forms of the animal, vegetable and mineral creation, which are representative of the divine order of truth and love. In the natural mind or lowest degree, they are perceived as symbolic representations of great moral principles and truths. As these descend into the corporeal or animal mind, they fall into the educational habits or literal facts and words. The mind, that does not ascend above mere literals or the signification of words, has made no progress in Masonry or a divine life; for words are the signs of ideas, and ideas are representative of the interior things of thought and affection, which are contained in the divine descending spheres.

Just in proportion as the transparency of the degrees is darkened by evils and falsities, the divine light from within is shut out; and just in proportion as the light is deprived of its heat, or remains undecomposed, the heavenly affections are cold and chilly, and remain unproductive of good. Divine order must be restored in the human mind by a life of faith and charity, in six successive days of labor or degrees of regeneration, in which man is instructed in the knowledges of the Word, and lives the life of charity or love.

This state of preparation first ascends in the regular orders of the degrees to the Royal Arch, when man comes to a state of perception of the interior things of the Word or the divine descending spheres, when he becomes a man angel and is led of the Lord.

Thus the written Word of God has supplied the place of the divine spheres in regeneration. The divine light constantly flows in by the red and blue rays, while the yellow or light principle is received from without, through the Word by the medium of the senses. The celestial love of truth and the celestial love of good, which are represented by the blue and the scarlet rays, form the two blades and angle of the square, by which all the motives, purposes and truths of life are tried, squared and prepared for the regenerate life. The compass represents the interior knowledges of science, and the interior perfections of the divine attributes, which serve to surround, clothe, enclose and protect our affections.

But when regeneration has taken place by the opening of the Royal Arch degree, the divine light, or science of regeneration, descends directly from the Lord, and the compass gives place to the attribute of wisdom, adding another blade to the sides of the square, forming an equilateral triangle, representative of the divine attributes of love, wisdom and use, which is the emblem of the Royal Arch degree. Thus the Holy Bible represents the divine descending sphere of the Lord. The square represents or corresponds to the celestial love of truth and the celestial love of good. The compass signifying the spiritual affectious of science through natural good and truth.

No. 66. The ornaments of the Lodge are the Mosaic pavements, the indented and tessellated border, and the blazing star. Mosaic work is made of pebbles of different colors, neatly cut and set in cement, arranged in the most beautiful manner, in different designs, agreeably to the taste of the artist. The utmost genius and mechanical skill have been exhausted upon this class of work; and many beautiful specimens of the handy work of our ancient brethren still exist throughout Europe. Indented tessellated work is made of different colored stones, cut in squares and so arranged and laid, as to represent small cubes or blocks. The stones of different colors are selected, and set so as to make them appear indented. These borders are of many patterns, of great variety and beauty.

The blazing or five pointed star, usually marked the center of the Mosaic pavement. The mental meaning or spiritual signification of these things, cannot be understood until something more is known of the progression, from state to state, of the human mind in regeneration. When man rises out of one state into another, the things of the former spiritually appear as the pavement, or street upon which he walks.

Hence the city of the new Jerusalem, seen by our Grand Master St. John, descending from Heaven, had its streets of pure gold. He also saw a sea of glass before the throne of God, like unto transparent gold.

The case with man is this—all things of the mind that are confirmed, cannot be destroyed, but remain with man to eternity. The principle derived from the mother, alone, is put off; but the works derived therefrom still exist in the human mind, and, so long as these remain active and uppermost in the mind, there is no progression from a lower to a higher state.

When regeneration is about to take place with a man, he is intromitted into a confused and darkened state of mind, in which he is dissatisfied with the past, and uncertain as to the future. In this state of mind, the Royal and Select Masters, or the descending spheres of celestial love of truth, and the celestial love of good, represented by the blue and the scarlet, are secretly at work in the hidden vaults of the mind, preparing all the confirmations produced by the conjunction of the will and understanding, and arranging them for the foundations of the new Temple.

The things of natural science in the mind, which have been confirmed by the will, whether true or false, are beautifully arranged by the Entered Apprentice, Fellow Craft and Master, agreeably to the design or prevailing loves of the man. Those things which are most true correspond to to white stones. Falsities and errors are represented by black and grey, with every variety of shade, color, hue and tint, from black to white. These colors and shades, arise from the deceptive appearances and falses of the senses. The five senses are represented by the Blazing Star, in the centre of the pavement.

Every state of the human mind, should be fully bounded, and finished before the mind proceeds to another. This bounding and finishing, is represented by the Indented and Tessallated Border. This border is the work of education in youth, and represents the manifold blessings of divine providence; which every Mason hopes to arrive at, through a good life and virtuous education.

Much of the harmony and beauty of the regenerate life, arises from the patient labor and finish bestowed upon this Pavement. It is one of the principal ornaments, of the Masonic mind. Rude, indeed, would be the Lodge without it. It requires much labor and education to fit and prepare the true and the false, so that they can dwell together in harmony. Representatives take place both by the animal, vegetable and mineral kingdoms.

In the animal kingdom, this state of mind is represented by the ringed, streaked and speckled of Laban flock, which were the share of Jacob. See Gen. 30, 32. A similar state is also represented by the coat of many colors, which Israel made for Joseph. The same state of mind is represented by the candidates being reclothed. The mind of the youth is developed in regular order, first by the observation and study of facts; secondly, by the inculcation of the principles of science, during the time that the hereditary principles of the father are brought forth, from twelve to eighteen years of age. The final finishing and surrounding of this state, with the beautiful Indented Tessellated Border, takes place during the completion of the scholastic education, from the age of eighteen to twenty-one; at which time the natural rational principle assumes control of the man. He is then said to be free born, of lawful age, and under the tongue of good report. At this period, the light of the five senses, gives place to the greater light of the natural rational or intellectual principle of the mother.

Hence, the Blazing Star that represents the light of the five senses, which is said to have shone on our Savior's nativity by Christian Masons, is placed under the feet of the man in the centre of the pavement.

From the foregoing, it will be seen, that the Masonic Pavement represents the affections of science. The Indented Tessellated Border represents the consummation of the natural sciences. The Blazing Star in the centre, signifies the light of the five senses, made subordinate to reason, so that all things of the senses are as a floor on which the spiritual rests for support. No man can ascend into spiritual things, until this floor is complete.

No. 67. The lights of a Lodge are located in the East, West and South. A light signifies an instructor, and light itself represents instruction. But there can be no instruction without a candidate to instruct, and no reception without the candidate is in a condition to receive. Light also signifies the receptive state and condition of the candidate. These states in general are three; first the state of morning or intelligence, when the truths of intelligence are received into the memory, and stored up in the mind. Morning, therefore, signifies the time or state of reception.

The second state or high twelve, represents the light of science. Truths are first received into the memory, and afterwards elevated into the middle chamber of the understanding, and lastly into the will, which is the work of the three first degrees of Masonry. A certain likeness exists in each continuous degree. The Entered Apprentice degree is the initiation of truth in the memory; the fulness of which takes place at high twelve, when the sun is at its meridian light.

Hence, high twelve signifies the fulness of reception, in which there is a certain likeness of a state of science : yet the Entered Apprentice cannot be said to be introduced into true science, notwithstanding, there is, to some extent, an arrangement of truths in the memory. The third state is the close of the day. When the love of memorising and arranging the things of faith, declines to the shade of evening, collecting the experiences of the day, from which arises the power of correct judgment or choosing the right, which is wisdom. These three states of reception in general, signify the light of intelligence, the light of science and the light of wisdom ; but these cannot in particular be applied to the Entered Apprentice, there being but a certain likeness of them with him, but refer in general to the Lodge, or the operation of the human mind, of which the Lodge is an exact representative. The will or celestial principle can do nothing of itself. The love or desire is first put forth in the East, through the light of intelligence or the knowledge of history and facts. These knowledges go forth from the East as a command, in which the will of the Worshipful Master is expressed.

These are referred to the light of reflection and experience in the West; from which they are referred for action to the light of science and mechanics in the South; having passed the several stations of the mind, they receive their full force and power from the scientific and mechanical principles. Every action must first be referred to the two extremes of the mind, and reflected or thrown back upon the centre, from which there is action.

This is equally the case, in regard to the parts

of the brain; the central portion just above, and in the region of the ear, is the centre of the muscular motion of the limbs, which is a kind of complex of the combined motion of the brain; upon which all the ideas concenter for action or operation. The will principle of the man is first brought forward into the light of intelligence, located in the right frontal portion of the brain; whence it returns and is thrown with great force into the left, being concentrated upon the ultimates of intellectual order in the left and frontal lobe of the brain, which, like precious stones or gems, sparkle with light of intelligence; by which the light is decomposed, and its internal principle set at liberty, and reflected upon the central portion or commissures of the brain for action.

But, these are mysterious operations of the mind, that can only be perceived and understood from the higher and more exalted states of perception, which arise from the opening of the Royal Arch degree of the mind, or rather the transparency and opening of all the degrees. The reader must bear in mind, that all thought substances are organized, being used by the brain in an electric form circulated through myriads of different channels; the brain being a microcosm or image of the universe itself.

From these three lights of the Lodge, arise three orders of men. First, those in whom the will principle acts, mainly, through history and facts. The second, are those of the reflective order: these break loose from the old and beaten tracks of the world, and constantly strive for new arrangements of thought; they are the philosophers. The third and last discrete class or order are scientific, mechanical and operative. To the close and accurate observer, these classes of men are as distinct as the three principal orders of architecture, differing in personal form, appearance and action. They are the manifestation of the celestial, spiritual and natural principles in man. One or the other of these takes the lead in all the various styles of persons, although the individual may belong to the higher middle or lower celestial, as the case may be; for each discrete degree has its three continuous degrees, in which the celestial, spiritual and natural are manifested in different individuals, marking these characters in each discrete degree.

When the human mind stands in divine order, through regeneration, the discrete degrees act by induction from the highest to the lowest. The celestial faculties induce action on the spiritual, and the spiritual on the natural. The perceptive faculties, discrete or separate, the sensual and corporeal, form the scientific or rational degree of the mind. The natural rational is separated from the spiritual, and presided over, by the Master's degree, the Master receiving the influxes of the spiritual, and the spiritual is discrete or separated from the celestial by the Royal Arch. Thus all things of the mind ascend and descend by three discrete and six continuous degrees, acting and reacting on each other.

No. 68.   The Jewels of the Lodge are six.   A jewel is an ornament of great value, usually set with precious stones, from which its name is derived. A precious stone represents a spiritual truth. Hence, the Lodge has in general, six spiritual truths, which are fundamental or primary, and which are represented by the Plumb, Square and Level, the Rough Ashler, the Perfect Ashler, and the Trestle Board.   The three former are said to be moveable, and the latter immoveable.   Motion or action is predicated of life, and inertia of death.

The Plumb, Square and Level, are representative of work or action.   The Rough Ashler, the Perfect Ashler, and the Trestle Board are representative of either inertia or reaction, for all motion in the universe is manifested by resistance or reaction.

The Plumb, Square and Level, are the active principles of the universe, through which the Great Architect causes the planets to revolve upon their axes, and rotate in their orbits. By them the earth is covered with its beautiful foliage, and man and beast move upon its surface. This cannot be readily understood, without an intimate knowledge of the laws of attraction and gravitation. All attraction arises from affinities, and affinities arise from the combination of light and heat. The law of light and heat is expansive, when free caloric prevails, and contractive, when the ethereal or light principle is in power. Every ultimate marriage of light and heat establishes an attractive force, so that there can be no drawing together or condensation of light, or the ethereal fluids, without establishing in each particle the law of attraction. The more numerous the particles, the greater is the power of attraction and condensation. See No. 44. So that all the minor formations are drawn or attracted to the larger. This attraction is called gravitation.

Supposing all things to be in an ethereal condition, and the law of attraction established in any considerable number of particles, they will be drawn together with equal force on every side, forming a sphere, under equal pressure. If any caloric be set at liberty within the body thus formed, it would become expansive, producing motion, and the law of action and reaction would commence. The fluids being under equal pressure on every side, the motion of necessity, among its parts must be circular, and hence, every contraction or expansion in a fluid body, tends directly to make it revolve upon its own axis. This motion, being once established, continues after the body has become ultimated into solids. Every motion of the atmosphere about it, which is being condensed and elaborated into ultimate forms, tends to produce and keep up its rotary motion.

Supposing the vast ethereal fluids themselves to be partially condensed and drawn together from the same causes, the contraction and expansion of parts would cause a rotary motion to take place upon a vast and extensive scale, including all the various minor bodies formed within it, so as to waft them into orbits and counter orbits around particular centres, and these again would all revolve around a grand centre, forming a universe of suns and planets, all subject to the same law of attraction and expansion, which originated in the combination of two particles of light and heat, extending in a geometrical progression, until suns and planets are drawn together; all held by the universal affinity of light and heat, moving in one grand harmonious whole, operated upon, and caused by the single law of attraction and expansion, all their principles agreeing with the Plumb, Square and Level.

Thus it is that the powers of attraction and gravitation, arise from the affinity of light and heat, the marriage of the two producing an offspring which is electricity, through which light and heat ultimate themselves in the animal, vegetable and mineral kingdoms of nature. Three discrete degrees are contained severally in light, heat and electricity. Heat being the soul of light, and light the body of heat, electricity is their garment or active sphere. The discrete degrees act and react upon each other, producing decomposition and recombination, agreeably to the will of the divine mind, which is present with every molecule through the spiritual light and heat of the great central sun, which is divine love and wisdom from the mind of the great Creator. Thus it is, that mind and matter are connected, working through fixed and positive laws which are necessities. These laws have no controlling power in themselves, but are instruments, like the Plumb, Square and Level in the hand of the Mason, which we shall now proceed to explain.

No. 69. From a marriage or intimate union, portions of light and heat are combined, forming the ethereal fluids in which are established the laws of attraction and gravitation. In the combining of light and heat, there is a partial decomposition and setting at liberty of other portions, which give rise to an electric sphere, around the particles thus formed. These spheres of various particles coalesce and conjoin them in other forms, establishing the power of cohesive attraction. The combination of all the particles impinges or concentrates upon one particle, the centre of gravitation, to which every particle tends. From the centre of gravitation, there is a reaction or resistance to every other particle.

This reaction takes place by the positive and negative spheres of electricity, attracting and combining negative particles, and rejecting the positive. Thus, the ethereal fluids flow together, each particle being stamped with the likeness of the mineral, vegetable and animal kingdoms, which are to come forth in the onward course of creation. These nebulous and gaseous forms, being free to move in all their parts, assume the spherical or globular form.

The contractive and expansive motion within, caused by the decomposition and recombining of parts, gives a general motion among the particles, which of necessity, must be circular and spiral, causing the whole body to rotate upon the centre of gravity. This motion, being once established, continues, although the different parts of the globe may be drawn together and solidified. The attractive power impinging upon the centre is called the Plumb. The constant pressure upon every side by this power, causes the earth to assume the spherical form, which is at right angles, at the surface, to every point of the Plumb or line of gravitation. This in Masonry, we call the Level.

If two opposing forces be exactly equal, opposing each other in one direct line, the action and reaction give rise to a second motion, which is at right angles to the line of the opposing forces. Thus, the gravitation and pressure upon the centre of gravity, of every particle of the earth, is equally resisted by the reaction from the centre, giving a second or lateral motion, forming the Square or right angle.

From the foregoing, it will be seen, that the Plumb, Square and Level are the result of action and equilibrium, and hence, agree with the action and counter action themselves. If a body be let fall upon the surface of the earth, it is resisted from the centre and brought to an equilibrium, giving a horizontal motion and momentum, which is a Square, and also a Level, from which it is seen that evey circle is composed of the Plumb, Square and Level, extending in myriads of directions, Hence, the equilibrium, that exists between the Plumb, Square and Level, causes the squares of the base and the perpendicular to be equal to the square of the hypothenuse. The formation of every stone in the quarry, the growth of the cedars of Lebanon, and the bounding of the hart upon the mountains, are by the Plumb, Square and Level.

The center of gravity being established in every animal and organic form, it is the ruling principle and reactive force of motion, constantly changing with every step. Every power of locomotion centres upon it, establishing a plumb line in the body at every movement. By a perception of this Plumb line, man is able to rise and stand upon his feet ; and by the opposing forces of the Plumb, Square and Level, the body is held in equilibrium, and has the power of motion, for without an equilibrium of parts, there is no freedom or will. To destroy this equilibrium, is to take away freedom and action.

Hence, every thing in nature tends to equilibrium. All motion is by the contraction and expansion of parts from a source or power, higher than nature. It is from the world of mind, through light, heat and electricity, regarded as agents or connecting links. The progressive states of formation in nature, are its Rough Ashler, Perfect Ashler, and Trestle Board. See No. 44.

No. 70. The Plumb, is an instrument used by operative Masons, to try perpendiculars. It consists of a small piece of metal, cast in a spherical and ornamental form, to which there is a line attached. This line is attached to a parallel rule ; and when the rule is applied to the side of a stone or building, the Plumb line determines at once whether it is perpendicular to the horizon.

If two right angles be attached to the bottom of the Plumb Rule, the instrument is called the

24

Level, and is made use of to determine horizontals.
The common Square can be temporarily used for
all these purposes, if a Plumb line be attached to
it.   But it is more convenient and perfect as a
Level, when the additional right angle is attached
to the opposite side.

From what has been said in the previous articles,
No. 68, 69, it will be perceived, that both the
Square and Level arise from the  single power of
the Plumb or gravitation.   We are therefore prepared to understand the correspondences of the
Plumb, Square and Level.   There can be no correspondence of natural things, with natural things,
for the operation would be a simple agreement of
parts, like applying the Plumb to a verticle line.

But in all representatives and  correspondences,
one side of the parallelism, must be in the natural
world, and the other side in the mental or spiritual
world.   In the spiritual world all attraction is of
love or affection. The Plumb in the natural world,
corresponds  to the  love  of God in the  spiritual;
for, by the love of God, the  whole heavens are
formed and held in their place.   As the power of
attraction gives rise to  the formation of the natural world, (as has been  shown above), so the love
of the Lord governs the  entire  societies  of  the

heavens. As a man's knowledges and loves are, as to the attributes of the Lord, so is his entire religious life.

The second great natural power of the world, is the power of cohesive attraction, which arises from the electric spheres. These spheres blend together and cause the organization of all substances. This power, in the natural world corresponds or agrees in its uses, to the love of the neighbor in the mental or spiritual. By this love, every society is drawn together and bound in the bonds of mutual love and friendship.

The love of God, or the scarlet ray of light, as it flows into the natural world, divides like the branches of a great tree, spreading and ramifying in every department of life. So it is with mutual love, which is represented by the blue. It spreads and divides into a thousand channels, drawing together every useful society upon the earth; and all heavenly and useful societies are but branches of the great home, the uses of which are derived into different heads, over which are presiding angels in heaven.

The great sphere of architecture or civilization flows down with a mighty current into the Masonic world or Lodge, through it, establishing order and mutual love.

Masonry is but a great branch of the universal church, having the same Lord, faith, doctrine and charity, the love of the neighbor, being the universal end. Its great use in the world is to foster and encourage civilization, for the benefit of man, in the universal heavens. As the Level is the combination of the Plumb and Square, resulting as a third instrument of use, it corresponds to the equal combination of the red and blue rays, with the perceptive or yellow, which results in the universal principle and life of charity; which is Masonry itself.

The Rough, the Perfect Ashler, and the Trestle Board, are the immovable jewels of the Lodge. Like the natural formations of the earth, they are the result of action or a life of use. The Rough Ashler is the rude stone as it comes from the quarry. The Perfect Ashler is the Rough Ashler, prepared by the hand of the Fellow Craft, to be placed in the building. The Trestle Board is the instrument on which the Master draws his designs. The Rough Ashler, in the natural world, corresponds to perceptive truths in the mental or spiritual. Hence, the Rough Ashler, is the plane of perception. The Perfect Ashler, in the natural world, is the same stone, prepared by art and science, to take a place in the building. In the spiritual world, it corresponds to the plane of science and art, or the scientific mind represented by the Orange.

The Trestle Board contains the designs of the Master workman; and corresponds to the reflective and rational faculties, represented by the Orange and Citron. In these faculties, appear the divine and natural order, contained in the devotional and domestic faculties. They are reflectors, or mirrors in the frontal portion of the head, in which the order of our affections appear; they are the light of the human understanding, supplied with all the forms of truth, by the natural world.

They become the mirrors in which our affections may see themselves; for all divine order flows in by the affections of celestial good and celestial truth. But these can only come forth into active life, as the intellectual and wisdom principle is perfected by education and the divine word of God, which is our spiritual and moral Trestle Board.

No. 71. The affections of the man are arranged in nine groups, agreeable to the groups of organs in the head, explained in plate 1, fig. 1. These affections are opened in their three discrete, and six continuous degrees by regeneration, in which they are arranged, and act and react by their attractive force in the likeness of the universal heavens. The love of the Lord, becomes the great light or central sun. The love of the neighbor, which is represented by the blue, with its blue and silvery rays, is like the light of the moon. As all the affections begin to revolve around these grand centres, they are drawn together by the power of attraction, and are organized by their cohesive forces, in likeness of the universe. Nos. 63, 69.

The sun rises in the east, to open and adorn the day, in every progressive state of the man, ascending until high twelve, when it declines to the shade of evening; and the moon, or the love of the neighbor, governs the night. These are the great lights spoken of, in the first chapter of Genesis.

Thus, it is, that the Plumb, Square and Level, govern all things in the regenerate mind. The Plumb, or attractive power, is the love of the

Lord ; the Level or grouping power, is the love of the neighbor. The two blades of the Square are, justice and judgment. With the unregenerate man the Plumb, or attractive force, is the love of self. His Level or cohesive power, is the love of the world ; and the angle of his Square, is self interest and pleasure. He belongs to a different world ; his universe is the hells. Between him and the regenerate man, "there is a great gulf, so that no one can pass."

In his universe, darkness, death and decay reign supreme. His east, is selflove and pleasure; his west is hatred and revenge, and in his south is the meridian light of self-intelligence. The east of the regenerate man is justice and judgment. His west, is the wisdom derived from the love of the neighbor, and his south, is the meridian height of science and intelligence. When the unregenerate man has confirmed himself in a life of evil, he passes beyond the bounds of regeneration, and becomes a devil or a satan, a devil if the love of self prevails; and a satan if the love of the world is his sun ; and sinks down into endless darkness and decay. Being first devastated of all good, and finally the decomposition of all the confirmations of life or substances of the spirit take place, until there is no memory of the life left, when the seed germ of the soul returns to God who gave it.

For God is all and in all, and those that oppose Him as the supreme ruler of the universe; however fierce and terrible the conflict that they may wage against his kingdom, must ultimately sink in despair. This is the second death. It is not the province of this book to speak of the evils and disorders of this world, or of the world to come, farther than is necessary to illustrate the grogressive Masonic and orderly state. There being evil in the world, it is necessary in the commencement of regeneration, that a door or way of escape should be opened to man, so that he can pass from evil to good. The opposing forces of the hells, are so arranged by the divine Providence of the Lord, as to counteract and hold the evil man in liberty, by placing him in an equilibrium between good and evil; so that he has freedom or will, and can spiritually move in any direction.

This power is like the power of attraction or the Plumb, which is opposed or reacted against from the centre, all things being held in equilibrium, so that man and beast, can move upon the surface of the earth. Thus it is in spirit with the unregenerate man.

The evils from the hells below, resist the goods from the heavens, and hold man in equilibrium, so that he can turn to either, and as he makes his choice, seeing the good, and fearing the evil, he gradually ascends, by a life of good, to the heavens. Or if he turns to the hells, he gradually sinks beyond the reach of the heavenly spheres, and is no longer at liberty to turn to the heavens, but is brought under the attractive force and power of the hells, which react upon themselves; giving the man the apparent power of freedom of action. Yet he is unable to rise or ascend from the hells, any more than man can bodily rise out of the world to another planet, and *vice versa.* The man who ascends to heaven, is gradually drawn spiritually into the range and power of its attractive force, so that every thing within him reacts from the ultimates of good, which have been inwrought into his spiritual life. These are his immoveable jewels, represented by the Rough Ashler, the Perfect Ashler and the Trestle Board.

Man, now, has become an inhabitant of the heavens, governed by all the attractive forces of that world, in which there is full and complete liberty to do all things that are good, through love, whereas, in the nether world of the hells, man cannot will, to do rightly, but is held in apparent order by the force of law and fear of punishment. This equilibrium or balancing of the heavens and the hells, is not at all necessary for the existence of the heavens; and neither was it necessary for the existence of man in his unfallen condition ; but fallen as he is, it exists by the divine mercy of the Lord, for the sake of freedom, of thought and action in the first commencement or starting point of regeneration.

No. 72. The Lodge is said to be located due East and West, because Solomon's Temple and also the Tabernacle of Moses were so erected. This was done by a divine command, the reasons of which were not made known. The early Christian Churches, and Cathedrals of the middle centuries, were always erected due East and West.

The Masonic Lodges, in all ages of the world, when a convenient location could be obtained, have been likewise so erected; and when circumstances have changed their position, the Master's seat is always called the East, the Senior Warden's the West, and the Junior Warden's the South. The representatives of these things have always been partialy understood in the Lodge ; but we shall now proceed to make known their more interior significations.

The points of the compass signify the relative states and conditions of man, in relation to the Lord; for all the societies of the heavens are arranged in a progressive order.

The Lord being the East or place of light, always appears to the celestial angels in a middle altitude, between the South and the East. In the morning of their progressive states, His divine love goes forth from East to West, and his divine wisdom from South to North.

Hence, the societies of the East are in the morning or spring of their love ; and those in the West are in the decline of love, which is a state of wisdom from love ; for love declines to wisdom. The wisdom of the South at its meridian height, is the wisdom of intelligence and science, which declines in the North, to the natural corporeal and sensual principles.

Thus, the interior intellectual and scientific principles of the angels of the heavens, as they are located in their progressive societies, constantly revolve, like the universe, around the great central sun. Drawn and held by the attractive force or love, they are conjoined and organised by the force of cohesive attraction, which has been explained above. Nos. 68, 69, 70. These two forces are love and wisdom, or will and understanding. Length spiritually, is predicated of love, and breadth of wisdom and intelligence.

The first regenerative power of the human soul, as it proceeds from the Lord, is the celestial love of truth, in the spiritual man; and in those that are of a celestial nature, the first effect of love, is the celestial love of good. The first putting forth of all love, is in a direct line from the Lord, which is East and West. Hence, is it said: "Straight is the gate, and narrow is the way, that leadeth unto life, and few there be that find it."

The first putting forth of the attractive cohesive power, is the drawing together of particles which give breadth. Its direction is North and South. By this principle alone of intelligence and science, none can be saved. Hence, it is said: "Wide is the gate, and broad is the way, that leadeth unto death, and many there be that go in thereat." The breadth is equal or less than the length; it cannot be more. No truth can be received and ingrafted into life, unless there is a ground work of love to receive it. The continuous degree of the intellect is such, that it may be elevated by instruction into the highest heavens ; and, for the time being, see and comprehend the truths thereof.

But as quick as the stimulating force of love from the instructor ceases, the mind again relapses into its former state, and the intelligence imparted, that is above the condition of love in the recipient, is ejected from the mind, like bubbles of air from the water; so that intelligence or breadth can never be greater than the length, or love. All worship is of love, and all instruction of wisdom.

Instructing a man in a Lodge does not save him, unless the instruction is received into a ground of love; and no love can save a man except it is brought forth into substance by breadth and depth, or by truth and action. All order proceeds from divine love, flowing forth into truth, and from truth into life. Since the descent of the Lord into the world, opening the power of spiritual thought in man, through regeneration, no representative worship is allowed. All conjunction with the Lord, is through love and a worship therefrom.

Representative worship leads directly to idolatry, for so soon as the mind is darkened, man looks to the representative, instead of the Lord. But it is orderly and permitted to teach by representatives

and correspondences.  Therefore, the entire Holy
Scriptures, as to their instructive principles, are
representative and correspondential.  Any attempt
to worship by representatives, is forbidden and
rejected of the Lord, which we learn from our
Ancient Grand Masters, John 4. 21 to the 24.

Therefore, the representative arrangement of a
Lodge, or a Church, and its correpondential instruction, or the arrangement of the society in its
officers and work, must not be considered any part
or portion of worship; and he, who so regards it,
is in thick darkness, and is so far rejected of the
Lord.  All representatives and correspondentials
are purely instructive, and no man can be saved by
them without love.  They are the broad gate that
leads to death.  All worship is by and through the
emotions of the heart and will, coming forth into
utterances and acts in keeping the ten commandments.

The arrangement of Lodges and Churches due
East and West, with altars and chancels and Holy
places, are matters of instruction and convenience,
but not of the divine order of worship.  That
order is not considered by its representatives, but
is a life of charity, through the precepts of charity
from the divine Word.  There is always a tendency

in the unregenerate mind to temple worship by correspondences, which to the regenerate man is like looking from the light into thick darkness. See what our Ancient Grand Master St. John says, John, 4. 20, 24.

No. 73. Masonic tradition inform us that Lodges Anciently were dedicated to King Solomon, but that Masonry had well nigh fallen into decay at the approach of the Christian era, that our Ancient Grand Master, St. John the Baptist, by his temperance and fortitude, nearly restored the order to. its ancient glory ; and that our Ancient Master, St. John the Evangelist, by his prudence and justice, completed what St. John the Baptist had commenced, and thus, is said to have drawn a line parallel.

Ever since his time, in every well governed Lodge, there is said to be represented a certain point within a circle. The circle being bounded on the East, and on the west, by two parallel lines, representative of St. John the Baptist, and St. John the Evangelist. On the top of the circle rest the Holy Scriptures, Square and Compass, above which is Jacob's ladder, the three principal rounds of which are Faith, Hope and Charity. Over these

is the all-seeing eye.   A brother, in passing round
the circle, touches as well the line of St. John the
Baptist, and St. John the Evangelist, as upon the
Holy Scriptures, and while he keeps himself thus
circumscribed, it is impossible that he should ma-
terially err.   The principal tenets of which are
Brotherly Love, Relief and Truth.

These tenets and the four cardinal virtues, temperance, fortitude, .prudence and justice, are well
and beautifully explained in every Monitor.   But
the representative meaning of the figure drawn,
has always been a matter of opinion.   The laws
upon which representatives and correspondences
are based, not being sufficiently understood, various
Masters have given their own interpretations.

But if we reflect upon the change that Masonry
underwent in its transition from a Jewish to a Christian institution, as well as the passing away of the
manners, customs and religions of the world,
which gave place to the great central doctrine of
the divine human or God with us, which was the
subject of all prophecy, and the Sacred Scriptures
themselves; we shall see at once, that the central
point within the circle, is the representative of the
doctrine of the divine humanity, so beautifully
illustrated by our Ancient Grand Master, St. John

the Evangelist, in the first chapter of the book of John, where he breaks forth, under the inspiration of the Holy Spirit, and declares : "In the beginning was the Word, and the Word was with God, and the Word was God." This doctrine is the central and pivotal doctrine of the Christian religion. It is like the great centre of gravitation of the universe, or the sun of suns, around which suns and planets of the starry heavens revolve in glory, harmony and beauty. The circle described from this centre, signifies that the circle of Masonic science and smybolism was completed with St. John the Evangelist. He was the apocalypse of Masonry. The Lord says that the law and the prophets prophesied until John the Baptist : he was the beginning of the Christian era, which St. John the Evangelist, by his revelations is its sublime fulness. The circle of Masonic science was complete in the doctrine and precepts of the Christian religion, upon which rest the Holy Bible, Square and Compass. Without the Jewish doctrine of the Emanuel, and the Christian doctrine of the divine humanity, there is neither sense nor reason in the Jewish institution and the Sacred Scriptures.

25*

# OPENING OF THE LODGE.

No. 74. The first duty of a Mason, is to see the Lodge tiled. The Tiler is a guard placed without the door, with a drawn sword, which signifies the protection of the Lord's divine truth. The instant that evil entered the world, all things that were good, required protection against it.

Therefore, man, when he had sinned, could no longer remain in the garden, but was driven out, and the Lord placed a Cherubim, with a flaming sword, at the East of the garden, to guard the Tree of Life. The Tree of Life signifies the most interior will principle in man, which is receptive of the Lord's divine mercy by which man has eternal life. Were it possible for evil to gain possession of that tree, man could never be regenerated.

Evil first gains admittance into the most exterior sensual principle of man, which causes a separation between the divine principles of the will and the senses. For this reason, man is said to be driven out of the garden of Eden, garden signifying a perception and understanding of divine truth. This perception and understanding is closed by evils, so that the senses no longer perceive the divine operation which takes place within.

The separation between the senses and the most interior will principle, or tree of life, was, at first, partial and gradual. This period is called by the ancient poets, the golden age of man. But as evils increased in the world, and were procreated in the offspring, the proprium, thus procreated, became entirely evil and false; so that man lost all perception and knowledge of the inward operation of the divine Providence, and could only receive and understand the ideas and forms received through the medium of the five senses.

It then became necessary that he should be instructed altogether by an exterior way; yet he still lived and moved by the interior powers of the tree of life. In this state of things, it was necessary that the human body should be put off by death, or man would have remained forever upon the surface of the earth, held by the powers of natural gravitation; so that there would have been no spiritual heaven created from the human race; and man would have lived upon the surface of the earth, in a worse condition, than any animal now existing; whereas, if evil had not been introduced into the earth, there could have been no such thing as death.

The interior will principle, or tree of life, would have came forth in the natural order of progression, until the most interior spirit, or soul principle of the father, pervaded every particle of the body, putting off all the grosser portions of matter, and assuming to itself a clothing from the electric, aromal and magnetic spheres of the earth.

The man would have been translated and taken up to the heavens as Elijah was. This is perfectly possible and orderly when man is brought into a state of regeneration, in which the most interior will principle, or tree of life, can be opened and adjoined to conscience, coming forth and subduing the sensual principle, and taking to itself the whole man.

The case with the unregenerated man, is this : that when the tree of life is locked up within his interior, all perception of truth, by an interior way, is lost. This is done by eating of the fruit of the tree of the knowledge of good and evil, which signifies to appropriate the perceptions of evil by submitting them to the senses for their approval. When man lives according to the dictates of the senses alone, all the knowledges of .faith are destroyed, so that a full and complete separation takes place between the soul and the body. The spiritual principle of the mother, which is receptive of evils, intervenes and completely separates the soul from the senses, so that the spiritual principle of the father cannot be brought forth into the senses.

It becomes necessary that the man should be instructed in the principles of faith by an exterior way, commencing with the truth of the Word, and elevating them into the rational principle, and finally into the will and life of charity therefrom, whereby there is a spiritual, rational principle, which is a new will or conscience, and lastly, by opening the interior will principle, or tree of life, into the conscience, and from the conscience into the rational, and through the rational by the scientific, into the sensual. Thus the great circle of regeneration is complete. The opening of the interior principle of man, is represented in the Royal Arch degree.

In order to instruct man in the things of faith,

by an exterior way, it became necessary that the Lord should fill the body of a man with his presence, and communicate the things of heaven, in the language and representative history of man ; that this instruction should be identified with the history of a people that it might be received by the nations of the earth ; that man might live agreeably to the laws thereof. Thus, gradually changing the hereditary principle of their children, until the fulness of time should come, when the Lord should take upon himself a human form in the womb of a virgin, and be born as a man ; [and taking upon himself a nativity and life in the world,] by which he has established a direct and positive communication, through an exterior way, with the tree of life or most interior will principle of man.

From the moment of the glorification of the Lord's human, accomplished by putting off the spiritual principle of the mother, but retaining the life therefrom, and making it divine, man became susceptible of spiritual thought, and representative worship ceased by being unacceptable to him. The Temple of Solomon was destroyed, and the Jewish nation scattered to the four quarters of the earth, never again to return; and thus, it will be with every church, that worships by an exterior Ritual of representatives, without the internal principle of worship, which is charity. The Lord ever guards these principles as the Tiler with the drawn sword.

No. 75. All truth, knowledge and education, exist for the sole purpose of enabling man to do good. Good is the ultimate end of knowledge. Therefore, no man can be made a Mason, until the Lodge is satisfied, that he has the desire of usefulness ; and then he is not permitted to scale the walls, but must enter the door, as all true and lawful brothers have done, that have gone that way before him.

A great evil is done to a community, when we educate a child that has no desire of being useful. It only places the means in his hands of avoiding the law, perverting order and injuring his fellows. Such should be put to manual labor, which tends to implant the idea of usefulness in the will. No greater calamity can befall a nation, than to have a great many educated men, that have not the good of the state at heart.

When evil minded men are educated into the knowledges of faith, charity languishes The family that introduces the seducer, will have its sanctity destroyed. Profound secrecy is the order of heaven, to all who are not in the love of the neighbor. Charity is first in the heart, although, faith is first in manifestation.

For these reasons, every Lodge is guarded by a Master Mason placed without the door, armed with the proper insignia of his office, to guard the approach of cowans and eave-droppers, and see that none pass or repass, except those that are duly qualified and have the permission of the Worshipful Master. These rules are not only enforced by the Masonic fraternity, but are the laws of our very existence.

Our most interior will principle, separates itself from the lust of the voluntary mind, sinking deep within the nerve cell and fibre, guarding every portal to the false and the lustful voluntary mind, still retaining control over the interior organs of life, with which it does not suffer the lust and falsities of the exterior mind to meddle with impunity. The brain sends forth its vitalizing influence, the lungs inhale the aromal spheres. The heart vitalizes the blood and forces it through the vascular system. The stomach and other vital organs perform their duty under the direct influence of the tree of life ; and yet the Cherubim, with the flaming sword, still guards that tree from the profane gaze of the evil and false.

In vain the anatomist inspects the tissues of the body with a magnifying glass, to discover the soul, which the Lord only reveals through a psychological and interior sight.

No. 76. Every man when he becomes regenerate in the first discrete degree, including the three continuous degrees, represented by the Entered Apprentice, Fellow Craft and Master Mason, is, as to his interiors, a Lodge in its least form ; and every man that is being regenerated, is placed under the care of a Lodge, or a society of angels, which is represented by a Lodge ; and hence, when we say a Lodge, we refer to the interior state and condition of a regenerate man and the order of the Heavens.

There are six Lodges, representative of the six days regeneration. These Lodges were held in different parts of the Temple during its erection. So it is with the various states of the human mind while undergoing the process of regeneration. Above these Lodges, we have the Chapter degree of Royal Arch, which represents the opening, and bringing forth of the most interior will principle,

26

which has been separated and locked up by the evils and falses of the exterior mind. The two degrees of Cryptic Masonry represent the secret working of the most interior principle of the will in constructing and arranging the nine arches of the brain.

· Hence, these degrees can only be conferred after the secret vault has been discovered in the Royal Arch, and the Divine Law, together with the pot of Manna and Aaron's rod, (that budded, blossomed and bore fruit in twenty-four hours) ; and the three Jewels of our most Ancient Grand Masters have been brought forth and introduced into the life of the man. From the secret vault, or most interior will principle, there constantly outflows, from the divine law of the Lord, an influx of good, or divine order. This influx is constantly met and reacted against by the affluxes of the evils and falses from the external mind ; so that the interiors of the man cannot come forth into exterior life.

The Lord, therefore, came into this external world, thereby connecting himself with the exteriors of man, adjoining the influx in the natural mind with the tree of life, thus completing the great circle of redemption ; which is represented in every well governed Entered Apprentice Lodge, bounded upon the east and west by two parallel straight lines, representative of Sts. John the Baptist and Evangelist. The Entered Apprentice Lodge is held in the sensual principle of the mind. The Fellow Craft in the rational, and the Master's Lodge in the exterior will principle or conscience of the man, from which there is a spiritual rational.

No. 77. Every love that comes forth from an interior way, has use for its object; and every divine truth from the Word of God, that is introduced into the exterior memory, is the servant of a love, until it is adjoined and married to the love, when it becomes a wisdom. The offspring of love and wisdom is intelligence and science.

Therefore, every regenerate mind, in the first discrete degree, is arranged in the order of love, wisdom and intelligence, or science.

Love, is the Master, and occupies the east of the Lodge. Wisdom, is the Senior Warden, and holds the west. Intelligence and science in the south.

All things that enter from without, come from the west, and are first presented to the Junior Warden, then to the Senior, and lastly to the east. And all things that go forth from the Lodge, proceed from the W. Master, by the way of the west, and lastly the south. Entering salutations should be made in the order of initiation.

The Master and Wardens are representatives of the divine attributes in man, by which he is regenerated. These are love, wisdom and use or science. Love refers all things to truth and experience, which is wisdom or the west; and wisdom refers them to intelligence and science, which are the operative principles in man; and *vice versa*, with the truths of the Word. They are first received by the intellectual and scientific principle which is the south, and are referred to the truth and experience of the past for examination, and lastly, to the most interior loves.

This order is the reverse with woman; all things are first presented to her loves, and lastly to truth and intelligence. Hence, woman is not a representative of a Lodge, and, therefore, cannot be made a mason. Her exterior is love, and interior truth. But man's interior is love, and the exterior principles of his mind are wisdom and science.

The celestial love of truth, which is represented by the blue, is the east of the Lodge, and presides in all the lower degrees of the mind. Therefore, the Master's Lodge is called the blue Lodge.

The celestial love of good, which is represented by the scarlet, presides in the higher degree of the Royal Arch; and is the High Priest of the Chapter. There is an arrangement and order extending from the highest to the lowest things that constitute the heavens. God is the highest, and man is the lowest. The regenerate man in the celestial and spiritual degrees is a likeness and image of the divine. And hence, there is a certain likeness and image of God in the organization and arrangement of every Lodge or heavenly society.

No. 78. In every rational man, some particular love hold the reins of government in his mind. This love begets to itself its own wisdom and intelligence. These are represented by the Master and Wardens of the Lodge.

Each love has its interior memory, where all things that are transacted within the mind, are recorded and stored up; so that every love has its own book of life. All the acts of charity that are performed to the neighbor are also treasured up; so that they become the riches and treasures of the love itself. This recording and treasuring up of spiritual riches, is represented by the Treasurer and Secretary of the Lodge.

26*  N2

The presiding love of the mind, makes use of such other loves and intelligence as may be required for the ends of use and purposes of the mind. These are the Deacons of a Lodge. And, in arriving at a solemn conclusion, every love and intelligence of the man is consulted. Thus, every human intellect is organized for ends of use, and in likeness of an empire, where the emperor presides immediately through his court over all the subordinate governments.

The ruling and presiding love of the brain is like the Grand Lodge of a State or Realm; around it are consociated all the minor loves; which hold their power to work from the Grand Master. So that every regenerate man is in likeness of a Grand Lodge, and its subordinate Lodges. The subordinate Lodges become represented by their uses or presiding officers in the Grand Lodge. Heaven only deals with uses or means which are truths, wisdom and science.

Truth, when it is adjoined to the love of the neighbor, gives the power of choosing the right, which is wisdom or the west. Through the power of wisdom, every fact is referred to its proper principle and arranged into its order, which we call intelligence and science. Truth, consists of three degrees, or in other words, is susceptible of being divided into its component parts, which are termed facts, principles and truths, truth being the bodily form of the parts, which we arrive at by the most solemn conclusions of the mind.

When these conclusions are adjoined to the love of the Lord, or the love of the neighbor, for the sake of the Lord, and brought forth into life, begetting experience, they become wisdom. And every collection of facts, which is intelligence, when arranged according to its appropriate principles or agreement of forms, becomes a science. Love is that heavenly and divine order which is induced upon the most interior principles of the will ; or, in other words, it is the Lord's divine mercy in man, and includes all the power of truth and science. When facts are introduced into the mind, through the medium of the senses, they induce a chemical change upon the thought substances of the will, producing a change upon the forms of the will itself, enabling the will, ever after, to assume such forms at pleasure. Hence, the sight or impression of any object, through the subtle fluids of light, heat and electricity, enable the will principle to assume the form, shape and quality of the object.

The pleasure that the will feels in assuming these forms and qualities, is called affection. The will principle exists in three discrete degrees, each of which contains three continuous degrees or powers of love, wisdom and use. These discrete degrees, correspond to the nine degrees in Ancient Masonry; arranged according to a three, six and ninefold order. The most interior will principle or tree of life, is called the celestial principle in man, by and through which all things in him subsist and exist. The celestial principles flow into the middle discrete degree or spiritual principle, where wisdom, or the Senior Warden, bears rule. The love, wisdom and science of the spiritual principle, as derived from the celestial principle, flow down into the natural will of the man, which is the Master's Lodge.

Thus, there are three distinct wills in man, consisting of three continuous degrees. These wills are successively opened in man by regeneration, through the divine influxes of order or love from within, and the knowledges of the Holy Word from without, through the medium of the senses. Therefore, no Lodge can be opened without the Holy Bible.

Evil and sin enter the mind from without, good and love from within. The reaction between these opposing forces, destroys the goods and truths of the external mind, and prevents the loves with their divine order, from coming forth into the external mind. Therefore, the natural mind, consisting of the outer degrees, must be re-arranged by faith in the divine Word. This order is conferred upon the external mind, by the knowledge and truths of Masonry contained in the Word of God.

Were it not for evils and falses, the most interior will principle would flow through the middle or intermediate will into the natural, enabling the external will to assume at pleasure, all the forms and qualities of both the interior and external worlds ; so that, heaven and earth would meet in common knowledges, and regeneration would be as orderly and as natural as the growth of man.

But owing to evils, some cannot even be prepared for regeneration ; for the opening of the will is now, by the Word, from without.

No. 79. The nature of a Lodge in its various degrees, cannot be understood until the degrees are unfolded. We have, therefore, made such general remarks upon the opening of a Lodge, as will enable the mind to apply the general principles hereafter.

Before a Lodge can be opened in the mind, the entire mind, in its trinity of parts and attributes, must be prepared, so that the influxes may flow in an orderly manner, from the interior outward to the external. This is done by the conferring of the degrees, and a life agreeably to the knowledges given. In regeneration this is done by the Lord himself, who, in ancient times, descended into the prophets, and spoke through them to the world, whereby all that received their words into a living faith, and life, could also receive the Lord by an interior way through the medium of angels.

To such, all worship was by representation. The Jewish church, being only a representative church: the Ancient Lodges established by King Solomon, were altogether representative. But in the fulness of time, the Lord appeared in the world in person, conferring the degrees of regeneration upon his Apostles and followers; completely adjoining in the regenerate man, the most interior will principle or tree of life, with the exterior mind, illuminating the rational faculties, so that the mind could perceive and understand spiritual truths. As this state of mind through regeneration, becomes transmitted to the offspring, a preparatory work is performed in the human family, by which the

Lord can descend more fully by an interior way into the external mind, in the new age.

This state was completed during the last century, when Masonry changed from a practical and operative society to a spiritual or speculative one ; and the brethren began to perceive more clearly the symbolic meanings of the ceremonies. This power of spiritual perception is now increasing, and will continue to do so until the representative meaning of the rights and ceremonies of the institution, will form the land marks of the Orator, through the pulpit and press, and guide the mind in all of its practical and useful conclusions, both in the Church and State.

The principles of Masonry will cease to be exclusive, becoming more generally diffu sed among every class of the community ; but not without opposition from a sectarian and perverted religious faith. Every principle of truth and love, that flows forth from the Lord as a divine sun has use for an object. The divine order in which uses come forth, is first, through love into wisdom, and from wisdom into intelligence and science. It is therefore necessary that the human mind should be prepared for their reception. This preparation is represented by our Ancient Grand

Master, St. John the Baptist. The complete state of preparation and uses is represented by St. John the Evangelist. Every consociation and arrangement of individuals into societies must be for ends of higher use; and each use must be performed by an officer, who is spiritually and naturally prepared to perform the uses of office. Hence, the officer is a representative of the uses he performs.

Therefore, the Lodge is an exact representative of the regenerate mind of man. When the nature of the Lodge is well understood, we can clearly comprehend the three, six and ninefold order of man. The same principles extending through all the heavenly societies, up to the Creator himself. In the Master's Lodge, the love of the neighbor presides through wisdom and intelligence over all the duties of the Lodge.

These attributes are distinctly one, although different in manifestation; for wisdom is of love, and love is of wisdom in the creative mind, and intelligence and science are their operative principles. Hence, when these three attributes take their seats in the human mind, and become operative, the Lodge is called to order and opened, in likeness of the divine mind, to perform all the uses that charity requires; before this can be done, however,

all the lusts and passions of the external will principle, must be broken off and put aside. The
spiritual or middle will principle which is conscience,
wherein truth reigns supreme, must be prepared
for the reception of the divine truth of the Word,
by putting away the errors of false doctrines. For
in vain, does any man worship the Lord, teaching
for doctrine the commandments of men.

It is not unfrequent that the external mind is
rational, being properly educated in natural things;
and yet, the spiritual principle or plane of conscience, is entirely perverted by false doctrines, so
that the spiritual mind is insane, and hence,
there can be no regeneration. For all influx
from the interior will principle or tree of life,
is by or through mediums established in the mind.
Hence, no Master can preside over a Lodge until
he has been made a Past Master, which is the
second continuous degree of the middle or spiritual
discrete degree, and so on throughout the entire
order of the degrees, the higher always presides
in and over the lower.

## OF THE FELLOW CRAFT'S DEGREE.

No. 80. The first section of the Fellow Craft's Degree, was conferred on the ground floor of King Solomon's Temple, and the second section in the middle chamber. The Mark Master's degree is only a continuation of the Fellow Craft's, and its final completion takes place with the Most Excellent. Thus it is that the Fellow Craft's degree, is a bond of union and connection between the higher and the lower degrees.

At the first sight, this arrangement may appear arbitrary; but when we reflect, that our Ancient Grand Masters were both Prophets and Seers, we are forced to conclude, that the arrangement has some important symbolical representation, which we will now explain.

The unperverted faculties of the human mind are arranged in a natural, spiritual and celestial order, in likeness of the universal heavens and the Divine attributes, which are represented by the Lodge, Chapter and Council ; and the various progressive states of the human mind in regeneration are represented by the degrees in Masonry.

The order of each discrete degree of the human mind, like the Lodge, Chapter and Council, is simultaneous, requiring every part to be properly constituted and joined together ; so that the full power of the degrees, may be present in every act, with all the natural forces of the mind, acting and reacting upon each other, like the various parts of a wheel on its own centre. Every rational conclusion is brought into science, and every knowledge is referred to its own principle and class, so as to be present in each act. Thus it is that simultaneous order, proceeds together as it were, acting and reacting from the outermost or periphery, upon its centre and from the centre to the circumference.

The natural, spiritual and celestial degrees of the mind are discrete. Yet each discrete degree, is composed of continuous degrees, among which there is a progression. This progression from one to the other, constitutes the degrees of longitude, which from the natural to the spiritual and celestial of the same discrete degree, like the higher and lower degrees of the same jurisdiction, which to distinguish, in a philosophical view, the progression among the continuous degrees of the same plane, is called the progression of the degrees of longitude.

The progression by continuous order from the lower to the higher discrete degrees of the mind, as from the natural to the spiritual and celestial degrees of altitude, both ascending and descending, takes place by influx, and not by the action of parts upon each other; so that the higher faculties may be entirely closed, while the lower faculties of the mind are in force and power. The degrees of the mind are successively opened like the degrees of the Lodge, Chapter and Council. The natural degree of the mind, by which there is a perception of things, is first opened ; which corresponds to the Entered Apprentice degree, and is located in the frontal portion of the base of the brain.

The first section of the Fellow Craft's is conferred in the central portion of the base of the head.

The second section was conferred in the middle chamber, or rational faculties of the mind, by which there is a union and progression of parts, successively and simultaneous.

In the depraved condition of the human mind

before regeneration, the discrete degrees act and react against each other, the celestial degree reacting against all the other portion of the brain; and hence, there is a continual warfare between the animal, spiritual and celestial minds, until it is terminated by a full and complete conquest by one or the other; if the animal conquers, the spirit to eternity is natural: if the spiritual degree conquers, the quality of the man is spiritual; if the celestial degree gains the ascendancy, the quality of the spirit is celestial; and the affections and understanding are opened in the sphere of causes, and the mind comes into a full perception of the divine ends of the Lord. This warfare between the natural, spiritual and celestial degrees of the human mind, is represented by the wars and conquests of the children of Israel, in driving out the Canaanites from the promised land. The war that exists between the spiritual and celestial degrees, is represented by the warfare that existed between Israel and Judah.

The similarity that exists between the first section of the Entered Apprentice, and the first section of the Fellow Craft, arises from the fact that they both represent the natural principle of their respective degrees,—therefore, such portions of the

27*

first section of the Fellow Craft, as can be easily inferred from similar portions of the Entered Apprentice degree, will be passed over ; there are, however, a few points in the first section of the Fellow Craft's degree, that will require a minute explanation.

No. 81.  Every rational state in the human mind must be complete, before there can be any orderly advancement to a higher condition ; and although the man that is undergoing regeneration is in darkness, and does not perceive the operations of the heavenly societies which he is in, yet every state and condition of the man, is clearly perceived by them, which is represented by the examination of the Entered Apprentice in open Lodge, to ascertain his proficiency in the preceeding degree. Every fault is corrected and the candidate properly instructed, before he is permitted to advance to the second degree ; which in the regenerate life, corresponds to repentance and acknowledgment of faults.

When it is clearly perceived that the regenerating man, is in proper condition of faith and repentrace, he is intromitted, by a state of preparation, to the second degree of Masonry or regeneration.

No. 82. Every Lodge room is provided with two ante-chambers. The Lodge is decorated and beautifully adorned with all the representatives of the degrees, which signify and represent the faith, doctrines and states of the heavenly societies, that preside over the regeneration of the man in their degree. The ante-chambers represent the preparatory states of those who are about to enter the Lodge. These rooms are guarded by the Tyler, treated of in Art. 74, 75.

The case with the man that is being regenerated, is this—that when he has served his full time and probation in a state of faith, and has passed through his examination spoken of in No. 81, he his intromitted into a state of humiliation and innocence, by repentance of all the faults of life, which are revealed and brought to light in his examination, in which he feels his own ignorance and want of more light, for no man can be taught any truth, and neither can he receive further light, as long as he thinks that he understands the subject.

His own pride of intelligence and self reliance resist any light that does not come from his own mind, as any one may perceive, who has ever undertaken to instruct a proud and arrogant man ; let him contrast the case with a humble and innocent child. The former will reject all truth, while the latter will receive it with avidity, pleasure and delight. The angels receive the greatest enjoyment, while instructing a humble and innocent minded man, although the man is ignorant of the source from whence his thoughts and affections come. Yet, there is an inward joy and gladness, which are like the commingling of oil and wine. In the state of humiliation to which the Entered Apprentice is reduced, before he is in a condition to receive the second degree, the light of faith seems to fail, and darkness comes over the mind, which produces a longing desire to understand the principles, and enter into the rationality of faith. The affections of truth which flow into the organs of the left side of the brain and body, treated of in No. 86, are clothed with the truths of faith, which is a state of grace, represented by the lamb skin and clothing of the left side, while the right side remains unclothed; for all clothing is of the exterior truths of the Word, which have been received and conjoined to the affections of good, which flow in by an interior way.

These affections remain naked and unclothed, until they are adjoined to the rational principles of faith, which have been lived, and brought into experience, in the life of the lower degree; so that every elevation from a lower to a higher state, is by the adjoining and marriage of the higher affections of good, with the rational truths derived from the experience of the life of the lower degree.

For the foregoing reasons, the right side in the preparation of the Fellow Craft is said to be unclothed. The good of hope, which is represented by the green, being unclothed by the rational faculties, having as yet never been clothed upon by the rational principles of faith, so that, as yet, there is no rational understanding and perception of the principles of divine order, in the light of the human understanding.

No. 83. Door signifies communication and introduction from one state to another, and is peculiarly representative of the spiritual boundary, that exists between the degrees of Masonry, wherein the spiritual good of the higher degree, unites with the intellectual of the lower. No. 87.

The connection and continuity of the continuous degrees is such, that when a man lives agreeably to the principles of faith contained in the Entered Apprentice degree, he acquires to himself, through work, a life of usefulness from which there is an increment of good or charity; which is subject to trial and temptation, from the intellectual principle of faith, by which it is confirmed and purified; this good or power of usefulness is really derived from the higher degree, it being the power of the higher which is secretly working in the lower degree to regenerate the man, for all regeneration is by the good of the higher degrees, secretly working in the lower.

By the benefit of this good, when man has attained to a life of usefulness, he is entitled to alarm the door of the higher degree; which is regular, and well known to those that hear it.

The good acquired in the lower degree, is the pass-word or benefit, which entitles the regenerate man of the Entered Apprentice degree, to enter upon the higher life of science and rationality of the Fellow Craft's degree. It is by the life of truth, that man is regenerated, and not by the truth itself; the intellectual principle always referring itself to truth, and the will principle to good or usefulness.

The good of the Entered Apprentice degree, by which there is increase, denotes plenty, represented by a sheaf of wheat, suspended near a water ford.

The intellectual principle, arising from the perceptive faculties is always endeavoring to rise by the degrees of altitude, and take possession of the rational and sympathetic principles ; and, also, to flow backward, by the degrees of longitude, and pervade the will principle of the cerebellum. These two influxes that have their center in the perceptives, like the angle of the Square, are reacted against both, by the domestic and devotional faculties, by which they are resisted, and properly balanced in the rational and sustaining faculties, by which they are appropriated, and directed to the useful purposes of life.

But when the perceptive faculties gain the ascendency over the laws of order, resisting the cerebellum and devotional faculties, the objects of life are diverted from the channels of use, and terminate in the mere sharpness of the intellectual principle of the mind. This principle of the mind is represented by the Ephraimites, who were not called upon by Jephtha, Judge of Israel, to take part in, and share the rich spoils of the Ammonitish war.

This whole subject is spiritually treated of, in the 11th and 12th Chapters of the Book of Judges.

The land of Canaan represents the human mind,

which is to be conquered and possessed by regeneration. The Canaanites represent the evils and falses to be driven out. The wars between the tribes of Israel, were representative of the action and reaction between the degrees of the mind; which are the principles from which all wars originate.

Those represented by the Ephraimites, cannot advance. Their regeneration terminates in the intellectual principles of the various degrees; those that terminate their regeneration in the intellectual of the Entered Apprentice degree, can never be made Fellow Crafts. Therefore the password of good, which is represented by a sheaf of wheat, suspended near a water ford, is introduced to prevent their ascension.

All the affections of the various states of regeneration are manifested in the tones of the voice. The tones of those that are in love are like those of the ancient Israelites, deep and sonorous. With those who are only in the truths of faith, without being adjoined to good; the tones of the voice are shrill and sharp. Hence, they are instantly known by their intonations of voice, for they can never frame the vocal organs to pronounce the deeper sounds.

This at once proves conclusively that they are Ephraimites, and that their state of regeneration has terminated in the intellectual principle, without the higher use and motives of good, which alone entitle any man to ascend into the science and rationality of faith.

The man's state is not perceived by himself, and hence the pass-word is not in his possession; but with those of the higher, which the candidate has the benefit of.

Gilead represents natural good, which is initiative to a higher state. A water ford is representative of a change of state; the river Jordan was the boundary of the land of Canaan, upon the East, which was entered by the fords of the river Jordan.

A sheaf of wheat signifies rational science arising from good, in the scientific principle of the mind.

The various principles of truth which have been used as productive of good, are collected and referred to their general principles; being collected into bundles, by the formation and opening of a plexus of vessels in the brain, which constantly undergo changes and reformations, as science is perfected in the mind. Therefore a sheaf of wheat is the peculiar emblem of science, derived from the good of experience.

The mere acuteness of science, which is derived from learning, is called Ephraim, and no Entered Apprentice Mason, that partakes of this quality in an eminent degree, can be made a Fellow Craft. Goodness and work are inseparably connected ; to be a good man and true, every principle of science, must be wrought out through the hands. All the faculties and powers both of body and mind, must be made the subjects of the scientific principles.

Nothing can be more injurious to the states of man's regeneration, than the amassing of science by the memorising of principles, without a direct end and object of use, such are Ephraimites. The purpose of life should be formed at an early period, and the study of sciences made subservient to it in the natural pursuit of life.

A definite business is the first thing to be considered, and the study of sciences made a collateral. Then the mind moves steadily forward with a fixed purpose, and all things of the memory remain, and are referred to their proper position in the mind.

In order to more fully illustrate the subject of Gilead and Ephraim, it will be necessary to state the difference between the brute creation and man.

In the animal creation the brain is small, and consists mainly of the basular region, represented by the yellow, blue and green, in Pl. 1, Fig. 1, of the human head, which receives the influxes from two discrete degrees; one is external, and the others interior. The external influxes are received in the perceptive faculties through the medium of the senses. The internal influxes of the animal mind are received into the cerebellum, and which are derived from the lowest ultimate degree of nature.

These influxes give the power of procreation, and all the affections of natural life, from which are derived a perception of the requisite means for the procuring of good, and the preservation of the young; together with means of defence, and shelter from the storm.

These perceptions or instincts come forth in order with the natural growth of the animal; but, with man, there are two additional planes of thought and perception; namely: the spiritual and celestial planes.

The spiritual plane occupies the central belt of the head, represented by the orange, the purple and the russet, from which is derived all the powers of rationality and spiritual thought.

The celestial plane occupies the upper region of the brain, represented by the scarlet, the citron

and the olive, from which we derive all the perceptions of divine order, the laws of Providence and
the notions of God. These flow in through the
devotional faculties, descending by two ways, to
meet the animal affections and thoughts in the base
of the brain.

The influxes of the perceptive faculties flow
backward, meeting the influxes of the cerebellum
in the sustaining faculties, as a general centre from
which all animal life proceeds. At the same time,
the perceptive faculties are elevated through the
plane of memory, and meet the descending influxes received through the devotional faculties in
the rational, represented by the orange ; by which
we have the power of ratiocination or talking about
truth. By the flowing backward of the perceptive
influxes, adjoining themselves with the influxes of
the cerebellum in the sustaining faculties, we have
the power of doing good ; for all action proceeds
through the sustaining faculties, which descend to
the body and are outworked in ends of use.

Thus, rationality and usefulness make the good
and true man ; but there is always a tendency in
man, to terminate the influxes of the perceptive
faculties or scholastic education in the rational
principle alone, without performing the labor of

usefulness, which descends through the sustaining faculties, into the ordinary operations of labor and mechanics. Those who thus terminate their education in the mere scientifics of the rational faculties, are Ephraimites.

No. 84. A spiritual conscience is an increment derived from the truths of faith. Previous to a state of faith, there is a natural conscience derived from the truths of nature. This conscience is superseded by the spiritual conscience, formed by science and rationality of faith, which are from spiritual truths, and when fully formed, it takes the ascendency over all the affairs of life. Thus the natural conscience is put away, which is represented by death and resurrection to life in the Master's degree. Previous to a state of faith, the natural conscience is violated by the breaking of the laws of nature; but the spiritual conscience is tortured by a violation of spiritual truth, as well as natural. Therefore, all the offices of life, are brought under the control of the new will. When the candidate first enters a Masonic Lodge, in the Entered Apprentice degree, the natural conscience which contains the first germs of the affections of truth, which is called a state of grace, is pierced by contrition and repentance, and lacerated as through the point of some sharp instrument, touched the vital organ of the heart. But in the Fellow Craft's degree, the candidate enters upon the course of science and rationality, under the approving smiles of the first germs of a spiritual conscience, which is represented by the angle of the Square, or the delights of virtue, which are felt in the right breast.

As no man can attain to rational science and understanding in the natural relations of life, without fixed and honest purposes, neither can the spiritual man take one single step in the path of spiritual science, without an honesty of purpose, the conscience being first purged by repentance and examination.

By a natural conscience there is an understanding of natural truth; by the spiritual conscience, or the germs of a new will, which is implanted in the intellectual part of man, which takes place by the separation of the perceptions, derived from the tree of good and evil, there is an understanding of spiritual things through science and rationality; so that the general embodiment of truth is perceived without its particulars.

But when the celestial principle in man is opened by the formation of a perceptive conscience, which is done by the introduction of the truths of the Word, into the most interior will principle, by a life of obedience to the principles of faith, rationality and science, the interior will in the Master's degree thence comes forth into the external mind; by which there is a state of wisdom, in which the principles of truth are seen, as with a vivid and palpable sight, in which not only the principles and forms of a truth, are seen in their correspondential and representative beauty; but when the Royal Arch is opened, the details in their various combinations, are also perceived; by which darkness is made light, and crooked things made straight.

But previous to this state of regeneration, the way appears tortuous and winding, the details of the operation being not understood; but the Lord leads the blind by a way they know not, and never forsakes them.

All spiritual science is derived from the influxes that flow in through the devotional faculties, adjoining themselves to the truths of the divine Word. These influxes are greatly aided by the proper and legitimate exercise of the devotional faculties in prayer, which directs and places the entire mind upon Deity ; and hence, every faculty is thrown open for the divine influxes to enter. But when man looks to himself, and strives t ) comprehend the principles of spiritual truth, the faculties are closed above and opened below, so that every thought is turned downward to the ultimates of nature, terminating in the science of quantity, geometrical forms and chemical affinities that adjoin with the blue ray when the scarlet is closed. But when the doors of the devotional faculties are thrown wide open by prayer, the natural sciences serve as a resting point for the natural faculties, upon which the spiritual faculties rest, as stone laid upon à sure foundation, to which the Plumb, Level and Square, can be applied, and the building erected agreeably to the rules of the great Architect; which are perceived through the devotional faculties.

Thus the rules of natural science, adjoined with the perceptions of divine order, constitute the angle of the Square, and the true dignity and science of the spiritual man.

The internal mind, should be constantly elevated to the Lord in devotion and prayer. No duty of life, however small, should be engaged in, without elevating the mind to Deity, and asking his direction.

When this course is pursued, the mind will soon perceive the influxes of divine order, and unite them to the principles of natural science, from which there will be a perception of the exact course to be pursued; and when this percep-tion comes, let it be acted upon in full confidence with energy and vigor, and the entire life will be one of divine order. Natural science will join hand in hand with the spiritual, and the mind will be constantly elevated into a pure and serene light. The laws of divine Providence will unfold with beauty and splendor to the mind.

Therefore, the candidate in the Entered Apprentice degree, is first taught to kneel and invoke the blessing of Deity, before entering upon any important understaking, and this is equally the duty of the Fellow Craft.

Prayer, presents our wants before the throne of God through a true and living faith in Him ; not that God is not good, constantly perceiving our wants and supplying them from his bountiful hand, even to the evil as well as the good ; but it sanctifies the grace to the receiver, and enlarges the devotional faculties of the head, and prepares them as receptacles for greater and higher blessings. It trains them to receive the influxes of heaven and makes them intuitive, so that the divine will is perceived by a brilliant light; but in order to accomplish this, the motives must be pure and unselfish; a prayer uttered from a selfish heart, in a dictatorial spirit, closes the devotional faculties and opens the faculties located in the base of the brain, for the inflowing of every carnal and selfish desire; such prayers are heard and answered by the devils, and not by the angels from the Lord.

But where there is an humble and contrite spirit, submitting the will to the laws of divine Providence, there is an opening and growth of all the upper and higher faculties of the head, until at last the man is governed in all his ways by the laws of divine Providence, and is able to illustrate their principles in the clearness of science.

Thus it is that the virtue, which is represented by the angle of the Square, is derived from the marriage of the laws of divine order, which flow in through the devotional faculties, with the truths of the Word, which are received through the external perceptive faculties. The love arising from the domestic faculties being yet silent and unperceived, preparing however, the foundation for the erection of the Temple, which will be explained in its proper place. The combination of the perceptive and devotional faculties gives the power to reason, from which is derived rationality and science, or the blades and angle of the Square. See the secondary color or orange, Pl. 1. fig. 1, and Nos. 23, 24, 27, as illustrative, also 47.

The blue ray, that flows in through the cerebellum, governing all laws of the natural life, is common to the brute, as well as the man; but the scarlet ray belongs to man alone; from one is the science of natural things, and from the other is the knowledge and science of divine Providence; by the marriage of these two loves, or rather the blending, proceeds a middle or intervening combination of affections, from which there is a spiritual rationality and science. The natural sciences, through a natural rational, being first opened; when the perceptions of the mind ascend into the spiritual affections, developing a spiritual rational plane, which is adjoined to the perceptive plane, which flows in through the scarlet ray.

When this conjunction takes place, another side is formed to the Square, and the great triangle of the mind is complete. The celestial perceptions of the devotional faculties penetrate the spiritual and natural sciences, quickening every principle, so that the celestial principles terminate in the natural, with its full force and power, but with a different degree of strength in each individual.

The divine order of the opening of these faculties with man is first through the natural; so that when he intensely desires the spiritual, he first obtains the natural, and when the celestial affections are strong, he next acquires the spiritual, and lastly, by the Lord alone, he obtains the celestial, when the details of regeneration are then perceived.

No. 85. We shall make a few remarks on the working tools of a Fellow Craft, and pass to the second section of the degree.

The working tools of a Fellow Craft, are the Plumb, Square and Level. The Plumb is used to try perpendiculars, the Square to form right angles, and the Level to lay horizontals. The Plumb admonishes us to walk uprightly, in our several stations of life, squaring our actions by the Square of virtue, ever remembering that we are travelling upon the level of time, to that bourn from whence no traveller returns.

The corner-stone of every Masonic edifice is laid in the north-east corner, by the application of the Plumb, Square and Level. The Grand Architect lays the foundation of the universe by these implements ; they are the foundation of all science and knowledge ; by the application of their principles, the terrestrial and celestial bodies are held in their positions.

There are two universal fluids in the natural world, ether and caloric; when these chemically combine, they set at liberty light, heat and electricity, producing the molecules of matter, establishing the universal power of attraction, which is the Plumb. The power of attraction established in these molecules react upon their centre, inducing a force which acts at right angles or upon the Level. This force is the power of cohesive attraction. The force of attraction, established in the molecules, produces the power of gravitation to the larger bodies, the various substances being adjoined agreeably to their affinities by the power of cohesion.

The power of attraction enters into every force; hence the momentum of all moving bodies is in an

exact ratio to their weight and velocity ; every
oblique or horizontal motion is induced by gravitation and reaction, upon these as a foundation,
rest the forces of nature. It is also a law of necessity that any current or motion, proceeding in a
right or curved line by reaction, induces a force at
angles.

This is beautifully illustrated in the magnet of
the electric telegraph : if a current of electricity
be passed around a piece of soft iron, or over it,
: t right angles, an inductive current is produced.
Thus it is that every force is induced by the combination of ether and caloric, setting at liberty
light, heat and electricity ; these forces combine in
the continuous degrees in a three, six and ninefold
order, in the likeness of the combination of colors
and sounds, in which are established all the laws
and affinities of the animal, vegetable and mineral
kingdoms of nature ; but these forces have no
power in themselves, being only the dead machines
which are acted upon by the Plumb, Square and
Level of the mental or spiritual world : there
being one world of matter, and another of mind,
the caloric of the mental world is love, which forms
the bond of every society ; the ether of the mental world is divine wisdom.

The combination of love and wisdom induces the mental power of cohesive attraction, which is the Level, the conjunction of truth and love, forms the angle of the Square; these are the foundations and starting points of every active mental force, by which we erect the Temple, not made with hands, eternal in the heavens.

# OF THE FELLOW CRAFT'S DEGREE.

No. 86. If there is any one doctrine that is well
defined in Masonry, it is the doctrine of works ;
every principle is taught for the sake of life, and
all knowledge is considered superfluous, that does
not embody itself through works or charity ; for,
although the doctrines of Masonry extend from the
centre to the highest heavens, they demand that a
Mason's charity should be equally extensive. By
charity, we mean every work derived from the love
of the human family, brought forth in the counting room, the workshop, the pulpit, and on the
bench, in justice and judgment.

Our ancient brethren wrought at the building
of King Solomon's Temple, and many other Masonic edifices ; they worked six days, and rested
upon the seventh. There are six Masonic days of
regeneration, in which there is temptation and re-

sistance of the natural and spiritual man, to the celestial degree of the mind, No. 80. In the first three degrees of Masonry, the natural mind is subdued and brought into a state of death, and raised in the likeness and image of the spiritual man.

In the degrees of Mark, Past and Most Excellent Masters, there are three days of trial and labor, in which the spiritual Temple is completed. These six states of the spirit are states of preparation and trial, in which there is always a resistance to the celestial or divine principle; and hence, they are days of labor. The spiritual intellect conducts the work through faith and obedience ; it finishes the spiritual Temple, and brings forth the capstone with shouting and praise ; but this Temple is only an image and skeleton of the celestial. If the spiritual principle were to predominate, without the interior and controlling principle of the celestial, Masonry or regeneration would be a mere symbolism or representative without the spirit or life ; but this parallelism must pass away by destruction and captivity before the true celestial Temple can be erected. The building of this Temple is a labor of love, and every workman engages in the great undertaking, without the hope

29*

of fee or reward ; it is the seventh day in which God finished his work and rested from his labors ; for this day of rest were all created things made, and therefore, it is said that our ancient brethren wrought six days and rested upon the seventh, for whatever is done by love has not the appearance of labor.

No. 87. The plan of King Solomon's Temple was given by divine inspiration to David, and was in every way worthy of its author and so great a Prophet; for although the temple proper was small, being sixty by twenty cubits in the clear; yet it was approached from the West through two courts, which were surrounded by lofty ranges of magnificent marble columns. The space between the Western and middle courts was an exact square, covered in by a marble roof and surrounded by an entablature and supported by Ionic columns. The columns of the western court were in the Doric style ; the columns of the inner court were in the Corinthian style, and the center place, as before described, was in the Ionic order. In passing through these courts to approach the western entrance of the Temple, the beholder was impressed with an idea of power, grandeur and beauty, that has never before nor since been attained, by any architectural composition in the world.

The design of the Temple, in general, and in particular, was a representative of the mind of a spiritual angel, and, hence, it was an image of the Divine, representing the Church and the Heavens. The courts represented the degrees of longitude, and the three chambers, that were built round about the temple, the degrees of altitude. The western court represented the perceptive mind, and the colonnade between the two courts, represented the external memory. The inner court represented external action and life, the temple itself representing the will, from which alone proceeds all worship. The Temple was surrounded by three chambers arranged one above the other. Outside of these again, was a court inclosed by an outer wall surrounding the temple, and all the courts inclosed a space in the form of an oblong square, and having three gates, one West, one South, and one East.

The western gate was the general entrance, and opened directly into the western court, heretofore described.

The southern gate entered into a narrow space, inclosed between the outer wall and the wall of the inner court. This court led eastward by a narrow way, towards the eastern gate of the temple, and entered the middle court by a gate just in front of the temple, so that the Fellow Craft, on his way to the middle chamber, entered by the south gate and turned to the right, and passing along between the outer and inner walls, entered the middle court and passed between the two brazen pillars, and then entered the lower chamber of the temple on the right side, which was a hall sixty by five cubits. From this hall, he ascended to the middle chamber by a flight of stone stairs, winding around a central column, consisting of three, five and seven steps, separated by broad platforms, upon which the Fellow Craft was taught to pause, and reflect upon the principles of science, before he entered the middle chamber.

The Entered Apprentice, in his approach to the temple, entered by the West, passing between the outer and inner walls, entered the lower chamber upon the ground floor, on the North side ; without entering the middle court or passing between the brazen pillars, or beholding the form and beauty thereof. The Entered Apprentice had access to, and was permitted to enter the outer court, which included the large Western court, out of which, upon the North side, there was a passage between the outer and inner wall, running eastward along the North side of the temple, and southward upon the East of the temple, and turning westward along the South side of the temple, it returned, entering the western court again, upon the South side.

Thus, the Entered Apprentice was permitted to make the entire circuit of the temple, passing the East and South gates; and also to enter the nethermost chamber on the North side of the temple. The Fellow Craft Mason was permitted to enter the outer and middle courts, by the South and West gates, and also to enter the lower and middle chambers of the temple, on the right or South side.

The Master Mason was permitted not only to enter all the courts, but also, the temple and Sanctum Sanctorum. Guards were placed at the various gates and entrances, so that none could pass and repass, unless they were duly qualified and had permission. Between the two courts, and their outer and inner walls, were upper chambers, constructed for all the offices of the courts and temple.

The various descriptions given of the temple,

may seem to the superficial reader to be confused; but, if the intelligent architect, who has made a close study of ancient architecture, examines them, he will find no difficulty in understanding the general design.

The Temple of Solomon was built about two hundred years before the celebrated Grecian Temple of Theseus, which was one of the oldest and best specimens of the Doric style, and was built upon the same general plan as that of Solomon's Temple, without its courts, with this exception, that colonnades were built along the sides instead of the chambers.

The Roman Basilica, or King's House, in after centuries, was built upon the same general plan as the Temple. From this building originated the general idea of the cathedral now in use, with its nave, apsis and side aisles.

We find, therefore, that the general design of the Temple of Solomon is the foundation of all modern religious architecture. The orders were undoubtedly taken by travelling Masons to Greece and other parts of the world, and used in the construction of their temples, as we find them simultaneously springing into existence, directly after the building of the Temple, in their most perfect specimens.

Notwithstanding Grecian historians claim their invention, we think that they had a divine origin, in the plan of the Temple, through the Prophet David. "All this, said David, the Lord made me understand, in writing by his hand upon me, even all the works of this pattern." 1, Chron. 18, 19.

The order of the Temple, was of two kinds, namely : progressive and simultaneous. Progressive order, is represented by the winding stairs leading to the middle and uppermost chambers. Simultaneous order, is represented by the ground plan of the temple and courts, which proceeds as from a centre outwards, whereas progressive order ascends and descends.

The Entered Apprentice worked at the preparing of rough stones for the Fellow Craft, and was permitted to assist in erecting the exterior wall of the outer Court. The Square, and angle of the Fellow Craft's work, were the erection of the outer and inner walls of the Court, which were squared and hewn in the most perfect manner. The Master Mason worked upon the columns of the Courts and walls of the Temple. Those that distinguished themselves as workmen were engaged upon the Royal or kingly Arch, over the mercy seat in the Sanctum Sanctorum. It will be necessary to say something of the general plan of the Temple and its Courts, before proceeding to the middle chamber.

No. 88. We learn from the Sacred Scriptures, that Hiram Abiff, the widow's son, cast of molten brass, for King Solomon, two pillars, and set them up in the porch in front of the Temple. These pillars were cast hollow, a hand's breadth in thickness, and eighteen cubits high, and a line of twelve cubits, did compass them about. On the top of these pillars, were placed chapiters of five cubits in height, adorned with net work, lily-work and pomegranates, 1. Kings, 7, Jer. 52.

Masonic traditions further inform us, that on the top of these chapiters were placed two globes, on the exterior surfaces of which were delineated all the maps and charts of both the terrestrial and celestial bodies. These traditions may be questioned, if history did not confirm the fact, that the Ancients had a full knowledge of the rotundity of the earth.

We are informed by the oriental cosmogomy of of the Vedas, which is known to have existed eight hundred and eighty years before the Christian era, " that at the North-pole, the year consists of a long day and night, and that their long day was the Northern, and their night the Southren, course of the sun ; and to the inhabitance of the moon, it is said, one day is equal in length to one month of mortals."

Vitruvius, the great architectural writer, who lived in the time of the Cæsars, quotes Archemedes, who says that water is not level, but takes the form of a spheroid, whose centre is the same as that of the earth. God said to Job, "Canst thou bind the sweet influences of Pleiades, or loose the bands of Orion." Job. 38, 31. The Ancients were not only acquainted with the manner of representing the heavenly bodies, but mapped them out by the aid of animal figures, representing the various affections which flow from the different heavenly bodies; this could be only done by the globe.

Monumental architecture is of two classes, commemorative and allegorical. In allegorical composition, the leading idea is made the crowning object of the structure ; all of the other parts are representative of the various principles brought in, to sustain, support and adorn the argument ; these are introduced as the corner stone, the base, the column, the arch, the key-stone and entablature.

The monumental structures set up in front of the Temple, were two, which were exactly alike ; each consisting of a pillar and a chapiter, supporting a

30

globe, upon which was delineated maps and charts, one of the terrestrial, and the other of the celestial bodies, which were the crowning representative ideas, and these again were representative in themselves of natural and heavenly truths.

Both monuments being of the same pattern, shows that they were intended, to represent the parallelism and correspondence, that exist between the natural and spiritual worlds. No man can rationally enter the *sanctum sanctorum*, and offer up his devotion, without a knowledge of God, and neither can any man enter the middle chamber of science, without a knowledge of the correspondence of the two worlds. In religion and science they must both alike, in entering the Temple, pass between these two great pillars.

As the body is dead without the spirit, so the forces of the natural world are dead without the inflowing of the spiritual. These cannot take place without a parallelism and correspondence of the two worlds, and hence, the science of correspondences, is the science of sciences. In Masonry, we find this science locked up in a precious casket and handed down to us as the wisdom of the Ancients. The starting point and threshold of this science, is the two pillars. We will now consider each part of these monumental structures separately.

No. 89. The ancients held the doctrine that man was not only a microcosm, but an epitome of the universe, holding within himself all the relations of mind and matter ; the parallelism of the two worlds being seen and understood by all the seers and prophets of ancient times.

The doctrine of the microcosm is represented by the terrestrial globe, and the parallelism of the two worlds, by the two globes of both the terrestrial and celestial bodies. This is what our most Ancient Grand Masters understood and intended to hand down to posterity by the globes.

Universal space is filled with substance, emanating from the Divine Being, existing in an endless variety of states, and conditions, all of which flow onward, through discrete suns, to ultimate worlds of effects. Such portions of these substances as are amenable to the laws of gravitation, we call matter, but the more subtle substances, such as heat, light and electricity, we term forces, because all power is derived through them, yet they are devoid of any manifestation of will and understanding.

They are not forces within themselves, but are receptacles of force. Within these elements, again, reside the elemental substances of the spiritual world, but which do not in any manner combine with them, either by chemical affinities or infusion of substance. They are as separate and distinct from each other as mind and matter ; one is the substance of the animal spirit, and the other is the receptacle of a living soul. There is no agreement of geometrical form, but they act and react upon each other by agreement of uses, and hence, we use the terms parallelism and correspondence to signify their relations.

The substances of both of these two worlds are alike stamped with the laws of the animal, vegetable and mineral kingdoms in their respective, distinct and separate degrees. The kingdoms of the spiritual world live from the divine sun of mind, the rays of which are divine love, wisdom and action: the kingdoms of the natural world live from the rays of the natural sun, which are light, heat and electricity. The substances of the spiritual world reside within the natural, just as one gas resides within another. The sun of the spiritual world, derived from the divine mind, operates upon all the substances of the spirit-world, and these again , by juxtaposition, operate on the substances of the natural, giving life and order.

The forms of the spiritual world do not flow into the natural, but only the affections of the spiritual world, exciting the thought-forms of the natural, and hence, the parallelism of the two worlds only exists by uses.

Not one word of the spiritual vocabulary can be pronounced by the natural organs ; not a single form of a spiritual idea can be received by the natural mind; the affections alone of the spiritual world flow in, and excite the external ideas of thought, so that the affection is spiritual and the thought natural. Hence it is only through the parallelism of the two worlds, that there can be any communication, and this takes place by the affections of each, exciting the thought forms which belong to the other.

When a man prays, his affections only are perceived by the angels, and not his words: the Lord only is both natural and spiritual at the same time, and hence, perceives both. When a man has advanced in regeneration in an orderly manner to the seventh degree, the celestial principle assumes control, and the celestial senses of the spirit are opened ; so that he sees, hears and feels the substances of the spirit world, and is conscious of their actual existence, perceiving the inflowing of spiritual affections and their transmission into the natural, and the excitation.

The things of the spiritual world appear in vision by the most brilliant and beautiful light; and, with these things, there comes a perception and excitation of natural thought, so that the subject is clearly understood; yet the man, is not in a conscious condition in the two worlds at the same time, any more than work can be conducted in two degrees of Masonry at once; yet, the transmission is so rapid as scarce to be perceived, the affections of the spiritual world flowing into the natural, and the natur. ' affections clothing them with their own language and science.

Where there is no agreement or parallelism between the affections of the natural and spiritual worlds, the vision is seen like a dream, but not understood. In the case of the prophets, an angel, filled with the divine spirit, entered their bodies and used their organs, language and science to give manifestation through the parallelism of the two worlds.

In this case the affections and truths of heaven

were expressed by the external facts, history and science of the natural world. In order that the divine Word might be correctly given, a people was selected, their entire history presided over, and circumstances induced, to exactly correspond with the affections and truths to be revealed; when these were inconsistent, visions were given and related in the natural language of the prophet to fill the vacancy, or act as a connecting link.

The Temple of Solomon, being erected by divine command, each and every part thereof, is correspondential and representative; and therefore, the pillars, now under description form a part of the divine parallelism of the word of God, which is allegorical, representative and correspondential.

No. 90.   Faith is referable to truth, and truth to the understanding. Charity refers itself to the will, and hence is predicated of good works; but charity can do nothing without the intellectual principle, by which there is a perception of truth, and a marriage of the will with the rational faculties.

Therefore all the degrees of the mind, must

unite and culminate in the intellectual degrees of altitude. See No. 80, also Pl. 1, Fig. 1. where the discrete degrees of the mind are colored red, yellow and blue, and numbered three, five and seven, which are their combining powers. These powers entering into all the secondary and tertiary colors or faculties of the mind, show the manner in which the affectional principles of the blue and red, come forward and unite with the ascending scale of the yellow or perceptive faculties, which in the anterior lobes of the hemispheres, form the two great intellectual columns of the brain, on the right and left sides.

These columns are the combined intellectual powers of the mind, consisting of three degrees of altitude; namely: the perceptive, rational and sympathetic faculties. The perceptive are animal, the rational are spiritual, and sympathetic faculties are the wisdom principles of the celestial man, from which arise all the originality, unity and beauty of design.

The combined power of these faculties is eighteen, being nine multiplied by two, which signifies the conjunction of all things of the degrees. See No. 32. It also represents the combined power of the discrete degrees of three, five and seven;

as three and seven are ten, and three and five are eight, and ten and eight are eighteen.

For the foregoing reasons, the two pillars, set up in the porch of King Solomon's Temple, were made eighteen cubits high, to represent the parallel columns of truth in both the natural and spiritual worlds, by which, not only the world, but the universe is sustained.

The arrangements of numbers, powers and faculties of the human mind, may appear to the superficial reader as incidental, arbitrary or ingeniously devised in order to sustain some preconceived notion of Masonry; but, I do assure him, that they are not mere inventions; but have their foundation in the nature of things, and can in no wise be changed, altered and defaced without obliterating nature itself, which is a work of the divine Being, proceeding in series of degrees, as end, cause and effect; the nature of which was seen and understood by the Prophets David and Solomon, who were the founders of Masonry through the building of the Temple, the plan of which was given by divine inspiration to David, and executed by Solomon. Therefore, all things connected with that temple are parallels and representatives of things, that exist in the heavens and earth.

No. 91. And a line of twelve cubits did compass them about. Twelve signifies all the truths of faith. See No. 29. The periphery of the circle is complete in itself. Divine and natural order flows into the domestic and devotional faculties of man, culminating and combining in the social.

Therefore the social faculties are colored purple, which represents the kingly or royal principle, which is derived from truth by which there is power of judgment.

Twelve, in a supreme sense, represents the infinite perception and understanding of the Deity, by which all things are simultaneously present with him, together with their laws of divine progressive order, running in series of end, cause and effect. The ancients therefore used the circle to represent infinity and eternity; but our Grand Master Hiram used the line of twelve cubits, in compassing the columns, to represent all the principles of truth, both of the natural and spiritual worlds. The center of the circle represents Deity; the radiuses represent the proceedings of his divine affections, and the periphery the boundary of his divine truth. These columns were therefore cast hollow, to distinguish between the representatives of the finite and infiinite truths.

No. 92. Each of the pillars in front of the Temple supported a chapiter, of five cubits in height. Five, signifies the discrete degree of the celestial affections. See the devotional faculties, No. 23. There exist in these affections, all the laws of divine order and Providence proper to man.

Hence five signifies man in a celestial sense.

The affections of the celestial man are supported, maintained and held in position, by the intellectual principle in its degrees of altitude, the perceptive, the rational and the sympathetic. The lower or perceptive degree of the senses, is common to the animal and man.

The rational degree belongs to the spiritual man, the sympathetic being perceptive of divine ends, belongs alone to the celestial. These degrees of altitude, contained in the anterior or frontal lobes of the brain, must agree, in every particular with the degrees of altitude of the affections, which are located in the posterior lobes of the hemispheres; so that the spiritual degree of the understanding cannot be opened without the spiritual degree of the affections, and vice versa; and neither can the sympathetic or celestial degree of the understanding be opened, without the dignifying faculties, which are represented by the olive ; and neither can the dignifying faculties be opened without the aid of the celestial principles of truth of the sympathetic.

The central columns of the brain, which exist in the right and left hemispheres, in their three degrees of the sustaining, semi-intellectual, and devotional faculties, are the bonds of union between the degrees of altitude contained in the front and posterior lobes of the brain, and therefore, express the life and action of both the intellect and the will, which flow together by the degrees of latitude, the intellectual flowing backward, and the will flowing forward, meeting each other in the central lobes. Hence the central column of the brain represents the active principle of the man.

Therefore,the long head gives intensity of thought, but less physical action. The broad head gives breadth and activity of thought, with great facility of action.

There is a certain transparency of the intellectual degrees of altitude, which enables a man to perceive and talk about truths which he does not comprehend, because his affections are not in them; but, if the affections be at the same time elevated, by a life of uses, the divine order, contained in the affections, flows forth through the intellectual principle, like water from a gushing fountain.

As the sympathetic and dignifying faculties are both opened by the knowledges of the divine Word, and a life agreeable thereto, the celestial principles become adorned with all the beauty, unity and variety of the three discrete degrees, which are represented by net work, lily work and pomegranates, which, in their literal sense signify unity, peace and plenty. "Seek first the kingdom of God, and its righteousness, and all these things shall be added unto you." Mat. 6. 33.

By the lower faculties of the brain, we have the scientific bond of net work, which, like the skin or integumentary principle in man, binds together the whole form. The net work therefore covered the chapiters.

By the middle or spiritual degree of the man, we have the perception of truth, which is always pure, blossoming like the lily ; it gives that peace of mind, which none but the spiritual man can realize. The ancients were, therefore, fond of representing the spiritual principles by the lily work.

The celestial principle, when opened, gives the

perception, understanding and powers of intellect, from which there is increase of idea, thought and perception, as plenty as the seeds of the pomegranate. The pomegranate, therefore, represents the multiplication of truth from affections, as the stars of heaven, by which a subject is perceived and seen without argument in all its relations to things.

The celestial faculties of the mind cannot be opened in connection with the spiritual temple; but with the spiritual man the influxes from the celestial degree of the mind are strong, enriching the spiritual degree with great beauty and harmony of thought; but yet, the full degree of the celestial mind cannot be opened, except in connection with the second or celestial temple. Therefore, Father Hiram, or Hiram-Abiff, did not live to complete the representation of the pillars. The full opening of the celestial mind could only be represented by a winged angel, standing on the top of each of the globes. Could Hiram have lived to see the final completion of the Temple, he would have crowned the monuments with these representations. But this could not be, for correspondences and representations cease with the spiritual degree; and a perception of the divine ends and motives, together with a higher class of symbolism, commences, by which there is a direct communication with the divine mind. The thoughts of the celestial angels, as they flow into the spiritual degree, are correspondences and representatives of divine things to the spiritual. Therefore, these pillars were broken up, and the brass carried away to Babylon. Jer. 52. 17.

No. 93. Around the Temple, upon the two sides and the rear, were built three chambers, one above the other, which are representative of the degrees of altitude. See Nos. 80, 90, 91, 92. The lower and nethermost chambers were representative of the perceptive or sensual degree of the intellect, and the affections which are the basis and foundation of the natural science.

A man must first pass through this degree in his course of regeneration, after the Entered Apprentice, and first section of the Fellow Craft, before he can proceed in the course of instruction in which the middle chamber is treated of. The object of natural science, so far as it relates to the body, is its protection and support; but through the middle chamber of the mind, it has a higher relation. There it meets the influxes of divine order, that descend through the devotional faculties by which there is a knowledge of God and a deep, rich and full faith in the divine Providence. Thus the scientific principle of the Fellow Craft receives its natural light from below, through the medium of the senses, and a divine light from above, through the inflowing of the laws of divine Providence, by which he is enabled to attain to a true spritual science.

The man who only looks to the outer world for light, through the medium of sense, must forever remain in thick darkness as to the interior forces of the natural, without being able to attain, even the threshold of knowledge: such, however, standing firmly upon the negative principles, dispute every thing, and consider themselves most wise, calling for a demonstration through the sensual, they say, "we do not believe," which is an end to further perception.

At the back or far end of the nethermost chamber, on the right side of the Temple, was located a flight of stone stairs winding around a central column and divided into series of three, five and seven, by broad platforms; thence, they ascended to the middle chamber on the east of the Temple, from which there was another flight of stairs leading to the third, which the Fellow Craft was not permitted to ascend.

The first three steps in ascending to the middle chamber, in their most literal sense, were representative of the three degrees of Masonry. The three stages of human life, youth, manhood and old age, and lastly the trinity of divine attributes which are divine love, wisdom and action, or procedure in the divine creation, which the Christian Mason calls the Father, Son and Holy Ghost. But as Masons, we are taught that all things proceed in a series of degrees, as end, cause and effect, which are the three first steps of knowledge, by which the mind rises to a perception of the interior forces and laws of natural and spiritual sciences; and he who has not rationally ascended these steps, has no claim to the understanding of either. A man, who merely examines natural objects, and experiments upon them, without being able to array them in series, is only useful in preparing the way for the more intelligent who may follow.

All things of creation have a certain likeness of the divine attributes of love, wisdom and use stamped upon them, by which they flow into ultimate ends of use or effect. This effect becomes

31*

the first end or use which flows forth again through
the cause into a second effect.

Thus, the energies of the first series of three,
namely, end, cause and effect, are in their full force
and power in the effect itself. This effect becomes
another cause, and produces the second effect, and
the two series taken together, are five, which is the
spiritual and representative meaning of five,
wherever it is found. The second effect again becomes the cause, and produces the third effect,
which is seven, and thus the three discrete degrees
in all created substances are formed. Hence, three,
five and seven are representative of the various
states of creation in their several degrees, and as
such, have always been held in high estimation
among Masons.

Mathematics, in its natural sense, is a science of
quantity ; but, in its spiritual, correspondential and
representative sense, it is a symbol of states. One
being representative of unity or Deity, which has
two qualities or powers, those of increase by multiplication and addition, as twice one are two and
one are three, which represent marriage and
fecundation of the divine mind, or power of creation.

These proceed in their onward course to complete another family circle ; as twice two are four, and one are five. Again proceeding in its circle of discrete degrees, as twice three are six and one are seven, completing the series of three, five and seven. Each of these degrees contains the powers of the three first numbers, in different states of ultimate creation ; and therefore, each of the series consists of three continuous degrees, which we have illustrated by light, heat and electricity, and the red, yellow and blue of the natural light ; the three degrees of the heat rays, with their different chemical powers, and the three degrees of electricity, with their inductive currents at right angles, the three forces in matter, gravitation, cohesive attraction and affinities, by which there are the three kingdoms of nature in their ultimates.

No. 94. The number five represents the devotional faculties. The influxes of divine order flow in through the devotional faculties, and the influxes of natural forms flow in through the perceptive faculties, which are represented by the number 3.

These two influxes meet each other, by the ascending and descending degrees and conjoin in the rational faculties of the mind. This conjunction of the two influxes, gives the power of reason and rationality, which is the manifestation of the light of the five senses to the eye of the soul: whereby the soul perceives all the natural affections and forms of the outer world, arranging them in series and degrees in a spiritual form. The power of referring, every object and affection to its proper class is reason. When there is a proper arrangement of ends, causes and effects, the result obtained is order in a three, and five fold form.

From the foregoing reasons, the five steps of the winding stair case, are said, in Masonic language, to represent the five senses, and the five orders of architecture. The five senses are seeing, hearing, feeling, tasting and smelling; three of these are discrete in their character and have always been held in high estimation among Masons; namely: seeing, hearing and feeling.

The five Orders of Architecture are the Doric, Ionic, Corinthian, Tuscan and Composite. The Doric, Ionic and Corinthian, are primitive in their character. The Tuscan is a rude compound of the Doric and Ionic. The Composite is a harmonious blending of the Ionic' and Corinthian.

The Doric, Ionic and Corinthian orders have always been held in high estimation among Masons, because they constituted the orders of the outer, middle and inner courts of the Temple.

Vitruvius, a Roman author of the time of the Cæsars, gives a description of the five orders and attribute their invention to the Greeks. His works were made the foundation of the cinque cinto school of architecture in the fifteenth century; but modern investigations and discoveries of the Grecian Temple described by him, prove that his descriptions were merely ideal. We cannot therefore credit his assertion, that the orders were invented by them. The oldest Grecian Temple of the Doric order, was erected about two hundred years after the Temple of Solomon, and was undoubtedly designed by travelling Masons, in imitation of the Temple, the proportions being nearly the same; the only material difference was the introduction of side colonnades, instead of the chambers. We therefore, notwitstanding, Vitruvius' assertion to the contrary, conclude that the Masonic tradition of their origin in the Temple is true. The five orders are the perfection of the principles of design, which are universal in their character, existing in nature as well as in art. The human system is the perfection of every principle in series and degrees, combining the three, the five and the seven, which are equally important. Three represents the degrees which are complete in nine and twenty-seven; five represents the order of the affections, and seven represents the fulness of natural science, the completion of the former state and the commencement of a new growth. These states, represented by the three, five and seven, are like the prime factors in numbers, which always maintain their original powers whatever state they enter into.

The five, when multiplied by two, signifies the order and fulness of remains. (See remains No. 28.) But, when considered in itself, it represents the fulness of the five orders of the human system which terminate in five distinct forms of the human character. (See the orders of man, No. 15.) The temperaments belong to the degrees and terminate in three, nine and twenty-seven. The seven belongs to the science, growth, creation and pro-gression of natural things. The principles repre-sented by these numbers hold their distinct relations in the human body. The three is complete in itself in three general divisions, as the head, body and limbs. Each limb, again, is articulated in three general divisions, and their extremities into five. The limb itself, in its fulness, is again articulated by its joints into seven distinct parts, counting the fingers and toes. The human form, in its complete height, is divided into seven distinct parts, which are the foot, the leg, the femur, the abdomen, the thorax, the neck and the head. Thus, the three, five and seven, with their multiples, are beautifully blended in every part of the human system. The three, five and seven, as they relate to the degrees, orders and ultimations of the human system, have their beginning, growth, culmination and decay, as in youth, manhood and old age.

No. 95. The seven steps represent the ultimations of natural science. The three and the five unite to produce the rational principle, the truths of which are arranged into science by which every act of charity is produced. The order of the human body and mind, is derived from the affections, uniting with the intellectual principle, from which originate the growth, science and active force of the body and mind in their ultimate powers, which are represented by seven.

Therefore, in Masonic language, the seven steps are said to be representative of the seven days of the week, the seven sabbatical years, the seven years of plenty, and the seven years of famine, the seven years in which the Temple was building, and the seven golden candle sticks, but more particularly, the seven liberal arts and sciences, which we shall hereafter enumerate, and fully explain.

The most important changes of the human system, both in sickness and health, take place in periods of seven, as seven days, seven weeks and seven years. The full and complete state of the natural body and mind, culminates in seven times seven, or forty-nine, when there is a material change, either for good or evil, according to the combined powers of the degrees and orders of the affections. If the orders of the affections are full, and the remains of infancy fully developed (which is represented by the number 10), the seven and the ten are multiplied together ; this being the case at the fulness of forty-nine ; a regrowth, both of the natural body and mind, takes place. The physical form does not increase in height, but fills up and expands in breadth. The limbs become more elastic, the activity of the body and the forces of the mind are increased. These states again culminate in three score and ten, or seventy, and if the affections and degrees are harmoniously blended, the life is multiplied by nine and ten, or ninety years ; or if by reason of the conjunction of the principles of truth, by which there is strength of the affections, the period of life culminates with the multiplication of eight and ten, which are eighty years. But, if the order of affections, and the degrees of the mind, terminate in the fulness of the principle of faith, the life is multiplied by ten times twelve, which is a hundred and twenty, which was the case with the prophet Moses ; and yet the forces of the body and the eye, were not dimmed by age. All the important changes of the physical system depend on the combination of the three, five and seven, with the various multiples. These principles may be feeble and but partially developed in their degrees, or they may be full and well developed and strengthened by the hereditary principle and force of habit. Thus, there is an endless variety of forces and powers, which governs the natural changes of the human system and length of life ; and these again may be renewed by repentance and regeneration. Medicine will never be reduced to a science, until the natural changes of the mind and body are understood.

No. 96. Quantity in the natural world corresponds to state in the spiritual; therefore, the science of mathematics has within it, the parallelism of the two worlds as to quantity and state. The number 7, is the third series of multiplication and addition, and hence, spiritually signifies fulness, completion and the commencement of the state, in which the divine principle reigns supreme. It was therefore said in the Holy Scriptures: "Thus the heavens and the earth were finished, and all the host of them. And on the seventh day God ended his work, which he had made; and he rested on the seventh day from all his work which he had made: And God blessed the seventh day and sanctified it : because that in it he had rested from all his work which God created and made." Gen. 2. 1. 2. The work which God had created and made, in the natural sense, signifies the heavens and the earth. In a spiritual sense it signifies the regeneration of man, by which the spirit is prepared in the natural and spiritual degrees, and the third or celestial state is commenced, which is a day of rest. See No. 86.

For the foregoing reasons, the seven steps in Masonic language, are said to represent the seven days of the week, the seven sabbatical years, the years of plenty, and the seven years of famine.

The ancients also arranged their schools in a

series of seven, wherein they taught seven arts and sciences. The seven steps *were therefore said to represent the seven liberal arts and sciences, which are Arithmetic, Grammar, Geometry, Logic, Rhetoric, Music and Astronomy. It may be urged that the liberal arts and sciences represented by the seven steps, are arbitrary and not founded in the nature of things, as there are many more arts and sciences taught at the present day. But the number seven signifies the fulness of natural things and the commencement of a new state, wherein the Lord rules. It therefore signifies all the laws of natural order made subservient to the celestial state or condition of man in the last or lowest ultimate degree. This degree is located in the cerebellum in man; it being derived from the ultimation of the higher degrees, it constitutes a little brain itself, and receiving the influxes of the lowest discrete degree of nature, it is the seat of nature, order and civil life. Its combining power is seven. The preparation of the cerebellum to receive the influxes of the spiritual man, is represented by the Master's degree.

After this preparation of the cerebellum has taken place through faith, hope and charity, profanation ceases, and all things relating to marriage, procreatiŏn and civil order is felt to be sacred and holy, and really becomes so to us, as the seventh day or Sabbath is attained to, the laws of the conjugal relations being looked upon as most sacred, and never to be profaned. The man leaves all other women and cleaves unto one wife, and they twain become one flesh; but this state can never take place without the careful study and practice of the natural and spiritual sciences contained in the divine Word, by which the mind attains not only to the fulness of a natural, but also a spiritual rational: just in propor tion as the influxes of the celestial degree become strong, flowing into and perfecting the spiritual rational mind of a people or nation, they leave the plurality of wives and adhere to one.

They require no divine law upon the subject of plurality; but let that man who commits adultery, know and understand that he is not in a state of mind to understand or comprehend the truth, either in the natural or spiritual degree, and that he must remain in thick darkness until the commandments are obeyed. Such men cannot be made Fellow Craft Masons in heart, or pass understandingly the seven steps which bring them to the middle chamber of science, wherein they attain to the knowledge of God. 'All things that appertain to the love of God or the neighbor are holy; but all things that relate to the love of self and the world are profane. He, therefore, who studies literally the liberal arts and sciences with a sole view to himself and to the world, constantly profanes all that is sacred; but he who ascends the three, five and seven steps, through faith, hope and charity, receives as his rewards, the blessings of natural and spiritual sciences, and attains, both naturally and spiritually, to a knowledge of Deity.

We should be glad, at this point, to enter into a full and complete description of the laws and rules of design and their parallelism in the spiritual; but the limits of our work will not permit. We, therefore, pass on to the more important points, giving a short analysis of a few elemental principles of the sciences, developing the series and degrees which exist in them.

# ARITHMETIC.

No. 97.  Arithmetic is the most important of all the sciences.  By the science of numbers, in the natural world we arrive at a knowledge of quantity, and in the world of mind, the state and condition of things; the relation that they hold to each other and the Creator : number and state are parallels that exist in the two worlds.

Creation itself takes place by marriage and increase through chemical combination, by which we have the alletropical condition of the elements and their compound by mixture, which agree with the elementary principles of multiplication and addition.  All numbers consist of a series of one by multiplication and addition.  These numbers again, are resolved into their prime factors by division, and their elementary digits by substraction; and hence, we have the four elementary rules of Arithmetic, together with the modes of enumerating, which are five with the four rules. Two are negative and two positive.  By the positive, we increase the quantity ; by the negative, it is diminished into its constituents. Every number, greater than nine, consists of a series of nine, plus the sum of the digits contained in the number; and hence, every number is divisible by nine with a remainder, which is the sum of its digits. If this sum be divisible by nine, the whole number is also divisible by nine. The same is the case with three, being the prime factor of nine.

The digits of the numerals terminate with nine, with the addition of one for every series of nine, by which we have a system of decimals. Nine, therefore, constitute the series of degrees throughout nature and mathematical science, and also represents the fulness of the degrees of the mind.

Quantity in numbers, increases by multiplcation and addition; as twice one are two and one are three ; twice two are four and one are five ; twice three are six and one are seven ; twice four are eight and one are nine ; twice five are ten and one are eleven; twice six are twelve and one are thirteen; twice seven are fourteen and one are fifteen.

Thus the numbers continue in series and degrees, constituting all the prime numbers.

The third term from three, is divisible by three; the fifth term from five, is divisible by five ; the seventh term from seven, being divisible by seven. Thus the prime numbers continue throughout in series and degrees, and therefore, the reverse of this operation of division by two, and substraction of one, reduces any number to its elementary constituents ; and any division by the prime numbers that will divide the number, without a remainder, reduces it to its prime factors, or the prime factors and the prime number ; for every number is either a prime number or consists of prime factors.

Thus, all the numbers spring from one multiplied by two, and the addition of one ; multiplication producing all the even numbers, and addition the odd numbers.

The first three series of multiplication and addition produce the prime numbers, three, five and seven, and the even numbers, two, four and six.

The fourth series produces the even number eight, and the odd number nine, which is divisible by three.

The fifth series gives the even number ten, and the prime number eleven.

The sixth series gives by multiplication, the even number twelve, and the prime number thirteen by addition.

In the seventh series, we have the even number

fourteen, and the odd number fifteen, which is divisible by five :

thus :

| 1. | 2. | 3. | 4. | 5. | 6. | 7. | 8. | 9. | 10. | 11. |
|----|----|----|----|----|----|----|----|----|-----|-----|
| 2 | 2 | 2 | 2 | 2 | 2 | 2 | 2 | 2 | 2 | 2 |

| 2 | 4 | 6 | 8 | 10 | 12 | 14 | 16 | 18 | 20 | 22 |
|---|---|---|---|----|----|----|----|----|----|----|
| 1 | 1 | 1 | 1 | 1 | 1 | 1 | 1 | 1 | 1 | 1 |

| 3. | 5. | 7. | 9. | 11. | 13. | 15. | 17. | 19. | 21. | 23. |
|----|----|----|----|-----|-----|-----|-----|-----|-----|-----|

The foregoing brings to view the progression of one by multiplication and addition, developing the nine digits, in their series of nine and the addition of one, which divides the progressive numbers into intervals of ten ; it also developes the even numbers in the progressive order of two, four, six and eight, and the progressive order of the prime numbers as three, five and seven. Commencing from one, these follow in series of three, terminating with nine, fifteen and twenty-one, after which they change, running in series of two and one, three and one continually changing the series by fixed laws, thus bringing to view the numbers in series and prime factors; the relations of which are the elements of Arithmetic.

The intuitive perception of the relations that exist between the nine digits, the even numbers and the prime factors, constitutes the natural

Arithmetician. Persons are now and then· met with who can perform the most astonishing calculations without being able to explain the principles upon which they are done, which they are enabled to perform by an intuitive perception of these relations.

Rising above the five rules of Arithmetic into the higher branches of mathematics, we introduce signs to designate the operations to be performed, and letters to denote the quantities, and the nine axioms to give clearness of operation.

1st. Things which are equal to the same things, are equal to each other.

2d. If equals be added to equals, the sums will be equal.

3d. If equals be taken from equals, the remainders will be equal.

4th. If equals be added to unequals, the wholes will be unequal.

5th. If equals be taken from unequals, the remainders will be unequal.

6th. Things which are double of equal things, are equal to each other.

7th. Things which are halves of equal things, are equal to each other.

8th. The whole is greater than any of its parts.

9th. The whole is equal to the sum of all its parts.

For although more axioms are introduced into the science of Geometry, when analyzed, they are found to be only a repetition of the foregoing.

By the introduction of infinitesimal quantities, we are enabled to ascend by the science of Mathematics, to a comprehension of the minute particles of time, space and quantity Thus, we have given an outline on the subject of Mathematics, in its natural sense.

But there exists a parallel science of Mathematics, that relates to the changes of states and conditions of mental and spiritual sciences, in which all the numbers and quantities, with their operations, are representatives of divine thought and affection, which is like a great central sun of mind, wherein every thought and love substance is organized in the likeness of the animal, vegetable and mineral kingdoms of the spiritual world.

These unfold agreeably to the law of numbers, or rather the law of numbers arise from their unfolding simultaneously with the outbirth of thought and affection.

Jehovah is distinctly one Lord, in whom there is a trinity of attributes and a unity of person; therefore He is represented by 1. The first procedure of his divine attributes is divine Good, the second procedure is divine Wisdom, by which there is a marriage of the divine Good and Wisdom; which is represented by multiplication. From these proceed his divine power of creation, represented by addition which is 3.

These again proceed by multiplication and addition commencing with 2, producing the prime number 5, which is representative of all the laws of divine Providence, which is derived from the divine love of good. The next series of multiplication and addition commences with 3, and terminates with the prime number, 7, which is representative of all the science of the creative power derived from divine love of truth.

Thus, all things of the divine mind are organized in likeness of a divine sun of mind, wherein exist all the first ends of creation. The decomposition and recombination of the light and heat of this divine sun, flowing into ultimates, produce all the substances of the spiritual world. When these substances have descended into a state of death, they are repelled from the life substances of

the spiritual world, and descend into the first molecules of natural light and heat. These, by their
affinities conjoin, producing the power of attraction,
which gives the first ends or molecules of matter,
which are drawn into sun spheres, wherein again,
there takes place an organization of the worlds
which are the offspring of their respective suns.

Thus, the sun that is derived from the divine
mind, is life and power; but the sun derived
through the spiritual world is dead and inert; receiving all of its forces from the sun of the divine
mind, wherein the divine Creator proceeds to or-
ganize in the light and heat spheres of our natural
sun, all the substances of the planets in ther liquid,
gazeous light forms. These forms flow into world
spheres and become ultimated, as natural earths
prepared for the reception of man, all of which
takes place strictly according to the law of numbers.
See the Article on the Square, Plumb and Level.

We think it is clearly proved and revealed by
the power of the spectroscope that all the substances of the earth and their solid, liquid and
gaseous forms are organized in the sun spheres,
notwithstanding there has not as yet been the
discovery of water or the precious metals.

33          R

No. 98.  In the development of the numbers
1, 2, 3 and 4, with the even and prime numbers
as illustrated in Article 97, we have the series:

$$
\left.
\begin{array}{cccc}
1. & 2. & 3. & 4. \\
2. & 2. & 2. & 2. \\
\hline
2. & 4. & 6. & 8. \\
1. & 1. & 1. & 1. \\
\hline
3. & 5. & 7. & 9.
\end{array}
\right\}
$$

The number 1, signifies unity or the Divine
Being.   1, 2, and 3, represents the divine attributes which are Love, Wisdom and Action or Goodness, Wisdom and Power.   These divine attributes are stamped in a greater or less degree upon
all created things; and hence the number 3, when it
relates to any being, represents the divine attributes that are impressed upon it.   The being or
substance itself, containing three more series represented by 2, 3 and 4.   The number 9, represents the fulness of the three discrete degrees, 3,
5 and 7, which have been treated of, throughout
the work, but more especially when treating of the
groups of the human faculties.   See Pl. fig. 1. and
Nos. 22 to 31.

The number 3, signifies the natural perception of individual things, which are impressed upon the five senses from the divine attributes. The number 5, signifies man, or all the laws of humanity and divine order in man, by which there is a perception and understanding of the laws of divine Providence. The number 7, signifies the fulness and completion of the scientific principle, the end of creation, and the commencement of a new state in which old things are put away, and all things made new. Hence, the Temple is destroyed, the children of Israel carried away captive, and a new Temple, upon a different plan, is erected.

The number 1, 2, 3 and 4, with their series terminating in 3, 5, 7 and 9, are representative of the chemical changes that take place by the four elements, that in general constitute the animal body and the great mass of the solid substances of the world. These elements are Hydrogen, Nitrogen, Oxygen and Carbon, which are governed by the same laws in another degree, as the numbers before treated of, ultimating themselves in three discrete degrees in the blood, agreeing with the animal, vegetable and mineral kingdoms, which have been before treated of in Nos. 5, 6, and 7.

The first ends or molecules of matter, as derived

from light and heat, through the electric forces, may be considered like all forms, elementary and primitive in their character, susceptible of contraction and expansion to an almost indefinite extent ; each possessing the electric forces in their discrete and continuous degrees, and capable of entering into the three kingdoms of nature, and of readily combining with each other, under different states of the electric substances.

When in like states, or degrees, they mutually repel and separate from one another; and when in unlike states, they mutually attract, and chemically combine, forming into compound, gases, liquids and solids.

# GRAMMAR.

No. 99. Grammar teaches the correct use of words, and is divided into four branches, Orthography, Etymology, Syntax and Prosody. Words are the signs of ideas. Ideas are derived from objects, their actions and qualities. These three are fully expressed in nine parts of speech, which are divided into three discrete and six continuous degrees, which are like the degrees of the human mind, heretofore illustrated.

The subject, the action and the quality are separate and discrete in their nature, and yet, they cohere like end, cause and effect, or goodness, wisdom and action. The quality and action cannot be separated from the object, and yet the mind conceives them as having a distinct existence. Every object either performs an action, or is receptive of one. When the object performs an act, it is said to be in the nominative case ; when it is the object of an action, it is in the objective case ; and when the object is simply announced as, O, Lord, it is in the nominative case independent, and when

placed before a participle it is called the nominative case absolute.   Objects exist, either single,
plural or collectively ; and hence, objects or nouns
are said to be singular, plural, and nouns of multitude ; and, when treating of human beings, they are
supposed to be either speaking, spoken to, or
spoken of; and hence, we have the first, second
and third persons of nouns, from which arises the
rule.   The verb must agree with its nominative in
number and person.

Verbs or actions have two qualities, namely :
manner of expression and time of action.   The
former is called the Mood, and the latter the Tense
of the verb.   The modes of expression are five.

First, the Indicative Mood, which declares a
fact.

Secondly, the Imperative Mood, which implies a
command.

Thirdly, the Potential Mood, which gives permission.

Fourthly, the Subjunctive Mood, which implies
a condition, and lastly, the Infinitive Mood, which
signifies to do.

The times of action expressed by the verb,
are six,   First, the present time, as now. Second,
the Imperfect time, as not yet complete.

Third, the Perfect time, as have or has. Fourth, the Pluperfect Tense, as had or hadst. Fifth, the First Future Tense, as shall or will, and lastly the Second Future Tense, as shall or will have.

All the relations and qualities of objects are expressed in a series of nine parts of speech, which are :

First, the Article. A, An, and The, which points out the noun or object.

Second, the Noun, which is the name of an object, known by making sense in itself.

Third, the Pronoun I, Thou, He, She, It, We, Ye, You, and They, which add to the beauty of the language and prevent the frequent repetition of the noun.

Fourth, the Adjective, which expresses the quality of the noun, and always makes sense with the word, thing.

Fifth, the Verb, which expresses action or being, and may be known by making sense with the word, To.

Sixth, the Adverb, which is a word expressing the manner of the Verb, and known by, How, When and Where, and frequently ending in *ly*.

Seventh, the Preposition which connects words, as In, At, On, Under, Beneath.

Eighth, the Conjunction, which connects words
and sentences, as And, If, Because. Ninth, the
Interjection, which is a word expressing sudden
emotion, as, Oh! Alas!

Tenth, the Participle is a word expressing action, and known by ending in Ing. or Ed.

The reader will perceive that in reality there
are but nine parts of speech. The Pronoun being
only a word substituted for a noun, and that thus
the fulness of the degrees of our language is expressed by the nine parts of speech, arising from
the object, its quality and action, which are the
discrete degrees of the language, agreeing with the
three, five and seven of the numerals in Arithmetic, which culminate in the nine digits. The
Pronoun holds a similar relation, in the parts of
speech, to the number ten of the numerals, which
divides the language into intervals of ten, which
move on in an extended description, like the rotation of a wheel in endless beauty of time, manner
and quality of action. Each of the parts of speech
agrees with all the other parts, either governing or
being governed.

Whatever number of nouns in the singular
number, is preceded by the distributive, each, every
and either, must have singular verbs and pronouns,

notwithstanding they are joined by the copulative conjunction, as, every man and woman was there.

When singular and plural nouns or pronouns are joined by the disjunctives or, or nor, the latter noun or pronoun takes precedence, and the following verb is in the singular or plural number as the case may require ; as the Master nor Wardens were there, or, the Wardens or Master was there.

When something doubtful or contingent is implied, and future time is expressed, though the noun or pronoun be singular, the verb must be plural, as, Though he slay me, yet will I trust in him.

When two or more pronouns, joined by and, serve merely to describe one person or thing, the verb should be singular, as, this Philosopher and Poet was.

Adding s to a noun, makes it plural ; adding s to a verb, makes it singular ; taking s from the verb in the third person, makes it plural. A verb that ends in s, is singular.

Singular nouns or pronouns require singular verbs. Plural nouns or pronouns require plural verbs.

Two or more nouns or pronouns, joined by the

copulative conjunction, And, require plural verbs and pronouns.

, Two or more nouns or pronouns in the singular number, joined by the disjunctive conjunction or, or nor, require singular verbs and pronouns.

A noun of multitude, as, Church, Lodge. Army, Navy, may have either a singular verb or pronoun. If unity of idea is expressed, it should have a singular verb and pronoun. If plurality of ideas is implied, it should have a plural noun and pronoun.

The nominative case denotes the agent or actor The Possessive case denotes the possession of an object.

The objective case expresses the object of an action or relation, and is always governed by an active verb, active participle or preposition. It is governed by an active verb, as, I love the Lodge ; and by an active participle, as obeying the Master, and governed by a preposition, as, With the Master.

The nominative case is independent when addressed.

The nominative case is absolute when the noun stands before a Participle, as the Master having arrived, we proceeded to open the Lodge.

The nominative case is in apposition, when two names come together meaning the same thing.

There is a nominative case after the verb *be*, and its inflection *is*, when a nominative precedes it, as, It is the Master, it is *He*.

There is an objective case after the verb, *be* and *is*, when an objective case precedes it, as, He looked to be the Master, I took it to be *Him*.

A verb in the Infinitive Mood or part of a sentence, may be taken for a noun and put in the nominative case to any other verb, as *To see* the Master working, gives pleasure.

Verbs in the Imperative Mood always agree with *Thou, Ye* or *You*, expressed or understood. They however, never can agree with nouns or with the first or third persons of pronouns.

Verbs, following *dare, let, make, need, see, hear, feel*, are put in the Infinitive Mood, without the sign *to*, as, Let me go.

*Who, Which, What* and *That*, are relative pronouns. *That*, may be three parts of speech ; a relative Pronoun, an Adjective and a Conjunction.

*That* is a relative pronoun, when we can change it into, *who* or *which* : It is an Adjective when it joins a Noun.

*What,* may be three parts of speech: A compound relative Pronoun, an Adjective and a relative Pronoun.

*Who,* is used to denote the human species, instead of the noun or pronoun.

The order and manner of parsing the various parts of speech, is too extensive and will be passed over.

The rules for parsing by transposition are short, easy to recollect, and useful in composition:

First, Place the Article first in the sentence.

Second, Place the Adjectives before their nouns.

Third, Place the Noun or Pronoun next, that is in the Nominative case to the Verb.

Fourth, Place the Verb next. If it be Active Transitive, let the object of the action follow.

Fifth, Let Adverbs follow the Verbs they limit or qualify, and supply every ellipsis.

Sixth, When the word *That* occurs as a Relative Pronoun, change it into *who* or *which,* as the sense requires.

He, that is able readily to transpose a sentence, agreeably to the foregoing rules, will at once perceive the relations of the parts of speech.

We shall content ourselves, in this article, with giving a short synopsis of Grammar, which may be useful in every day life, and serve to bring out the principles of each degree, or part of speech; although the rules, in their condensed form, are not strictly philosophical.

Thus, the English language is founded in the nature of degrees and is adequate to their full expression. The Grammar of other languages differs as they are more or less perfect. The more complete Grammars express the same ideas, series and degrees only in another form.

There are many kinds of language. A combination of lines, according to certain rules, represents sounds, and sounds represent ideas; and ideas represent all the objects, actions and qualities of the animal, vegetable and mineral kingdoms of the world; and these again, in their turn, are representative of all the actions, operations, qualities and substances of the human mind.

The landscape, through the art of drawing, light and shade, painting and colors, represents, in the beautiful language of art, all the forms, qualities and actions of nature, the arts and sciences of civilization, and the religious emotions of man, at a single view, thus presenting to the eye what sounds do to the ear; and also there is a language of the feelings.

34

The external language of sounds, writing and printing excites the emotions of the mind in rapid succession, giving rise to combinations of thoughts and affections. These all have their parallel in the world of mind. The descending beatitudes of of Deity flow forth from his divine creative attributes, mirroring all the forms, operations and qualities of the animal, vegetable and mineral kingdoms, upon the first ends of existence and molecules of spiritual substance.

These are perceived by the regenerate man in vision, sound and feeling, as the divine Words descending from the throne of God, through a universal sun of causes, descending through discrete suns of angelic minds, to the sensorium of man, in the natural world. These, like the three primitive rays of light, the red, yellow and blue, are received into the cerebellum; the perceptive and the devotional faculties, giving the light or perception of the five senses; natural and civil order by the cerebellum; and the perception of the laws and ends of Divine Providence, through the devotional; which are received and understood according to the quality of the man and his state of regeneration, giving power of perception and thought.

Thus, in the regenerate man, the divine influxes flow into his feelings, prompting all the divine ends and motives of the Deity. These are expressed in the beauty and splendor of his external education, descending into the corresponding objects of thought. If these be ample and beautiful, his feelings will be expressed with beauty and richness of language; but, if his education be limited, and the scenery of life rugged, his feelings will be expressed with more force than beauty, and yet the same internal emotions, derived from the influxes of the divine mind, will be contained in his language.

When evils and falses have destroyed the virtuous affections of the angelic man, they are no longer excited to action by the divine influxes, but darkness reigns upon the face of the deep, and the spirit of God must again move upon the face of the waters, and Masonically say, "let there be light!"

# GEOMETRY.

No. 100. Geometry treats of solids, which have Geometrically, three properties; length, breadth and thickness. Every solid is bounded by surfaces.

The inclination of two surfaces forms an angle. The intersection of two surfaces gives a line, and hence, a line has length without thickness.

If a line be intersected by a cross plane, it gives a corner or point, and therefore, a point has position only, without length, breadth or thickness.

A square surface is a figure bounded by four equal parallel lines, with an equal number of right angles, and hence, it is called a parallelogram. If the length be greater than the breadth, it is called an oblong. These forms are more easily understood by the mind than any other figure, and, therefore, every measurement in mensuration is reduced to either a square, an oblong or a cube; as a square inch or foot, or a cubic inch, foot or yard.

Every surface is made up of one or more triangles. A triangle is reduced to a square or
parallelogram by multiplying the height, by half
of the length of the base. The height is found
by letting fall a line from the apex perpendicular
to the base. For the foregoing reasons, every
figure or solid can be reduced to a triangle, and
thereby, brought into a square or parallelogram,
reducing it to its simplest form, so that the mind
can readily comprehend its measurement. If a
square or parallelogram be divided diagonally by
a plane passing through the opposite corners, it
will be divided into two equal triangles. But
the surfaces and the angles being divided equally,
each triangle will be equal to half of the square
or parallelogram, and half of the angles.

Therefore, all the angles of any triangle, are
equal to two right angles, and its surface is equal
to half the legnth of the parallelogram, multiplied
by its breadth.

If the triangle again be divided into any number of similar triangles, all of the angles will be
the same, and their similar sides will be propor-
tional; but if the triangle be again divided into
dissimilar triangles, all the sides and angles will
be dissimilar; but, as each of these dissimilar

triangles contains two right angles, the length of their sides and the angles can be readily found, if one side and two angles be given.

The triangle is equal to half of the square, or parallelogram, formed by the multiplication of its base and perpendicular. The square of the hypothenuse, or long line extending to the diagonal corner of the parallelogram, is equal to twice the parallelogram. Therefore, it is said, that the square of the hypothenuse is equal to the square of the base and perpendicular.

Upon the foregoing principles and relation of the square and triangle, depend all of the operations of measurement of surfaces and solids.

Solids, are of three general kinds; first, the Pyramid, which has a flat base, and its apex terminating in a point. The form of the base may be triangular, quadrangular or polyagonal. The number of the sides may be increased to an infinite number, terminating in a cone.

The second solid is a Prism, which has three general forms which are triangular, quadrangular, and polyagonal, terminating with an infinite number of sides in a cylinder.

The third and last general form, is the Hedron, the simplest form is the tetrahedron, which is bounded by four triangles. The octohedron, is bounded by eight equal triangles, and the polyhedron, by many equal triangles, which may be increased indefinitely until the solids terminate in a spheroid.

Thus, the surface of every solid is composed of triangles, which commence with a simple triangular figure, and terminates in an infinite number, which is a circle, and, therefore, every solid and its surfaces, can be measured by the triangle.

The intersection of surfaces forming lines, are either straight, or curved. Any section of a spheroid is a circular figure ; also the section of the cylinder and cone, when cut parallel to their bases. If a cylinder or cone be cut by a plane passing through them at an acute or obtuse angle, with their axis, the figure thus formed, is an ellipsis. If a cone be cut parallel to one side, or its axis, the figures thus formed, are either a hyperbola or a parabola, and, if an envelope be thrown off from a section of either a cone or cylinder, a fifth curve will be formed, which has not as yet been named or defined in Geometry.

From the foregoing it will be perceived that a series of threes and nines runs through the science of Geometry, similar to that of Arithmetic. As every number in the science of quantity is either a prime number or composed of prime factors, so it will be perceived that every figure is either a triangle or composed of a multiplication and addition of triangles; and, if a triangle be divided into similar or dissimilar triangles, that the same law of ratio and proportion exists among the triangles as there does among the numbers in fractions, and therefore all the various operations in numbers may be geometrically performed with lines, angles and surfaces.

Mind is not the mere effect of matter, but a substance that belongs to the world of mind, derived from the great Creator, who is the source of all things. The forces that exist between the natural world and the world of mind, are like those that exist between the body and spirit, which act and react upon each other, there being a complete parallelism between the two. The world of mind has its geometry, and seven sciences and arts, like the world of forms ; as every object in the natural world has length, breadth and thickness, so has every substance of the spirit world. Love corresponds to length, and breadth to wisdom ; and hence, we say, in speaking of wisdom, the " broad principles of truth," the multiplication of truth and affection

produces wisdom ; and addition gives action. These
being the three primitive degrees or attributes of the
mind, namely, love, wisdom and action, which are
stamped by the divine Creator in a certain image
upon all created things ; and, therefore, creation
exists in series and degrees like the numbers and
regular solids.

The multiplication of a line produces breadth,
and addition gives thickness; these are terminated
by other affections and truths, which give the representations of angles and points. In every
affection, there is an effort to reproduce itself; that
reproduction is by intelligence. In the multiplication
of affections and wisdom, which are the male and
female principles, there resides an effort to action
or to reproduce themselves, which is addition.
This corresponds to a solid body in Geometry or a
prime number in Arithmetic, or marriage and increase in the animal world, or the seed and growth
in the vegetable kingdom, or to affinity and combination in the mineral.

The efforts and affinities, that reside in the substances of love, are ever endeavoring to put forth
their geometrical lines into bodies and surfaces, to
ultimate their own likenesses in the forms of the
natural world ; and thus, the geometrical princi-

ples of the spiritual world are always acting against their opposing principles in the natural, there being a parallel between the two; and hence, whenever the proper conditions exist in the world, the geometrical principles of the spiritual, are ever pressing upon the natural, forcing them to action. The natural world is a creation in itself, and can in no wise be elevated into the spiritual; and hence, death is a mere separation of the natural and spiritual, through the termination of the legitimate conditions of one or the other of the two worlds.

The first molecules of matter receive a definite form, according to the degrees that they are of, in the order of three, five and seven. If two or more molecules be joined together in one direction, they form a line. If the third molecule be added to the side of two others, falling into the interstice between them, the figure thus formed is a triangle, and every additional molecule that is added gives an additional triangle. This may be readily understood by bringing together a number of small shot on a table, or even other bodies of different forms, and taking a line from center to center of the various particles brought together. It will be readily perceived that the addition of every object gives an additional triangle.

Thus it is that the triangle becomes the foundation of measurement for every surface or solid.

When the molecules of matter chemically combine, the particles become polarized, joining together in right lines, triangles, cubes and polyagonal figures, agreeably to the direct and induced electric currents. There being in general, three currents, the direct current which produces an induced current at right angles, and another at forty-five degrees. These constitute the discrete degrees in the electric forces, which take place by decomposition, and agree with the three primitive colors in light. Each of these discrete degrees meet each other by continuous degrees, which form intervening angles ; each discrete degree of electric force repels the particles of matter, which are alike electrified, and attracts other particles of matter, which are electrified by the other discrete degrees.

These attractions and repulsions do not take place by undulations as sounds, but by direct lines, through points of contact, exciting light and heat, in every molecule of matter, through which the electric forces pass.

# LOGIC.

No. 101. Logic is the art of reasoning, and
every art, when intelligibly understood, is the exercise of science. Science, therefore, is the basis
of logic. All of our knowledges consist of facts,
principles and truths; facts are objects, circumstances and events, individualized from the observation of our own senses or the testimony of others.
Principles are facts reduced to order. Truth, is a
solemn conclusion of the human mind, derived
from an arrangement of facts or truths, that have
been previously individualized, arranged and con-
cluded upon.

To reason, therefore, the perceptive faculties
must first clearly perform their duty, by appre-
hending and particularizing every object and event
of personal observation, history or science. These
are united with the affections, extending into life,
and elevated into the middle chamber of the rational faculties where they are arranged in a certain
order, by chemical combination, with the influxes

and the electric forces, derived from the devotional faculties by the descending degrees of the mind, arranging them in the proper order that belongs to the loves of the man, which are represented by the number five. This order is perceived or seen by a kind of interior sight, which belongs to the higher faculties of the mind. By this sight, the quality of every object is perceived when it is elevated into the middle chamber, and immediately referred to its proper class. This operation. when perceived by the mind, is reasoning.

To exercise the art of reasoning, therefore, and to bring it forth into language, every fact and truth, previously received, must be clearly defined and arranged as to their universal principles ; so that when a proposition is presented it is immediately seen whether it is true or false, by referring it to its o\ n roper class, and seeing whether or not, the things asserted of the object agree with the universal principles known and acknowleged to belong to its class. This is the universal mode of all reasoning, and the means by which every conclu- sion is justly arrived at, whether it be perceived by the mind or not.

The deduction of every truth by a process of reasoning, can be reduced to a simple syllogism,

35                          S

consisting of three propositions; the first of which consists of a statement which is universally admitted to be true, of a certain class of things. The second proposition consists of a statement, that a certain object belongs to that class. The third proposition asserts, that the object of the second proposition, therefore, possesses the qualities of the first, as : —

1st. That every good Mason is a true man.

2d. Our brother Junior Warden is a good Mason.

3d. Therefore, he is a true man.

But the reverse of this proposition that every true man is a good Mason, would not be true, because it cannot be predicated of the first proposition, for there are many true men that are not Masons. It is, therefore, all important to see that the thing asserted in the first proposition is universal. If what is asserted, and the object which it is asserted of, be both predicated of each other in the first proposition, the reverse of the conclusion is also true, as : —

1st. That which is good is also true.

2d. Masonry is good.

3d. Therefore it is true.

The reverse of this proposition is equally true, because it is universally admitted that whatever is good is also true, and whatever is true is also good. We therefore say Masonry is good, because it is true.

The second proposition of the syllogism, in ordinary speaking and writing, is usually left out or concealed, and we say that every good Mason is a true man ; therefore, brother Junior Warden is a true man, but the second proposition is always understood.

The syllogism itself should never appear in the discourse, until all the facts of the two first propositions have been clearly stated, their terms defined and illustrated, and the universality of the thing asserted in the first proposition is made indisputable to the minds of the audience.

The second proposition should be clearly shown to be included in the first. Thus, step by step, the argument should advance to the final conclusion, which will be followed by an irresistible conviction. The plot, design and arrangement of the argument, so as to enlist the affections, adorn the statements and gain the assent of the mind to the first and second propositions, and the final climax are the Work of Rhetoric.

Goodness of heart and honesty of purpose are the two great pillars of logic. The hearer first examines into the motives and ends of the speaker, and if he is convinced that he is actuated by good motives, and honest in his purposes, he is at once ready to excuse any defect in the style or Logic, for, whatever is good is also true.

The science of Logic is also the science of the operations of the mind in reasoning; for whenever we discover the parts of the brain used in reasoning, we can at once infer how they combine in producing the result.

It is a well known fact that the animals have not the upper portion of the brain developed. We therefore infer, at once, that these portions of the brain give man the power of rationality and reasoning, which endow him with his superiority ; and yet the brutes have powerful perceptive minds, and their senses most acutely developed, and an intuitive principle, by which they are enabled to provide for their wants as to food, protection and care of the young. We find, in dissecting the brain of the animal, that the basular lobes and cerebellum are well developed. We therefore refer all of the brute faculties in man to these portions of the brain. In examining the forms and developments of the head in a class of men who are gifted with the power of discoursing about truth, with a considerable degree of facility and apparent understanding, and yet we find them unable to arrive at any important conclusion upon the great subjects of divine Providence and the immortality of the soul; the conclusion always terminating in a negation settling down upon the animal plane.

Thus a long lifetime of reasoning has been spent, and yet the mind comes to exactly the same conclusion with the brute, that the man dies, and that is the end of him. Such men have a well developed base of the brain and central belt, being devoid of the sympathetic, devotional and dignifying faculties.

We, therefore, can infer at once that the power of ratiocination, or conversing about truth, together with the social faculties, and the power of judgment upon civil things, reside in the central belt of the head; that the faculties, which give sympathy, devotion and dignity of use; together with an intuitive knowledge of human character, divine ends and purposes, and the exalted aims of man, reside in the coronal region of the head.

If we again, examine the head longitudinally, we shall at once discover, that the frontal region of the two hemispheres of the brain, are devoted to

35*

perception, rationality and sympathy ; and that the central columns are devoted to physical action, judgment and devotion, and that the posterior lobes of the brain, rising upon the back part of the head, are devoted to the love of family, friends, and the greater purposes of life, and any deficiency of brain in any one of these regions, is a sure and positive mark of a like deficiency of character, and any full development of any one of these nine portions of the brain, is a sure indication of a like exaltation of the corresponding faculty of the mind, as represented in Pl. 1. fig. 1.

Thus the head and mind are divided into nine degrees, in likeness of the degrees of Ancient Masonry, the degree of high Priesthood, constituting the tenth, which is in likeness of the entire celestial man. We have shown that three of the degrees of the human mind are primitive or discrete, that these act and react against each other. See No. 80, by degrees of altitude, longitude, and descending degrees. Thus there is a lower and higher perception of the organs which meet in the middle chamber or central belt of the head. That the perceptive faculties take cognizance of facts, circumstances and events, and also learn truth from other truths that have been previously ascertained and elevate them, by the memory, into the middle chamber of the understanding ; when they are arranged in series and degrees, according to the state of the affections, and where they are surveyed and passed upon, and a final judgment pronounced as to their forms and qualities. The left side of the head, takes cognizance of their forms, and the right side, senses their qualities.

Thus the devotional faculties look down upon their arrangement, seeing all their forms beautifully mirrored in the left side of the rational faculties, sensing the order of their affections in the right.

By the foregoing operation, we have the exact form of the syllogism of logic in the rational mind, consisting, first, of a perception of facts, their arrangements and qualities ; secondly, the examination of every new proposition, and its classification by the discovery of the class to which it belongs, and lastly, the judgment or conclusion of the mind relative to its appropriate place and quality. This operation is an exact likeness of the operations of the Lodge, corresponding to the Worshipful Master, Senior and Junior Wardens. See the opening of the Lodge, No. 74, 75, 76, 78, 79.

# RHETORIC.

No. 102.  Rhetoric is the music of oratory and the plot of Logic, combining the beauty and harmony of nature with the Logic of Mathematics, so as to convince the judgment, and play upon every cord of the affections; stealing upon the hearer with statements in soft harmonies, the sublime scenes of the mountain path, the rich verdure of the glade, and the silvery tones of the laughing water, until the mind is enchanted with the splendor of language and bewildered with the profusion of thought, when like the lion, with one mighty bound of logic, the orator rushes on his prey, and binds his hearers with a spell of enchantment that they would not break if they could.

True Rhetoric is a child of nature, and the out-birth of an honest conviction, combining the energy of action and the rhapsody of virtue.  Its rules may be taught, but the fire of genius alone makes it eloquent; (the bubbling fountain can be accurately described, but its sparkling waters alone spring from the truth.)

An intimate knowledge of the relations that exist between mind and matter, the parallelism and correspondence of the two worlds, is the foundation of all that is figurative in speech. The judgment is enlarged, matured and bounded by history and science.

No man can be an orator until he has passed between the two brazen pillars, and ascended the three, five and seven steps of science, and been admitted to the knowledge of God, in the middle chamber of the understanding.

The true orator has the general good of the community in view, as the chief end of his discourse; his purpose therefore, in every speech is, to convince his hearers and urge them on to action upon some proposition that has been well matured in his own mind and reduced to the form of a simple syllogysm; he therefore avoids deducing the general conclusion until the first and second propositions of the syllogism have been well considered. Every argument consists of three parts; first, the clear statement, and general classification of facts that constitute the first proposition; secondly, the identification of the subject of the second proposition as clearly included in the first, and lastly to show that the subject of the third proposition is qualified by the first.

The orator, to avoid exciting the prejudice of his hearers, endeavors to gain their attention by eloquent and pleasing statements, exciting emotions that are grand, sublime and beautiful in character. Every part of an object or scene that is introduced, is described by a sentence which is clear and distinct, and terminated by some well defined noun which serves as a land mark or point to separate it from the coming description of other parts.

Simplicity is the foundation of the great style in oratory, and refers to the arrangement, bringing forward and opening of the arguments in their natural order, in a clear full and rich expression of language.

Taste is the delicate exercise of judgment in controlling the grand, sublime and beautiful emotions of the mind, and clothing them with their appropriate language. Every tone of voice must agree with the character of the subject, and every motion must be true to nature. In the expression of passion, the mind rushes upon the words, leaving out every thing that is superfluous in the sentence.

In the grandeur and sublimity of thought, the mind rises with strength and vigorous sentences, one above the other, until the height of sublimity is reached, which is called a climax. In the bereft and plaintive tones of language, the orator dwells upon his words. In the description of the beautiful he touches every note and harmony of music in time and rhythm. Clearness, flexibility and strength of voice are indispensable to the orator.

The writers upon Rhetoric have divided and subdivided the foregoing general principles into many particular rules, all of which are useful to correct the habits and break off the evils of composition; but in themselves they are not sufficient to make an orator. The reader and the writer may consult them at their leisure ; but when the orator rises before his audience, he is actuated by no ordinary feeling. Suspended, as it were, between heaven and earth, the only rules that he consults are the laws of God and humanity, and yielding to the sublime influxes of the spiritual world, with a God-like inspiration he becomes an instrument in the hands of his Creator, for the promulgation of great and undying truths.

# MUSIC.

No. 103.   Music is to the ear, what light is to the eye.   As color is an interior property of light, so is harmony of musical sound.   Every simple sound is in reality made up of three, which are so intimately blended together, that they appear as one, which may be short or long, high or low, soft or loud, from which we have rhythm, melody and dynamics, length, pitch and power.

These nine properties of music run in series and degrees, like every other branch of knowledge and science.

The length of sound is regulated by equal portions of time, which is called measure.   Measure again is subdivided into double, triple, quadruple, sextuple measure, which are designated by bars computed by beats.   Double measure has two beats; triple measure three, quadruple four, and sextuple six.   One measure in quadruple, is equal to two measures in double time, and one measure in sextuple is equivalent to two measures in triple time. The length of sounds is indicated by notes which are of five kinds in common use, namely: the whole, half, quarter, eighth and sixteenth notes, and they have a further division in the same order, if required.

Melody arises from a series of sounds, called the common scale, consisting of one, two, three, four, five, six, seven and eight; eight being a repetition of the first sound in a higher degree. The seven notes of Music exactly agree with the seven colors of the prismatic scale, and if the keys of each octave on the piano be colored red, orange, yellow, green, blue, indigo and violet, the colors will exactly agree with the tones of the piano. The contrasting powers of different tones, from which arise certain harmonies, will also agree with the contrasting powers of the colors.

Thus, if the first and fifth be sounded together, the harmony produced will agree with the purple.

If these again be sounded with the fourth, the harmony will correspond to the russet.

If the second and fourth be sounded together, the harmony will correspond to the citron.

The first, third and fifth notes are the primitive or discrete degrees of Music, from which arise the tones and harmonies corresponding to the seven colors and tones of the prismatic scale, and the harmonies of the nine colors.

These notes in Music correspond, when sounded together, to the grey in painting, which gives value, depth and shade to all the other colors ; and, when sounded successively or separately, correspond to the red, yellow and blue.

The seven notes of the scale also agree with the vowel sounds, which are *a, e, i, o, u, w* and *y*, of which *a, i* and *u*, are the discrete or primitive degrees of the vowels, which, in a greater or less degree flow into the other sounds, and constitute, in oratory, what the first, third and fifth notes do in music.

If a man be an orator, musician and painter, with a knowledge of the series and degrees that run through these arts, he will instantaneously discover their precise agreement so as to be able to correct one by the other ; and if he be an adept in music and painting, a brilliantly colored landscape may be set before him, instead of his notes ; and he will produce the most brillant harmonies on the piano, first executing the fore ground, then the middle, and lastly the distance, with all their soft and beautiful greys, contrasted with their lights, shades and half tints, their rich and beautiful colors of the first, secondary and tertiary hues with the mild olive and cutting russet.

And also, if the eminent professor of elocution be at the same time eminent as a painter and musician, he will produce the most thrilling eloquence from like combinations in music or art, or, if he be an adept in all the sciences, through the knowledge of degrees, he will discover their exact relations; or, if he is an eminent Mason, he will at once discover the relations that exist between universal nature and Masonry.

It has been frequently said, that there is music in all things. The same is true of all the arts and sciences. They combine with each other, and beautifully blend through the discrete and continuous degrees, which are in likeness of the attributes of the divine Creator, and which he has stamped upon all created things.

The various tones in Music psychologically arise from the different groups of the faculties in the head. The first, third and fifth notes are the three, five and seven of the discrete faculties, called the perceptive, domestic and devotional. The devotional faculties correspond to the trumpet and wind instruments, which are celestial in their nature.

The three, and seven of the faculties correspond

to the stringed and percussion instruments, which are spiritual and natural. Thus the full orchestra reacts and produces pleasurable emotions in all the affections of the soul. This is the secret of Music.

In the human voice, there is a higher and lower scale, which arise from the male and female principle represented in the man, by the base and tenor voice; and in the female by the alto and soprano.

These two voices, in both the male and the female, react upon each other, producing an intermediate or middle voice, namely: the barytone in the male and the mezzo soprano in the female.

Thus, the male and female have, each, three distinct or discrete voices, agreeing with the three, five and seven of the numbers; and the red, yellow and blue of the colors, and the a, i, and u of the vowels, the three propositions of the syllogism in Logic, the grand, sublime and beautiful of Rhetoric, and the three points or sides of the triangle in Geometry; and also the perceptive, domestic and devotional faculties in man, See Pl. 1, Fig. 1. These also agree with the noun, verb and qualities in language.

All of these discrete degrees, in the sciences, correspond or agree with the three discrete degrees

of Masonry, which are the Entered Apprentice,
Master and Royal Arch degrees; and also the three
kingdoms of nature, and the attributes of the
Divine Being, which are Love, Wisdom and Use.

# ASTRONOMY.

No. 104. Astronomy teaches the distribution, position and magnitude of the various heavenly bodies, their physical structure, mutual relations and influences upon each other.

Astronomy displays in a wonderful manner the infinite goodness, wisdom and power of the divine mind. Unnumbered suns with their planetary systems revolve in endless beauty, grandeur and sublimity around us, all framed by the hand of the Divine Architect, for the abode of man ; their bond of continuity and unity of design bespeak the same Creator, at the mention of whose name we bow and worship with reverence and awe.

The motions of the heavenly bodies are well understood, but the forces and causes of their motions yet remain to be explained. We shall proceed to explain them on the theory of the electric forces, which appears the most reasonable.

Electricity is the machine that moves the universe in its smallest particles and molecules, as well as in its largest bodies.

Light and heat are the motive powers which are the receptacles of the mental forces of the Creator, and clearly mark the limits and boundaries of the natural and spiritual worlds. Between these there exists a discrete degree, by which there is an obvious separation, as distinct as that, which exists between the Creator, and the thing created.

There are two universal fluids, namely ; ether and caloric, which are male and female, or positive and negative to each other. See No. 69.

The marriage or connection of these two fluids begets the electric forces, by which there is the sensation of light and heat, action and reaction, contraction and expansion.

Heat, light and electricity are each primitively composed of three discrete degrees. These discrete degrees in their action and reaction, have three continuous degrees of altitude, and three continuous degrees of longitude, by which there is ascension, descension and horizontal action, or expansion and contraction.

The discrete degrees of heat are seperated by the prism, as is manifested by their different chemical powers. The prism also separates or decomposes the white light into its three primitive or discrete rays of red, yellow and blue, from which we have the well known prismatic and negative colors, by combination producing nine.  See Pl. 1, Figs. 2, 3, and numbers 5, 16, 17, 18 and 19.

Light and heat descend from the sun, and act alone through the electric forces, which are derived from the combined power of each ; so that, whatever excites light and heat, also excites electricity.

The decomposition of electricity separates it into its primitive, discrete degrees, producing one direct and two inductive currents, which are at different angles to each other.  Each of these currents is a discrete degree in itself, each repelling the subtance of its own degree, by which there is repulsion of parts, in direct lines from a center.  The discrete degrees at the same time attract each other with a force equal to their repulsion ; so that, if any body be partly negative and partly positive, it will both repel and attract any other body that is either positive or negative, tending to produce a rotary motion in itself upon its own axis, which will be balanced between the angles of the positive and the negative forces.  Hence any decomposition of the electric force among the molecules of the universe would cause the whole to revolve around a given center by mutual attraction and repulsion.

The law of gravitation being established in every

cell or molecule, by the affinity of light and heat, causes all the particles of matter to mutually attract each other, and hence the larger combinations of molecules exert the greater power over the smaller, drawing them together upon a single center, producing the spherical form by which there is action and reaction; if any number of the molecules become polarized, they unite through their poles, producing the power of cohesive attraction, partaking of one or the other of the discrete degrees of the electric forces, thus establishing positive and negative spheres, which attract and repel, from both within and without, the spherical body to which they belong, causing a rotary motion of the secondary body upon its own axis.

Thus it is, that all the suns and planetary systems are drawn together within one vast field of nebular matter, revolving around a single central sun and their polar suns from West to East; therefore all the other suns sweep onward in their great orbits, revolving upon their own centers. Around these again, in the same direction, revolve their innumerable planets; around which, again, in the same direction, revolve their moons, all of which are held together and moved onward by the mutual laws of attraction and repulsion, derived from the decomposition and recombination of the electric forces.

The different currents of the electric degrees caused by the decomposition of their forces, are at different angles to each other.

Therefore, no one of the heavenly bodies can revolve upon its own axis with its equator in the same line as its ecliptic, and neither will the ecliptic of any of the planets be exactly in the same plane, each being nicely adjusted and balanced between the different angles of the various electric degrees, by which they are acted upon.

The atmospheres and substances of the various bodies continually decompose the light, heat and electricity of their suns, by which there is continual warmth, growth and decay of their animal, vegetable and mineral kingdoms, and the seasons return with endless variety and beauty.

Each of the primary suns and planets sweeps on with an unerring certainty and with a rapid motion around the suns to which they are second ; around these again, revolve their planets and moons in the same order ; as the planets and moons come within the orbits of their primaries, their motions are in the direct line of their great centers, to which the planets and moons tend with full momentum, they hesitate and slacken their motion until their suns and planets have passed, when they retrace their courses, and again recross the tracks of their planets and suns in the rear, and then again, with an accelerated motion, sweep past their planets and suns upon the outside of their orbits in a rapid manner, running far ahead, crossing the track of their primaries. Turning to the inside of their orbits, they again wait their passage. These motions may be illustrated by a noble steamer that is sailing down the gulf stream, around which the fish are playing with sportful glee, speeding past the steamer on the outer side, and crossing her bow toward the shore, they stop and float with the current and wait for the steamer to pass, turning backward then crossing the stern to the outer side, they rush forward again and pass the steamer in her speed.

These motions in the heavenly bodies are so timed with each other, that the primary planet or sun appears to stand still, and their secondaries to revolve quietly and steadily around them, slightly elliptical; maintaining nearly equal distances at the various seasons of the year.

It is a law, that like electric states, repel and unlike attract. The heavenly bodies, as they are warmed and electrified from their

suns, are repelled; but when cooled and nega-
tively electrified, they are attracted; so that, if
any planet by an extraneous cause, should be
thrown off into space, it would be immediately
brought back by the negative forces, and should
it approximate any other planet, it would immediately be repelled.

The planets and the secondary bodies at once
find their legitimate distance from the primaries,
around which they revolve by their centripetal
and centrifugal forces. Yet these forces in themselves are not sufficient to hold the planets in
their orbits, for, however, nicely they may be adjusted between these two forces at certain points
in their orbits, they could not remain so, any
considerable time, without the aid of the electrical forces, which are sometimes repulsive and at
others attractive.

The motions of the heavenly bodies are calculated with great certainty, by the aid of experience and science. It has been demonstrated, so
far as mathematics have been applied, that the
deflection of the moon in its orbit from a straight
line, is, in one minute equal to that of a falling
body in the same period of time. From this
fact, the theory that the planets are held in their

orbits by the centripetal and centrifugal forces, has been universally received.

It is also well-known in the science of Astronomy, that all the planets revolve around the sun in their ecliptics from west to east. Around the planets again revolve their moons, nearly in the same planes and direction, forming a series of concave segmental lines around the sun. That every time the moon passes in front of the earth, at a certain point in its orbits, its motion aproximates a line to the sun. Thus, if it was thrown from its orbit at that point, it would be precipitated in a more direct line upon the sun, with its full momentum, and its increased velocity from its attractive power. Instead of yielding to its own momentum and the direct attraction, it passes inward and changes its course turning outward, and again revolves in a segmental line with an increased velocity around the earth, upon the outer side of its orbit.

These motions and the addition of the attractive force of the sun to the momentum of the moon at a certain point in its orbit, and the fact that the moon turns outward again without going backward on the orbit of the earth, while under the attraction of the sun, are facts which invalidate the theory that the moon and planets are held in their orbits by their centripetal and centrifugal force alone, and show conclusively, that they are only made use of to economise power.

Practical astronomy is divided into three parts, namely, Spherical, Theoretical and Physical. By spherical astronomy, we arrive at a knowledge of the various points and circles of the celestial spheres, the constellations and position of the stars with respect to these points and circles, and also the phenomena accruing in the spheres of the heavens.

By theoretical astronomy, we are enabled from observation, to determine the true path of the earth and planets around the sun, the apparent path of the stars, and infer the general rotation of all the heavenly bodies around a central sun.

By physical astronomy, we determine the laws by which the heavenly bodies are regulated, showing how their motions are calculated, and all that is known of their physical character.

From the foregoing it will be perceived, that astronomy is the science of sciences, enlarging as we progress in the knowledges of science and art. It cultivates the rational powers of the

mind, and elevates the understanding into a clearer
light, by which we are enabled to appreciate the
works of the divine hand, and to perceive the
parallelism that exists between mind and matter.

Each terrestrial and celestial body has its
magnetic, electric and aromal spheres, No. 5,
which are the embodiment of the electrical
spheres of the animal, vegetable and mineral
kingdoms. These are continually renewing, ex-
haling and growing in the active operations of
the three kingdoms of the earth, and any operation produced upon them is attended with a like
change in the growth, fruitfulness and health of
the earth.

These spheres act, and are reacted upon, by the
mental forces of mankind, which stand directly
connected with the mental forces of the spiritual
world, which are entirely separate from the natural, being of a different substance, and subject
only to the laws of the heavens, and to the
divine mind. The light, heat and electricity, and
the gaseous and liquid substances of the heavenly
bodies, are but the mere dead machinery through
which the life forces of the spiritual world act.

The animal life or spirit has an electric body
in man, which is receptive of the spiritual, and

the spiritual is receptive of the soul, in which reside the mental forces of heat, light and electricity, or the love, wisdom and action derived from the great mental sun of the divine mind. The spirit at death is separated from the electric body, with which it will again be clothed at the final restitution and purification of the world.

There is a memory of the natural body, and there is also a memory that belongs to the spiritual, so that when the spirit is separated from earth, it retains the life and all the events of the natural world. This life and the events belonging thereto, the Lord at his resurrection glorified; and engrafted together with the electric body, upon the divine natural ; so that he is not only God, but man, standing directly connected with all the electric spheres of the terrestrial and celestial bodies, by which every regenerate man is made susceptible of spiritual thought and affection, and by which all the thought forms of the natural world, are receptive of the thought forms of the spiritual, through the natural affections.

The spirit of man, upon leaving the world, takes with him, by the internal memory, all the knowledges of the natural world ; so that there is no idea or thought of any good man that has ever existed on the earth, that is not now in the heavens.

Thus the heavens, which are around and near each terrestrial body, become the repository not only of the heavens, but of the earths in all time.

For the foregoing reasons, there is a parallelism and correspondence between all things of the natural and spiritual worlds. The things of the natural and spiritual worlds, agree with each other as parts of the same creation ; but the natural and spiritual worlds are two distinct creations, and, therefore, can, in no wise, unite by chemical combinations. Yet the substances of the natural world were created from the spiritual, and the spiritual substances from the sun of the divine mind ; and hence, there is a correspondence, but no agreement, between the substances of the divine Being and the divine or spiritual sun ; and also a correspondence, but no agreement, between the substances of the natural and spiritual worlds. The correspondence or parallelism between the two takes place by uses, and not by any geometrical form of parts. But the uses of the spiritual world excite the geometrical forms of the natural to action.

Around every heavenly body, there exist innumerable societies of angels in the three, six and ninefold forms of the heavens. These are all connected in one general heaven, lighted by the divine sun, in which dwells the divine Architect of the universe. The societies around each sun and planet are of different orders of affection ; so that the influxes of mental thought and affection that flow in from each are different, and are represented by every beautiful form of the animal, vegetable and mineral kingdoms, which in some measure were represented by the signs of the Zodiac and the constellations represented in the maps and charts of the heavens by the ancients.

These things being understood and perceived by the most ancient people, were handed down to their offspring, and, as the human mind became darkened, their representations were worshipped by those who had lost the idea of one Jehovah, in whom dwells a trinity of divine attributes of love, wisdom and use ; but this idea cannot be received until the final opening of the seventh degree of regeneration. Before this, the mind dwells in the idea of the creative power, which it conceives to be nearly related to nature and the sciences of geometry and astronomy, which are taught by the three, five and seven steps of the stairway that led to the middle chamber of King Solomon's Temple, which every Fellow Craft must ascend before he can attain a knowledge of God.

The heavens that surround the terrestrial and celestial bodies are represented by the Grand Lodge, and its subordinate Lodges, over which the Grand Architect of the universe presides.

No. 105. The spiritual degree of the mind, which is located in the central belt of the head, above the organs of the base and below those of the coronal region, represented in Pl. 1, fig. 1, by the rational semi-intellectual and social faculties, and which was represented by the middle chamber of King Solomon's Temple, has no generative or productive power in itself of elementary forms. It possesses only the power of arranging the thought forms and affections, which are supplied from the three primitive, discrete and elementary degrees of the mind, which are the perceptive faculties, the domestic and the devotional; two of these are below the spiritual degree, located in the base of the brain, and one is above.

The affections of the domestic faculties, which contain the laws of domestic order, ascend by the posterior degree of altitude into the social faculties. The thought forms, which are received through the medium of the senses, flow upward, by the anterior, or frontal degree of altitude into the rational faculties, whence they flow backward by the degrees of longitude, and adjoin with the spiritual affections, which flow forward from the social faculties, and conjoin with the thought forms of the perceptive in the semi-intellectual faculties.

The influxes of divine order, which descend through the devotional faculties, located in the coronal portion of the head, descend by the posterior and anterior descending degrees, into the rational and social faculties, adjoining with the influxes of the domestic and perceptive faculties in the spiritual degree of the mind.

If the divine influxes, descending through the devotional faculties to the middle chamber from above, be entirely cut off by removing the staircase between the third and middle chamber of the mind, the spiritual degree would only be supplied with the thought forms from the perceptive faculties and the domestic affections from the cerebellum. These forms and affections would be laid hold of by the spiritual degree of the mind, and arranged into apparent sciences, to suit the animal appetites and affections, without any regard to conscience, religion, or a God; all the sciences of the mind being arranged without any regard, feeling or knowledge of divine order.

Thus, the man would become an atheist and a rascal of the deepest dye. If the rational and social faculties be large, he would be polite, plausible, and, with a seeming order, would use the rational faculties to arrange all the facts presented through his perception, in the most graceful manner, without any regard to conscience or divine order, with as much facility as a fanciful workman would arrange his pattern to suit the occasion. Such a man can never be made a Mason, for, although he may deceive the Lodge, and take the degrees, and even become zealous in the cause, yet he will never have any conception of its true principles.

If the lower faculties of the two discrete degrees, namely, the perceptive and domestic faculties, be in any manner impaired by mal-formation, injury or education, so that they do not yield their proper influxes and stimulus, by the degrees of altitude, to the middle or spiritual chamber of the mind, the connecting link between the outer and inner world of the mind will be broken, and the intellect become idiotic ; but if there be at the same time, a strong influx through the devotional faculties, the person, instead of being an idiot as he grows up, will become religiously insane. Therefore, the Lord is ever operating to maintain an equilibrium between the higher and lower faculties, restraining the influxes of the devotional, until the mind is properly educated, step by step, in the scientific principles of faith, hope and charity; for if the influxes of the devotional faculties are strong, flowing down with power into the middle chamber, and if, at the same time, the rational and social faculties be large, the scientific principle will lay hold of the principles of divine order, and arrange them into theories that have no foundation in facts ; but if, at the same time, the base of the brain be large, well organized in conjunction with a healthy and well-formed body, and both culti-vated by labor and proper education, the upper and lower faculties of the mind will be equally balanced and practical in all their operations. Th ? mind will be illuminated by the light of the two worlds.

If an angelic spirit descends into the middle chamber, and speaks by the organs of a man, it becomes inspiration, and heavenly and divine things are revealed by a parallel arrangement of natural objects and truths ; but, if the mind of the angel flows into the middle chamber, through the electric forces of the spiritual world, meeting the electric forces of the natural world, and arranging the thought forms, so that they are seen by a rational sight the operation is called illumination, which is the highest state of the human mind known to man ; for, although the mind may be inspired, the inspiration passes away with the angel, but illumination is derived from both the state of the mind and of the angel, which are from the Lord.

We have colored the different groups of the faculties : Pl. 1, fig. 1; so that their operations can be presented to the eye. The primitive and discrete faculties we have colored red, yellow and blue, and given them their combining numbers of three, five and seven. The combination of these colors are the orange, green and purple, the citron, russet and olive, in which all the forces of the faculties are represented by their combining numbers being equally balanced. For instance, if a slight quantity of yellow be mixed with a large quantity of red, the red is changed, and tinged with the orange. If the amount of yellow be gradually increased, until the composition consists of three of yellow and five of red, the composition will have passed through all the phases of a dark to a perfect orange. If the yellow still be increased gradually, the orange will become lighter until it apparently terminates in the yellow. The same law of compound force exists between the perceptive and devotional faculties, meeting and combining in the rational; and thus it takes place in all the compound faculties represented by the secondary and tertiary colors.

Thus, we have briefly described the uses and operations that take place in the middle chamber of the mind, which were represented by the middle chamber of King Solomon's Temple, into which every Fellow Craft must enter, before the ideas of faith.through spiritual science,can be united with the affections, for neither the affections nor truth can be made operative in producing charity, without science.

The affections are blind without truth, and truth is inoperative without the affections, for all classification and arrangement of truths are done by the affections. See the Article on Logic, 102. The perceptive faculties from the outer world supply all the thought forms, which are arranged in series and degrees by the affections, in which reside the laws of Divine Order; and no idea of form can be introduced into the mind by an interior way through the affections, neither can any truth of the natural world, by an exterior way, produce an affection of the mind, and therefore when once the law of Divine Order had been broken between will and the understanding, the world was rendered entirely incapable of perceiving and maintaining the idea of one Supreme Being without a Divine revelation of the fact given by an angel, who descended into the middle chamber of the understanding in the prophets of ancient times, using the language, circumstances and history of the times, to communicate the fact by the thought forms of the individual through whom he communicated ; for all the influxes of the spiritual world, that descend through the devotional faculties, fall upon the ideas of the natural world, and arrange them in a representative form.

Therefore, every idea of God and the spiritual world, without a Divine revelation, terminates in the representative forms themselves, and hence, these forms appear as God and spiritual things, and therefore, the whole world worshipped the representatives of their own affections. Those who admired the astronomy, and the wonders of the.Heavens, worshipped the sun, moon and stars, and the hosts thereof; and those whose affections terminated in agriculture, worshipped the beasts of the field, and the fruits of the earth ; and those whose delights terminated on the mere sensual plane, worshipped the serpent ; and those, whose affections terminated in a supreme selflove, and therefore a destruction of their fellow being by the arts of war, worship· ped their heroes, as Gods and demi-Gods ; and every family had its household Gods, who presided over their destinies, and to whom they sacrificed the objects of their affections.

The Jewish Church, through the administration of angels, could only be made a representative of a church, until the final descent of the Lord himself into the flesh, by which he imparted to man the power of spiritual thought, by which the spiritual idea of God, as a Divine man, in the person of our Lord, was imparted to the human family; and when his glorification took place, representative worship, with all believers in him, ceased. Yet it is allowable to teach by representation, but not to worship. The Lodge continues to teach these great truths by the letter "G," but not to worship, by sacrificing to any representative, the objects of their affections, nor to worship by any representative of the Lord himself ; for God is a spirit and seeketh such to worship him as worship in spirit and in truth. For the foregoing reasons, the Fellow Craft is introduced into the middle chamber, and taught the knowledge of God. But truth alone is not acceptable unto the Lord. Instruction is external, but the affections are interior. Through education and science, the affections open, as through a door, into the outer world; through faith they are elevated by an interior way, into the light and heat of the Divine mind, where they are warmed and expanded into action and growth. The elevation of the affections, by faith, to the Lord, in works of charity is an acceptable worship unto Him; but words appertaining to faith, instruction and science are edifying unto man, but not to God who requires the heart.

Therefore, representatives, in themselves, are not worship, but may be made use of for a confession of faith as the case is with the ordinances, in which all the representative ceremonies of the Jewish Church, relating to feasts and purification, are embodied in the bread and wine, and the ordinance of Baptism. In the bread and wine, we acknowledge that the Lord is the life of all. In the ordinance of Baptism, we acknowledge that the Lord is our purifier, instructor and redeemer.

These ordinances, in themselves, do not give us

a title to Heaven without a life of charity; we therefore perceive that it is the motives, ends and affections that sanctify them to us.

No. 106.   The committing of truth to memory, does not give the power of action or understanding. Action and understanding depend upon the states of science and the affections. If the affections are not in a state to receive the truth, there is no disposition to execute it, and when the affections are in a condition to receive the truth, they act by the plane of science already formed in the mind. This plane of action, so far as it relates to bodily action and the principles of doing, is altogether geometrical, although the science of Geometry may have never been studied.

The knowledge of God in the memory does not give the power of understanding his attributes, nor acting upon their divine principles; states of affections and planes of science, through the principles of faith, hope and charity, must first be formed in the mind.   The first idea of God, which is received from faith, is that of some vague creative power, which is to be feared rather than loved.   This idea of the creative principle is nearly allied to the ideas of Geometry in the mind; he, therefore, who is being regenerated in the second degree, holds the idea of God as a great universal principle, rather than that of a Divine person, and not until the middle chamber of the mind is opened, does he realize that God is a divine person. The middle chamber of the mind is opened by conferring states of affection and spiritual science through arrangement and divine order in the mind, which is done by the divine spirit, arranging the precepts of the Holy Word; first, in the memory, secondly, in the understanding, and lastly, by science, from which there is a life of charity, which is done through the middle chamber of the understanding. The letter "G," therefore, is both the Initial of Geometry and of God.

The divine attributes of Deity, known as Jehovah, can only be conferred, received and acted upon, by the celestial degree of the mind. The spiritual degree can have no conception of the divine attributes of love, wisdom and use in their universal sphere of creation, as they descend from the divine mind. These can only be understood by the celestial degree of the mind, which is opened in the Royal Arch. The christian Mason, who has not been introduced into the middle chamber by the second degree of regeneration, has no conception of the fulness of the God-head in Jesus Christ.

He therefore divides the God-head into persons, and if he is simply instructed in the truth of religion, he destroys, by the idea of a plurality of persons in the God-head, all notions of a Divine Being; so that, when he is examined before the Holy Angels, they find in him no idea of a God.   But if he has lived a christian life, he is in a condition to advance in knowledge and virtue, and finally to come into a knowledge of the fulness of the God-head in the Lord, and to understand his divine attributes.

The foregoing principles are represented, so far as they relate to the knowledge of God, by the middle chamber of King Solomon's Temple.   The divine attributes of Jehovah, which include the knowledges of God and his self existence, designated by the name, "I am that I am," are represented in the erection of the new temple or the Royal Arch degree.

No. 106.   The wages of Fellow Craft are corn, wine and oil.   Nourishment is predicated of corn, gladness of wine, and joy of oil.   Corn signifies the good that is begotten of the natural principle of truth, for, by the art and science of agriculture, the field is cultivated and the corn produced; so, by the exercise of the truths of the Word in the

Lodge, good is produced, by which the mind is strengthened and nourished.

From the good that is begotten through the natural of the divine Word, there springs a true faith in God, by which life and immortality are brought to light. This is the source of all true gladness, which cheers the spirit like wine.

Oil is the good that is derived from the spiritual love of truth, which delights the affections, and is called joy. Gladness is the delight of the intellectual principles derived from faith. Thus the Fellow Craft is nourished from the good of natural science, gladdened by the principles of faith, and delighted with the joy of the affections. Seek first the kingdom of God and its righteousness, and all these things shall be added unto you.

# THE THIRD, OR,

# SUBLIME DEGREE OF MASTER MASON.

———◆◄◇►◆———

No. 107.  Love is the order of existence, and as it revolves in the circuit of its affections, it brings forth, like the seasons of the year, manhood and old age.  In the spring, it is warmed by the heat of the Divine mind into effort, and, like the fruit tree, it puts forth the buds, leaves and blossoms.  In the heat of its summer, or the full tide of manhood, every effort is brought forth into labor, which ripens into wisdom in the fall of old age, and is gathered by the harvest of death into the store-house of the spiritual world, for the food of angelic life.  Thus it is the order of the natural body and spirit.

The spirit is of a threefold order, natural, spiritual and celestial.  The second and third orders are angelic, but the first is natural and must die, before the spiritual angelic form can be born.  Its death and resurrection are represented in the Master's degree.

Evils destroy the order of love, and blot the face of nature ; so that the orderly changes of the body and spirit cannot take place without the process of death. Sin is a resistance to the order of the Divine mind and the love principle of the soul. Every transgression drives back the spiritual principle, causing it to retire more deeply within, and producing a false and fungus growth and order of the body, which gives rise to a diseased condition of parts and portions of the system. These diseases are hereditary, transmitted to the offspring, through the blood of the parents, so that the apparent normal condition of the child is a state of disease.

The divine and heavenly order of the spirit, which is derived from the soul, is driven back and separated, so that it can never be brought forth into the natural, without the restraining principles of truth, and death of the natural spirit by its own evils. If this death does not take place, the spirit continues in its natural state to eternity. The angelic order being destroyed, it sinks down, or lingers upon the borders of heaven.

There is a fierce and obstinate resistance of the

evil and perverted order of the natural to the
birth of the spiritual, by action and reaction.
The spiritual is always striving to come forth into
the natural principles of the body, and to subdue
its sensual, scientific and rational principles, and
bring them into subjection to the spiritual degree
of the mind. In opposition to this, the perverted
orders of selflove and the love of the world, pride
of the eye and lust of the flesh, through the falsities and evils of the body, react with great power
againt the spiritual degree, begetting a general
scepticism and disbelief in all things, that cannot
be tested by the senses. Thus, all the higher rational faculties, by which there is a faith in immortality and perception of the laws of Divine
providence, are restrained and driven back,
shutting out all the light and love of the soul,
which lives directly from the influxes of the
celestial world.

The orders, arising from the love of self, and
the world, beget a false and perverted growth of
the tissues of the body, so that there are different
orders of life for the body and spirit, so that
when the spirit flows forth into the body, its entire order of action is changed, like the juices

of a noble tree that is engrafted upon by the thorn.

This exterior order, having once obtained the ascendancy, can never be overcome, from an interior way, by the influxes of the spirit, any more than the influxes of the root can change the fruit of the engrafted limb. Therefore it was necessary for the salvation of man that the Lord should give a Divine revelation through the prophets, and ultimately, come into the world himself to establish counter influxes through the Divine Word and his assumed body with man, thus restraining the natural disorders of the body, learning man to subdue his passions and improve himself in spiritual knowledges.

When perversion or sin was once established through the sensual principles of the mind or the serpent, it became immediately necessary to restrain the wanton pleasures of evil by labor, sickness and death. Therefore the Divine influxes of the spiritual world, were partially withdrawn from the natural, and the earth brought forth its thistles and thorns. Man was under the necessity of eating his bread in the sweat of his brow. Fierce and turbulent pains were the results of a disordered state of the body. The hemlock and belladona brought forth their poi. sons, which found a deadly access to the tissues of the body through its perverted order. But when the spiritual and celestial order reigns supremely in the body, as was the case with the Apostles and Prophets, these deadly poisons were as harmless as water.

In the fierce conflicts of the opposing loves of the body and soul, the two great powers of the heavens and hells are opposed to each other, the spiritual powers of the soul coming forth into the body to destroy the fungus and abnormal growth of the tissues. The soul is encouraged and sustained by faith and love through the sympathy of friends and the influences of the Lord. Poisons are introduced into the system in the form of medicines, which hasten on the crisis, to decide the question for weal or woe.

If the perverted order of the body gains the ascendancy, the spirit is driven back, and the mind relapses into scepticism and doubt. The perverted orders of selflove and the love of the world regain their normal condition, which we call health; but, in reality, it is one point gained for an endless death of the soul.

When the spiritual principle of the mind gains

the ascendancy, it puts away and destroys the perverted order of the body; a new growth of the tissues take place ; the spirit advances in power and energy; faith revives ; the love of the Lord and the neighbor warms and vitalizes the physical system; and one step has been obtained towards the death of the old man and the resurrection of the new.

There is one order of the physical system, another of the natural mind, and another of the spiritual. These are more or less dependent upon each other, following in successive order ; yet the natural mind may come to maturity and die before the body, and the spiritual order of the mind may be brought forth, grow and be perfected while the natural body lives in the world. Thus, the man is really an angel, while he yet lives in the body.

No. 108. There are three loves that bear rule, with the different degrees, with the unregenerated man. These are the love of self, the love of the world, and the love of mammon. Opposed to these, in the regenerate man, are the love of the Lord, the love of the neighbor, and the love of usefulness. The character of one is angelic, and the other satanic; one is of heaven and the other of hell; " for the kingdom of God cometh without ob- servation; it is in you :" Luke 17. 20, 21.

The three primitive and elemental loves of the natural man, by the law of compounds, branch into orders of three, five, seven and fifteen. See the law of numbers, Article 97. The order of architecture and the human form, Nos. 95, 94, 15. Every truth, that is received and retained in the human mind, is adjoined to a good affection, and every falsity that is confirmed by habit, is adjoined to an affection of evil, by which the falsities are arranged in series and degrees, being grouped to- gether in distinct orders, agreeably to the affections to which they are adjoined.

In the fall of man from his regenerate state, the sensual principle gradually gained the ascendancy over the natural mind, introducing its apparent truths and falsities, arranging them in the mind as apparent truths, by which the affections of good were perverted, distorted and changed into positive evils, until at length they appeared to the angels as thick and dark clouds in the human under- standing, shutting out all light that flows in through the celestial degrees of the mind. Thus the spiri- tual and celestial principles that shone forth as a

sun and moon, enlightening the natural degree of
the human understanding, were entirely shut out
and reflected backward upon themselves, so that
all knowledge of God, and his laws of Divine Providence, were expelled from the external mind, and
thick darkness, as an eternal night, reigned supreme. This darkened state of the mind had its
beginning, rise and gradual progress in the descendants of Adam, down to the flood, so that every
generation was a representative of the progressive
heresies that followed the fall of man.

There is no such thing as a perception of pure
and essential truth, except, in the celestial state.
As this degree becomes closed, truth is only perceived representatively: again, when the spiritual
degree is closed, the mind is only opened to the
external world through the medium of the senses.
The perceptions which the natural mind calls truths,
are the mere necessities that arise from the operation of natural things in the growth and progression of nature. These are called its laws, whereas
these appearances are mere effects arising from
the growth and outbirth of nature, there being no
perception of the interior laws by which there is
life and motion; but, when the spiritual degree
of the mind is opened and restored, the laws of

life and motion are representatively perceived, and as the celestial degree is restored to the control of the mind, there is a perception of essential truth.

The mind then, gradually extends to a perception and understanding of both the generals and particulars, which are more or less perfect as the natural spiritual and celestial act in harmony with each other, all truths being arranged into principles and sciences agreeably to the order of the various affections. When there is a full harmony and correspondence between the different degrees of the mind, the powers of the understanding are equal to the perception, and every thing beheld elevates the mind to the Creator. That was the case with man before his fall, and will again be, when he is fully restored to the celestial state.

No. 109. The object of the Mason is to attain to a knowledge of the Divine attributes of Jehovah and to receive his name ; this can only be done by entering into his quality by regeneration, in each discrete degree of the mind, through which man is restored to Divine order. Religion is true or false with every man, just in proportion as there is a true perception of the Divine attributes and a life of charity agreeable to the Word.

The influxes of the Lord, through the celestial degree, restore the entire mind to a divine and heavenly order, just in proportion to the removal of the evils and falses of the exterior mind. When man resists evils as sins against the Lord, the former evils and sins are forced to one side and put away by the divine influxes of the Lord, which flow in through the celestial and spiritual degrees of the mind. The power to resist evil is derived from the conjunction of the Divine with the truths of the Word. The first visible effects being contrition, repentance and humiliation, without which no evil of the mind can be put away.

Every faith is true or false as it serves to illustrate the Divine attributes, and leads to repentance and humiliation. In every progressive state of the human mind, there is an enlarged and perfected view of Deity, and this increases to the full opening of the celestial degree, in which there is a perception and understanding of the divine attributes. As the celestial and spiritual degrees of the mind are closed by evils and falses of the sensual principle, man loses the knowledges of God, and the laws of his Divine Providence, and sinks into

30*

a state of darkness and obscure perception of the truths of faith until they are finally lost; for, although they may be repeated a thousand times in his hearing, the perception of their truth is lost in scepticism and disbelief.

Thus it is, that the various states of regeneration and darkness of the mind, give rise to the various different faiths and practices of the religious world. Therefore, the various heresies that exist in the religious world appear to their receivers as the very essence of true faith, whereas, in reality, there can be no real understanding of the divine attributes, except from the celestial degree of the mind.

Therefore, for these reasons, a substitute for the true faith is given in the Master's word, until future generations shall bring it forth; for the true knowledge of the divine attributes can only be given by the full opening of the three degrees of the mind, which form a living arch above, and a triangular pavement beneath, wherein all the faculties of the mind are joined in wisdom and understanding by three, and three times three.

No. 110. Every truth of the Word has the good of divine order for its object or ultimate end. Such truths, when received into the memory, are seeds of usefulness, and when vitalized and warmed by the affections of the celestial degree, spring forth and grow into perceptions, like trees, in the understanding, from which there is an additional growth of the tissues of the brain, which finally extend to those 'of the body, so that the whole bodily form would grow into a likeness of the affections and principles of truth which are confirmed by habit, were it not for the order of the hereditary.

The love of self, the world and mammon, prevails in every unregenerate man in his fallen condition, so that their hereditary principles are transmitted to the offspring, from which arise twelve principles or tribes of falsities which are opposite or opposed to the twelve principles of faith. See the twelve principles of faith, No. 29. These evils and falsities have a modifying influence upon the perceptions of faith; so that the doctrines of the Sacred Scriptures are understood agreeably to the state of regeneration.

The truths of faith are first introduced into the memory, which is the Entered Apprentice degree, and secondly, into the understanding, by which is represented the Fellow Craft's degree, and thirdly, they take root and are brought forth by

the will into the active principles of life, which are
represented by the Master's degree. Thus every.
truth of the Word passes through three degrees or
stages, before it becomes a part of a man, by
bringing forth its fruit into life. The experience,
arising from a life of truth, begets other and higher
perceptions, from which spring other affections
and truths. This operation is continued in the
course of regeneration until all the principles of
truth culminate in the twelve principles of faith,
and of the affections in the ten principles of charity,
Nos. 28, 29, 32, 134 to 144.

As the mind progresses through a state of memory and science, before the true rational of the
spiritual principle can be brought forth in the
Master's degree, the principles of memory and
science must pass through a transition state by
which the exterior principles of truth and science
become subject to the principles of conscience, by
which there is a higher perception of truth, from
which arises a new spiritual rational principle.
This transition is represented by a state of death
and resurrection to newness of life, the particulars of which are fully represented in the Master's
degree, which will form the subject of the following numbers.

## OF THE MASTER'S DEGREE.

No. 111. No change of state can take place, proceeding from a state of evil to good, except by repentance, and no higher truth can be received except in humility of heart. These principles are illustrated and represented, as has been previously shown, in Nos. 47, 48, 49.

The attention of the Master Mason is particularly called to the following passage of Scripture: "And Lamech took unto him two wives; the name of the one was Adah, and the name of the other Zillah. And Adah bare Jabal: he was the father of such as dwell in tents, and of such as have cattle. And his brother's name was Jubal; he was the father of such as handle the harp and organ. And Zillah, she also bare Tubal-Cain, an instructor of every artificer in brass and iron: and the sister of Tubal-Cain was Naamah." Genesis, 4. 19, 20, 21, 22, which we will now explain.

Every generation in the history of the world is remarkable for some idea that appears to be particular to itself. In fact, this is the case with every individual. Such is the infinity of the human family, that every person has his distinctive features and traits of character, so much so that he is unlike all those who have gone before him, and this continues to eternity. That, which is true in individuals, in this respect, is also true of each generation; for although the individuals of a generation are different in features, feelings and thoughts, yet there is some common bond of education and habit with each nation, kindred and tongue, which is but another phase of the great principles by which they are governed.

Principles, like individuals and nations, have their rise, growth, maturity and decay; when they become subservient to a lower or higher principle, in the ascending or descending scale of truth; this is also true of every church and religion, which have their peculiar faith and worship, and pass into a new state. Such was the case with the Hebrew, Jewish and Christian Churches.

Although the Christian Church still exists, yet

the close observer finds himself entering upon a new age, in which the receiver is unwilling to fol- fow any blind faith, but demands a reason for every thing ; even the Masonic Fraternity is not an exception to the rule. The Jewish Lodge fell into decay, and was well nigh lost, when it was revived by St. John the Baptist and St. John the Evangelist, who have been ever since considered the Patrons of Masonry.

From the years 1717 to 1760, the institution underwent a transition state, passing from the operative to the speculative, and it continues to unfold its interior principles; and yet, like a tree in the spring time, we see it putting forth its buds and blossoms, from which we may expect a rich harvest of golden fruit.

The ancients divided the world into periods, which they represented as the age of gold, the age of silver, brass and iron. The age of gold was the first dawn of the human faculties, while the celestial degree of the mind was yet open. The age of silver followed, in which the celestial degree of the mind was closed and the spiritual degree open.

The age of brass and iron followed, when the spi- ritual and celestial degrees were both closed and the natural degree alone remained open ; the leading principles of which are natural truth and good, natural truth being represented by iron, and natural good by brass.

This age, in the successive decay of the celestial and spiritual principles in the fall of man, commences with Lamech, wherein the celestial and spiritual principles were divided into celestial and spiritual sections, which were represented by Adah and Zillah, which were no less than a life of heretical doctrines, which finally close the celestial and spiritual perceptions of the ages of gold and silver.

The perversions, in the celestial principles were represented by Jabal, and in the spiritual principle by Jubal, from which follow the perverted ideas of the divine attributes represented by Juballa, Juballo and Juballum, which will be treated of in their proper place.

And Zillah she also bare Tubal-Cain, an instructer of every artificer in brass and iron. Tubal-Cain represents the spiritual of the natural principle in man, which was the condition of the offspring and quality of Tubal-Cain, from which arise all the knowledges of good and truth, which are represented by iron and brass.

An artificer in iron and brass represents a good

and wise man ; to instruct in goodness and wisdom is a peculiar quality of a Master Mason. The first operation of truth, adjoined to the new will in the regenerate man, is to instruct in natural goodness and truth. All instruction, before this state of regeneration is attained to, arises in part, or in whole, and is dictated by, the love of self, the world and mammon, in which there is a dictatorial spirit, which tends to divide into sects where it cannot bare absolute rule.

But when the Master's degree is opened by regeneration, all instruction is tempered with meekness and use ; there being a perception of the states of the hearers, and wisdom to adapt the instruction to their condition. This state corresponds to Levi, the third son of Jacob ; therefore the tribe of Levi was chosen to the Priesthood.

No. 112. Every natural truth exists by virtue of a spiritual and celestial cause. If the spiritual and celestial were removed, the natural degree would be inoperative and dead ; but if the natural degree were removed, the spiritual and celestial degrees would have no resting place ; yet their interior principles would still exist in effort. Therefore, the natural creation, like the rough Ashler in the foundation, is the base and fulciment of the whole.

Every spiritual and celestial principle is only operative through its natural, and the natural principle is inoperative without the celestial and spiritual.

The celestial and spiritual degrees of the natural may remain closed, manifesting no interior principle, yet the natural receives its ability to act from them.   But when the spiritual or celestial degrees are opened, the celestial degree through its motives, controls the whole.   Therefore, all things of the human mind are said to be natural, spiritual and celestial, according to the motives that govern the act.

With every natural thing there are two qualities in general, the form of the object and its use. These unite in a third, which is the operation. The use is called its good, and its form or adaptation, is called its truth ; and hence the terms, natural good and truth, which express the form and use of the object. To teach these great qualities, with a view to their spiritual and celestial ends, is the great office of a Master-Mason, and a man that is wise and skilful in the use of natural truth and good, is said to be an artificer in brass and iron.

As the compass is the principal instrument, in laying off and designing all constructions in iron and brass, as well as in stone, the vital tenets of the Mason's profession are said to be contained between the two points of the Compass.

The ruling principles of the human form are natural good and truth. These are said to be located in the right and left sides, the right side corresponds to good and the left to truth, a marriage of which takes place in every act which proceeds from the will. Therefore, all things that are done from the will, are first put forth from the right side, there being a tendency to use the left side first, in all things that are done through deception, and also to extend the left hand to an enemy, or where there is pretence to friendship. The right has ever been considered the seat of fidelity. With an evil man, when surprised, there is always a tendency to turn or look to the left.

For the foregoing reasons, the most vital principles of man's life are said to be contained between the right and left breasts, and the most sacred principles of his profession between the points of the compass, one of which represents natural good, and the other natural truth. These states of good and truth can only be implanted in the contrite and humble spirit, wherein a man is said to be neither naked nor clothed, appearing to himself to be in a state in which there is no usefulness nor truth. To such only, it is said, "seek and ye shall find, knock and it shall be opened unto you."

No. 113. The obligations of a Master-Mason, taken in the three several degrees of the Entered Apprentice, Fellow Craft, and Master, are representative of the principles that govern the natural heavens. The obligations of the Past Master, Mark Master, and Most Excellent Master, are representative of the principles that govern the spiritual heavens. The obligations of the Royal Arch, Royal and Select Master's Degrees, are representative of the principles that govern the celestial heavens, and exactly agree, when taken together, with the ten commandments, which are a universal expression of law, both in the natural, spiritual and celestial degrees, as spoken by God on Mount Sinai, Exodus 20th.

To these several principles that govern the heavens in their various degrees, are added the penalties arising from the profanation of the same, whereby all spiritual life is destroyed, and man dies the death arising from his own profanations. Truth is first received into the memory, in the Entered Apprentice degree, the profanation of which consists in turning the truth to selfish ends and motives, without regard to spiritual states, the effect of which is a universal falsification of the truth. Thus, as James says: 3d. 6th. The tongue is a fire, a world of iniquity; so is the tongue among our members, that it defileth the whole body, and setteth on fire the course of nature, and it is set on fire of hell. See the obligation of an Entered Apprentice, No. 19, and the subject of profanation.

In the Fellow Craft degree, the truths of the Entered Apprentice are arranged in series and degrees, which constitute the natural sciences, which is the peculiar quality of a Fellow Craft. To profane the truths of the natural sciences is to turn their principles to selfish ends without regard to conscience or spiritual states, which destroy all the principles of spiritual life, which are represented by the heart and vitals. The foul passions of the unregenerate man are represented by the beasts of the field, and his reasoning against truth by the vultures of the air. The foul passions and reasoning prey upon the vital principles of truth, until there is no life in it. Thus man spiritually dies the death of his own profanation, and is cast into hell while he yet lives in the body.

In the Master's degree, scientific truths are introduced into the will, for the sake of conscience and the spiritual condition. This state corresponds to the bowels. Bowels, in the most external sense, signify truth derived from sciences in their most interior and celestial sense; they signify the mercy of the Lord.

When the principles of truth are profaned by turning them to selfish purposes, the mind is unable to arrive at any conclusion upon the subject of faith from the scientific principles; but immediately negates all the principles of faith, through a general scepticism, coming to the conclusion that man dies and is dissolved into the natural elements of the earth as the brute. The mind of the brute being equally competent to arrive at the same conclusion. Thus, when the principles of science are profaned in the will, the mind sinks to the mere sensual and animal planes. All spiritual life becomes extinct, and the mercy of the Lord is withdrawn from the spiritual degree, and the man is led through all the shifting scenes of life by the love of self, the world and mammon, and every external means is used by divine

Providence to prevent the man from sinking into crime. The honors and emoluments of office and riches are held out as allurements, as preventative of sin. In this state, man is governed by the consideration of external principles, disavowing all belief in the government of a divine Providence. He is in continual fear of coming to want, and endeavors to amass to himself riches and to continually increase his wealth from usury.

The foregoing state of profanation should never be confounded with wealth that arises from a state of usefulness. This love is directly opposite to the love of mammon. The man that in this love seeks alone to be useful in every department of life; to him it is given frequently, to acquire great wealth, that he may open new fields of enterprise, and employ thousands and bring them under his direct control, by which they are clothed and fed, and their labor directed to ends of use, for the advancement of the world.

The love of mammon is satanic, and the love of usefulness is angelic.

The love of self, the world and mammon, burns with a lust that consumes the bowels, both naturally and spiritually, and scatters their ashes, as it were to the four winds of heaven. A large class of diseases in the human family, arise from the lust of these loves, and not only destroy the life of the parents, but hereditarily entail their diseases upon the children to the third and fourth generations. Thus it is that profanations not only destroy the spiritual life of a man, but cut short his natural existence. These profanations are represented by the penalties of the Master's obligations.

No. 114. The ability to understand, depends upon the state of the affections; when the affections are in the natural degree, there is no perception of spiritual truth, yet there is an influx into the spiritual of the natural degree, from the celestial, which elevates the mind for the time being, to the spiritual and natural truth of this degree; but there is no permanent increment of truth which can be called light. The celestial affections of each continuous degree shine forth in the understanding as a sun.

The East is the light of divine truth, the South is the light of science, and the West is the light of wisdom, which arises from experience, by which the Craftsman receives the wages of the day.

The states of light exists from the celestial,

natural and spiritual, which are contained in every state of the affections. For, in each degree of the Lodge, there must be present, Masters, Fellow Crafts and Entered Apprentices. Thus it is with each continuous degree of the mind. There is something of the celestial, spiritual and natural present; for nothing can exist, however small, without the presence of the three degrees. Yet, only one degree is said to be opened at a time. All influxes are from the higher degrees into the lower. But the effect of the influx is only perceived in the degree that is opened.

For this reason, influxes of thought and of love, which are of the Lord, are received through the interior degrees of the mind, and yet they appear to the Prophets as a voice, and as though the hand of the Lord was laid upon his person, or as a vision seen in all its glory and beauty; and frequently the presence of the Lord and the Angels were seen as though they stood before the Prophet, and spoke with him face to face, and sometimes the bodily form of the Prophet was caught up, and removed to another place as by physical force, as was the case with Phillip. Acts. 8. 39.

These effects all appeared to the Prophets as though they were external and foreign to themselves, and yet they were caused by the influxes of the divine spirit through the interior degrees of the mind, extending even to the surrounding substances, as was the case with Elisha and the axe. 2. Kings, 5. 6.

There is also an influx from the spiritual world, which is from without. It being first received into the electric forces of the natural world, and from thence to the physical of the man, by which his limbs are controlled and the organs of speech used without his will.

This is done by means of familiar spirits, and is called afflux. This is the great distinction between the work of familiar spirits and the spirit of the Lord. One illuminates the mind to see and understand heavenly things through the interiors of the mind, by which there is an opening of the heavens. The other effects the physical first, and controls the organs of hearing and sight, in which there is no perception of heavenly truths. This is obsession of spirits, which opens the mind downwards to the hells.

Influxes and Affluxes take place with every man, with more or less power, but are only perceived and understood as a man attains to the spiritual degree of regeneration. The influxes, that proceed from the celestial, are the sun of the human understanding. When these influxes are reflected from the truths of faith, they constitute its moon, and when they are received into the natural principle of the mind, they are represented by the Master of the Lodge. These are a likeness and representative of the divine attributes.

The glory of the Lord shines forth in the celestial degree as a sun, and in the spiritual degree as a moon. Thus, the sun in the celestial degree, appears with great brilliancy and beauty. In the spiritual degree, it is pale and silvery, and as that degree descends towards the natural, it becomes as the light of the moon. In the natural degree, the spirits receive their light from the instruction of angels through the Lord's Divine humanity. Thus the Lord is perceived by the angels according to the state of the degree in which they are, for each discrete degree has its natural, spiritual and celestial states, which are continuous.

With a man living in the natural world, when either the celestial or spiritual is opened, the Lord is seen in vision; but with a natural mind the humanity of the Lord alone can be seen, and not then without the Lord taking upon himself flesh and nativity, by which he would appear weak and infirm according to the state and condition of the man.

When the mind passes from one degree to another in regeneration, the interior affections are unfolded, by which there is a greater power to perceive, which, in Masonic language, is called more light, and is indicated by the elevation of the point of the compass, which signifies natural truth and good, by which there is a perception and application of the natural principles of faith and charity, which are represented by the first section of the Master's degree.

No. 115.   To the Master Mason belong all the tools of Masonry indiscriminately; but to him is recommended, more particularly, the trowel, which is an instrument made use of by the operative mechanic to spread the cement that binds a building into one common mass; but, as a Free and Accepted Mason, he is taught to make use of the trowel for the more noble and glorious purpose of spreading the cement of brotherly love, that binds the members of the Masonic Fraternity in a common bond of unity, among whom there is no disagreement, save that noble contention, or rather emulation, of who can best work and best agree.

The principles of mutual love like the powers of mutual attraction, bind every individual of the heavens into societies and Lodges, and these again are arranged in the general form of one man, in whom the Lord resides, as a spirit within its body.

The Divine love of the Lord appears, at an angle of forty-five degrees above the face of this man. The divine spiritual principle of the Lord appears as a moon, and his knowledges as the stars of the heavens. The rational principle of the Lord appears as the blue vault, and his natural principle as the earth beneath.

Thus it appears to every individual spirit, according to the state in which he is. Nine different groupes of societies hold a controlling influence in the brain, from which arise the degrees of Masonry. The breast is composed of societies of angels; also, the abdomen, which are spiritual in their character. The lower limbs are composed of societies of angels, which are in the natural degree. Thus the heavens, ascending and descending, are divided into three discrete degrees, corresponding to the head, body and limbs. These, again, are divided into seven distinct orders, ascending and descending. The right and left sides of the head, body and limbs, are articulated into degrees, which are

41                              V

both discrete and continuous, agreeing with the nine groups of societies, located on either side of the brain. These societies are duplicated on either side of the body, and are positive and negative to each other. Those, upon the right side, relating more to the will, those, on the left, to the understanding.

Thus the heavens are organized in the likeness of a human form, so that every angel, as he becomes instructed in the heavens, knows from each particular thereof the principles that exist in the natural body of man, so far as he is brought into divine order by regeneration.

Every affection has its embodiment, in its own separate degree, in an animal form. Thus it is, that all the various animals, that exist from the heavens, correspond with some part thereof, in their particular degree, the difference between the human and animal creations consisting in this, that the human form receives its influxes from each and every part of the heavens, in its three degrees, with infinite variety. Each species of the animal creation, which exists from the heavens, receives its influx of life and order, only in part, from one degree of the heavens. These animals, thus receiving their influxes of life from the heavenly degrees, are called clean, in the laws of Moses.

As the human family became perverted in its divine order, the love of self, of the world and of riches, distorted the divine order of the human family. Thus the love of self, of the world and of riches, which are diabolical and satanic, give rise to the hells in the spiritual world. These react upon both man and the animal creation, and also upon the natural earth. Thus, there are men, animals, and vegetation, that receive a false life from the influxes of the hells. The accumulation of disorderly spirits reacted upon the earth with such force as to darken the celestial and spiritual degrees of man, and turn the representative ideas of things into Gods, which they worshipped; but, after the descent of the Lord into the natural, these representative worships, in the more en-lightened portions of the world, were done away with, and the oppressed condition of the spiritual degree in man releived, so that he became capable of spiritual thought. A natural spiritual church was restored upon the earth, in the Christian re-ligion. This has had its rise, manhood and old age. The sun has declined below the western horizon, and the spiritual degree is now about to be opened. The mighty influxes of the heavens have pressed upon mankind for one hundred years past, like the waves of the ocean upon a dike, the waters begin already to seap through, and, before many centuries, the flood tide of spiritual knowledges will rush like a mighty current, sweeping away the falsities and errors of the past. The glorious sun of the celestial degree rises in the horizon of the east, to open and adorn the day. All sects of religion will be absorbed in mutual love, and the human family be cemented together, in the bonds of unity, no one shall then say: know ye the Lord, for all shall behold Him in his Word. If the gray light, before the dawn of morning, while the cock yet crows, has so illuminated the intellectual mind for one hundred years past, that it now numbers more improvements in the arts and sciences, and greater spiritual knowledges, than have been previously attained to from the flood, until the past century, with what shall we compare the full blaze of the meridian sun at high twelve, when every ray shall be a science and every heat a perception.

## THE SECOND SECTION.

# OF THE MASTER'S DEGREE.

No. 116. This section treats of the intimate relations that existed between our Ancient Grand Master Solomon, King of Israel, Hiram, King of Tyre, and Hiram Abiff, the widow's son.

Solomon, in a representative sense, represents the most internal principles of the celestial mind, brought forth into the natural, or the Lord in the earth after his glorification, by the resurrection from the dead. Therefore, to him was given wisdom, riches and honors, such as no king of the earth ever had before or since. His wives and concubines represented all the churches and religions of the earth. The great and crowning act of Solomon was the building of his Temple, which was honored by the presence of the Lord, speaking from between the wings of the cherubims, when fire came down from heaven and lighted the altar.

41*

The building of the Temple represents the regeneration of man, and the Temple when erected, represented the Christian Church, all things of the Jewish Church being representative of the Christian.

Hiram, King of Tyre, represented the goods and truths of the spiritual degree. In the more external sense, he represented the spiritual and celestial knowledges, which are known to the spiritual man.

In the east, from time immemorial, have resided the most populous nations of the earth. Their trade has always enriched the people of the west. Babylon was the great distributing city of that trade, for the central portion of Asia, and Tyre for the west. Hence, that city was the great center of commerce and trade. Her ships covered the Mediterranean sea, and bore the rich productions of the east to a thousand cities. Tyre, in her day, was like Venice and London in theirs. The King of Tyre, therefore, was representative of all the celestial and spiritual knowledges of the spiritual man that have been introduced into the science and knowledges of the world.

Hiram Abiff, the widow's son, was representative of the goods and truths of the mother in the natural degree of the mind, which are derived from the external world through the medium of the senses. His mother being a widow, signifies that his quality was derived from the good, and not the truths, of the church. Son is predicated of the intellectual principle of the natural. To be a son of God, is predicated of the intellectual principles derived from the spiritual degree. A daughter is predicated of the good, and affections arising from the will. A wife signifies the church, a widow signifies the affections of the church, which are unprotected by truth. These correspondences arise from the parallelism of the natural and spiritual worlds. A spiritual truth must be expressed by natural means; therefore, natural means are employed as a parallel of the spiritual idea, and this is the only way that spiritual things can be expressed.

For these reasons, Hiram Abiff, a widow's son, was chosen by Hiram, King of Tyre, and sent to King Solomon, to represent the natural good and truth of the mother, derived through the medium of the senses and natural affections of the world, which, by nature and education, he was in the highest degree prepared to represent by his office in the building of the Temple. As a general overseer and conductor of the work, he received his commands directly from King Solomon, and drew his designs upon the Trestle Board, which displayed all the wisdom and knowledges of Solomon, King of Israel, for the wisdom and science of the celestial and spiritual degree, can only be expressed by the natural; therefore, the natural degree must be prepared by natural science and education to receive the spiritual and celestial; either of the degrees alone, is incapable of expressing and teaching the divine attributes; therefore, there existed a close intimate compact between Solomon, King of Israel, Hiram, King of Tyre, and Hiram Abiff, the widow's son, never to confer the secrets of a Master-Mason upon any one, unless they three were present, this being for the best reason in the world, for the natural principle is incapable of understanding the mysteries of the divine attributes of Jehovah. Therefore it takes the presence of three Master Masons, in all ages of the world, to confer the degree, in its limited sense as given in the blue Lodge, and nine to complete it in the Royal Arch.

With every individual, there is a male and female principle, derived from the blending of the temperaments of the mother and father. See No. 46. This gives rise to the difference of their regeneration. In man, the will principle, derived from the father, holds a central and interior position. The female principle derived from the mother, is external and corporeal, from which the natural rational mind is first formed, which is successively put away by a state of death in the regeneration of man, when he comes into the hereditary of the father. The natural mind derived from the mother, is called the widow's son.

No. 117. In the natural degree of the infant, there reside the corporeal, intellectual and will principles, which are the three degrees of the natural. Still more interiorly, there resides the discrete degree of the spiritual, with its natural, spiritual and celestial degrees, in which there reside the innermost principles of the celestial degree, which are receptive of the divine influxes.

These degrees can only be opened successively, by uses performed through the truth of their degrees. Thus it is, that the truth is first operative in the man that is being regenerated; but when the celestial degree is opened, the ascending order is changed to the descending, by which the celestial love principle, in divine order, issues its commands and takes control of all the affairs of life.

The corporeal of the infant is operative at birth in its lowest principles, being successively strengthened and enlarged by exercise and growth. The affections of the natural degree in infancy, come directly forth into the corporeal and sensual principles of the child, so that the affections of surrounding persons and objects are sensed. The emotions, passions and feelings of the parents and friends, flow directly into the affections of the child. All the affections, manifested through the tones of the voice and gestures of the nurse, bring forth similar emotions in the infant. The affections, thus received by the child, contain something of the natural, spiritual and celestial, which flow directly inward, are absorbed and remain with these degrees, which serve for the ultimate opening of their intellectual principles into science, so that the entire life of the external world is found to be present when these degrees are opened. This storing up of the affections of external things, begets, with each degree, an internal memory of the external world, so that the spiritual retains all the events of its natural life after death, in whatever degree it may be, there being a complete recollection of friends, and the motives and ends that govern all of their intercourse in the world.

The influxes of the spiritual and celestial degrees, continually pour forth, as a breath, into the natural, by which all the affections and forms of the natural world are adjoined to the interior degrees. These influxes first produce an active life in the lowest principles of the natural, continually ascending as the man is regenerated, until the celestial degree becomes the active seat of life ; when the entire order of life is changed. The affections and understanding of the celestial degree, with all of its perceptions and science, flow forth into the natural, when there is an understanding of the divine attributes of Jehovah, by the natural mind. For the foregoing reasons, it is said that the secrets of a Master Mason are lost, until brought forth by future generations, the natural principles, before that period, being entirely incompetent to reveal the knowledge of Jehovah. The ideas of the Divine, as contained in the name of God, are conferred upon the Fellow Craft, in the middle chamber of the Temple. See Nos. 105, 106.

The natural degree of the mind derived from the mother, is represented by Hiram Abiff, the widow's son. The peculiar qualities of this degree, we shall now illustrate. In the fallen condition of man, there is a false life of the natural, derived from the distorted orders, springing from selflove, the love of the world and riches. See Nos. 111, 112, 113. These constitute the hereditary principles of the natural, which only can be subdued and brought into subjection by the divine truths of the Word of God, given through the Prophets and Apostles for this express end. These truths cannot be received into the will, unless the ground of the affections is first prepared by natural good and truth. See what is said upon this subject, in the first section of the Master's degree. The affections of the parents and friends flow into the child, and are stored up in the various degrees, to aid their scientific principles to come forth. This storehouse of the affections, in the natural degree, is located in the sustaining faculties designated by the green. See Pl. 1, fig. 1, and No. 28. To these affections are added the experience of life, the scholastic education of youth, by which the natural principles of good and truth are formed in the mind. These are united to the hereditary principles of the parents, which form the peculiar proprium or self-hood of the man through the combinations of the temperaments of the parents, by which they transmit a tendency in their children to their own qualities, graces and affections. These, united to the remains of childhood, form the governing principle of the natural mind, and when directed by the spiritual, they are a crown of grace to the family, friend and business man. They soften the asperities of life and make the genial friend, and lay the foundation of usefulness and science.

The rational principle, arising from the natural good and truth, is the ground into which the seed of the word of God is sown. Mathew 13th. 23. Natural good and truth restrain the evils and falses of the external mind, through the constant watchfulness of Divine Providence and the influence of friends; but when the natural mind is led away by the love of self, the pleasures of the world and the love of riches, the natural principle is clouded and darkened by the falsities of evil, so that the Word of the Lord is received with difficulty, and not being understood, it is choked by the pleasures of life; so that regeneration is impossible, unless the natural principle is restrained by sickness and adversity.

The natural principle derived from the mother in itself, has no power to withstand temptation. It can only be prevented through the influence of

42

Divine Providence and the protection of friends. No man is admitted into spiritual temptations, until the truths of the Divine Word are united with the will, which is the peculiar state of the Master Mason, represented by the first section of the degree, wherein the natural goods and truths of the mind are represented by Hiram Abiff, the widow's son.

The natural mind is led by the cable-toe of faith, hope, and charity: being protected from all spiritual temptation, until a spiritual conscience is formed in the mind. If a man was let into spiritual temptations before this period, he would be destroyed both as to soul and body, by the powers of the hells; but, when the spiritual conscience is once formed, the man resists by the power of truth confirmed in himself, and the evils and falses are only destroyed.

No. 118. Stone signifies spiritual truth. A Fellow Craft, who works in stone, represents the principles of faith, by which the ultimate truths of the mind are shaped and prepared for that living Temple not made with hands, eternal in the heavens. The principles and doctrine of faith, derived from the Word, are first introduced into the memory, and secondly, into the understanding, by which the natural rational principle, from a conjunction of natural good and truth, begins to reason about spiritual things, into which the influxes of the spiritual degree flow, begetting an increment of truth, which is called a spiritual conscience.

When this conscience grows and becomes strengthened and perfected, it assumes to itself the control of the intellectual mind; then it is that man begins to act from a new will, and the truths of faith are said to be introduced into the will. This state corresponds to the first section of the Master's degree. A separation now takes place between the new will and the old will, and also a separation takes place between the principles of the new spiritual science, derived from conscience, and all the external sciences, derived from natural good and truth.

The man now, for the first time, begins to perceive and understand, that all of his religion, heretofore, has been derived from an extended self love, the love of the world, and the love of riches; that he loved the Lord, because he expected to be saved by the technicalities of faith. He also finds that he desired to be saved for the sake of the pleasures and riches of heaven. Thus it is, that all the principles of natural truth and good have been brought in, and used by the principles of self love, the love of the world, and the love of riches, which form the will principle of the natural man. From these three principles of the natural mind, there spring twelve principles of natural science, corresponding with the twelve principles of faith, which make fifteen Craftsmen, who have heretofore been engaged in the building of the Temple.

These Craftsmen, perceiving that the Temple is well nigh completed, or, in other words, that a spiritual conscience is about to take control of all the affairs of life, perceive at the completion of the Temple, they will be turned off without attaining to the knowledges of the divine attributes of Jehovah, which they had hoped to receive, that they might travel into foreign countries and receive the wages of a Master Mason, by which are represented the delights and enjoyments of heaven, which they had heretofore hoped to receive, and control from their own selflove, the love of the world and mammon; but when they perceive that they are rejected by the spiritual principle, a separation takes place between the things of natural science and conscience. The principles of natural truth and good, retiring, determine on making the last effort to extort from the natural rational mind, through reasoning, the knowledges of the divine attributes of Jehovah.

We have shown, in No. 116, that there is no perception of the essential divine truth, without the orderly opening of the three degrees of the mind, which are represented by our three Ancient Grand Masters, who must be present and co-operative. As the celestial degree, in the most ancient times, became closed, the knowledges of Jehovah disappeared from the earth, and as the spiritual degree of the mind alone remained open, the knowledges of God were only perceived representatively ; and as the spiritual degree became entirely closed, the representatives themselves were worshipped as Deities. See No. 105. Traces were yet left of the celestial and spiritual doctrines in their disintegrated forms, which were represented by the descendants of Lamech, Jabal representing the celestial, and Jubal, the intellectual doctrines derived from the spiritual. These were brothers of Tubal-Cain, who, as has been shown, represented natural good and truth, arising from the uses and sciences of the external world, Jubal representing the perverted spiritual ideas of the divine attributes. From which were derived the attributes and name Jebusites, in the land of Canaan, for all of the ancient names represented qualities.  Further perversions took place, which derived their names from the parent stock, and, in Masonry, are called Juballa, Juballo, and Juballum.  These are representative of the perverted ideas of the essential divine good, the essential divine truth, and the divine creative power.  These attributes cannot be comprehended unless the lower degrees of the mind are opened upward into the celestial, so that they are all present with the conclusion.

The natural mind perceives these attributes as different divine personalities, which formed the ground work in ancient mythology of Gods many. In order to elevate the mind from this state of things, it was necessary, in the Christian religion, to represent the Divine attributes as the Father, Son and Holy Ghost.  It was further taught that the fulness of the God-head, bodily, is complete in Jesus Christ.   Col. 2. 9.

Our Ancient Grand Master St. John, the Evangelist, also taught that in the beginning, was the Word, and the Word was with God, and the Word was God.   The Lord also taught that he and the Father are one.   But the natural mind is so prone to the ideas of Gods many, that it perverted this doctrine of the divine attributes of the Father, Son and Holy Ghost into personalities, whereby all perception of a trinity of attributes was lost, and the idea of three distinct persons substituted in its stead. Thus the omnipotence, omnipresence and omniscience of the Creator were destroyed, being confined by the idea of persons, who in themselves are not infinite; for one infinite cannot include another. The mind may conceive of one person with an infinite will, power and understanding, from whom all created things proceed in series and degrees. But, as soon as the idea of distinct persons is introduced into the God-head, each person becomes limited in capacity, power and intelligence, and the idea of infinity is lost, and the Creator sinks to the level of Gods many in the mind.

These perversions are the natural offspring of the love of self, the love of the world, and the love of riches. The love of self will not permit or acknowledge any superior, and when it is forced to acknowledge a God, it still clings to the idea of its own superiority, and would dethrone the Creator, if permitted, and destroy the idea of infinite being. The love of the pleasures of the world combines with selflove; strives at a pre-eminent degree of self-enjoyment, and the control of the delights of others. The love of mammon is a continual effort for power, through the means of riches, for self gratification. Thus it is, that the divine good, the divine wisdom and divine power, are perverted into the doctrines of individual persons. Evil spirits seize upon these doctrines in temptation, and would destroy every person without the protection of a guardian angel.

Food or refreshment corresponds to the goods and truths of faith, which are the food of the spirit, and are received in a state of light; therefore, natural food is partaken of during the day, and not the night; morning, noon and evening, are the natural periods of refreshment, arising from the state of the spirit.

Food grows, and is prepared from the kingdoms of nature, for the support of the natural body, which corresponds to the growth of ideas from the affections, and their preparation for the use of the spirit.

The sanctum sanctorum of the Temple, from its location and use, corresponded to the new will in the man who is being regenerated. From the conjunction of the truth of faith in the will, proceeds the motives and ends of divine order, in the natural course of the regenerate man, which corresponds to the drawing of designs upon the Trestle Board. Without these ends and motives of divine order, the Craftsmen cannot pursue their labors and are thrown into confusion and disorder.

Craftsmen correspond to the principles of faith, and designs upon the Trestle-Board, to the principles of order. Order is of three kinds, natural, spiritual and celestial. External order proceeds from the natural affections of the will; spiritual, from spiritual affections, and celestial from the celestial affections, the will itself being threefold, natural, spiritual and celestial.

Order always implies three things, as the base, shaft and capital of the column, the architrave frieze and cornice of an entablature, or, in general as the pedestal, column and entablature. Thus, there are three, six and nine component parts in every order. There are three distinct orders proceeding from the natural, spiritual and celestial affections. The affections of the discrete degrees flow forth into wisdom, and wisdom into science, which takes upon itself forms which agree with the affection, wisdom and science of the love from which they arise, in its natural, spiritual and celestial degrees.

There are three fundamental loves of the heavens,

which are the love of the Lord, the love of the neighbor, and the love of usefulness.

These blend in every act of heavenly life, each existing in a threefold order, which constitutes nine ascending principles, from the natural to the celestial, by discrete and continuous degrees in wisdom and science. The science of each degree, in the intellect, developes twelve principles of faith, which arise from the divine attributes of love, wisdom and use, which make fifteen operations of the mind in a divine and heavenly order, which exist with the celestial angel in the natural, spiritual and celestial orders of his mind. Opposed to these, in the diabolical and satanic mind, there are three opposing loves which stand opposite to those of the heavens.

These are the love of self, the love of the world, and the love of mammon, which hold rule in the natural planes of the unregenerate mind, from which proceed a false and heretical notion of the divine attributes, by which the Deity appears to be an embodiment of selflove, pleasure and power, rewarding the human family with like conditions and qualities. These attributes of selflove, the pleasures of the world, and power of riches, occupy the south, the west, and the east gates of the natural mind, which are the affections of wisdom and science of the natural man, controlling every principle for their own ends, receiving the truths of the divine Word, and arranging them into twelve opposing principles of faith, which join in the building of the Temple for the sake of selflove, pleasure and power.

As the Temple progresses in its construction, the love of the Lord, the neighbor, and usefulness, flow into the natural from the celestial and spiritual degrees of the mind unperceived, and adjoin themselves to the truths of the divine Word, by which there is a spiritual conscience formed. There now begins to be a separation between the natural goods and truths that flow in, by the natural degree, from the external world, and the goods and truths of the spiritual. Thus there is a plane or expanse formed for their separation, in the second day of regeneration.

This subject is fully represented and treated of in true correspondential language, in the first chapter of Genesis, from the 6th to the 13th verses, inclusive. And God said, "Let the waters under heaven be gathered together unto one place, and let the dry land appear ; and it was so." This subject, so far as it appertains to the second degree, or rational plane of the mind, is represented by the two pillars and globes, set up in front of the Temple.

Before the introduction of the truths of the Word into the will, in the first section of the Master's degree, there is no power to resist spiritual temptations. While the truth is being introduced into the memory, understanding and will, the man is carefully guarded and led by the Lord, through the holy angels, who protect him from the assaults of evil spirits. But, when that state is attained, all protection is at once withdrawn, and the man enters into spiritual combats, fighting from the confirmations of the truths of the Word in his own life.

Evil spirits then enter directly into the natural good and truths of his mind, and seize upon the perverted and false doctrines and ideas of the divine attributes. By these, they assail the spiritual principles of faith, and endeavor to come into the spiritual knowledges of Jehovah, that they may destroy every principle of internal and heavenly life. Thus it is, that the doctrine of distinct personalities in the God-head, derived from the love of self, the love of the world and mammon, are made useful in the first stages of regeneration, and when the man is led into spiritual temptation, they are used to destroy, and put away, the natural principles derived from the mother, and in their turn, are destroyed themselves.

No. 119. A ground is formed in youth, in the natural mind, for the reception of a spiritual plane of thought, by the introduction of goods and truths. arising from education in the sciences and uses of business, from which there is a natural rational principle formed, and hence, there is a consciousness of right and wrong. This is not a real conscience, but a plane into which the spiritual principles of the divine Word are implanted. This plane also gives the power of reasoning upon natural uses and sciences, by which there is natural truth and good in the mind. These are the receptacles of spiritual goods and truths, derived from a life of faith, through the Word of God.

Regeneration cannot commence with the man, until there is a natural rational formed, by which the Word of the Lord may be understood, which is done by the inflowing into the natural of the spiritual and celestial degrees. These influxes rest in the goods and truths of the natural mind, like the fruit in its husk, which, as the fruit is perfected,

is burst asunder and cast away.   Thus it is with
the natural and spiritual; when the spiritual is
born, it supplies the place of the natural with a
more perfect understanding and higher good.

The spiritual is brought forth by temptation,
which casts aside the natural rational principle, by
a state of death to the old, and a resurrection to
the new.   This transition of life and death is progressive in its character, commencing with temptation, which destroys the natural goods and truths,
and precipitates the mind into doubt and scepticism, so that there is a confusion of ideas and loss
of understanding.  · The simplest principles of spiritual truth are not understood.   The memory
refuses to call up the past.   The ideas of the mind
are diffused and scattered.  A physical crisis ensues,
in which the natural powers are suspended, and is
frequently attended with a vision state of the
mind, in which, to some extent, the mind appears
to comprehend its own condition.

The powers of the hells, which are present in
temptation, destroy every thing of the mind to
which they can get access, and not unfrequently
natural death ensues.

But the most interior principles of spiritual
truth from the Word, which have been adjoined to

the will, are guarded by the Holy angels, as the tree of life, at the east of the garden, is guarded by the cherubim, with a flaming sword. In this state, all the heavenly and divine principles of faith are active in the putting away all the perverted affections arising from the love of self, the world and riches, introducing, in their stead, the love of the Lord, the neighbor and usefulness; so that the mind may be raised to newness of life upon the five points of Fellowship, which are expressed by brotherly love, relief and truth.

These principles are represented by the foot, the knee, the breast, the hand, the mouth and ear.

The development of principles attending the new birth, we shall more particularly describe, in the following numbers, by the mercy of the Lord.

No. 120. It was the custom of our Grand Master, Hiram Abiff, every day to enter into the sanctum sanctorum at high twelve, when the Craft were at refreshment, and offer up his devotions to Almighty God, and draw his designs upon the Trestle-Board, and retire at the South gate.

The sun, at the meridian height, corresponds to a state of affection and science, which is doctrine.

At this time, the truths of faith enter into, and are received by the will.

In the second degree of regeneration, the mind begins to perceive that there is a separation between the spiritual and natural minds. In the third degree, the rational principles of divine truth are introduced into the will; and a spiritual conscience appears, by which there is an affection of truth. Man, then begins to live and act from the good of truth as though it was from himself. The things of the natural and spiritual world, appear to him as distinct.

He who cannot form to himself a clear and distinct idea of the parallelism of the two worlds; but, when it is stated and presented to the mind, it appears as an analogy; let him understand distinctly that he has not entered upon the second degree of Masonry or regeneration; but, let him not despair, but persevere in the truths of the Word, for all these various states follow each other, in an orderly progression. The first degree must be completed, and he must pass his examination for the second, before he can be advanced. This is meant by the expression in the Lord's prayer, "Give us this day our daily bread."

No. 121. Every Lodge, to a certain extent, agrees with King Solomon's Temple, which had gates situated on the south, west and east sides. The gates of the Temple were representative of the receptive principles of the mind, which are memory, science and affection, by which the truths of the Word are received, first, into the memory, secondly, into the rational mind, where they are arranged into science or doctrines, and, lastly, into the affections by which they are implanted in the will.

Such is the nature of the Word of God, that it contains concealed, within it, the spiritual and celestial principles of the heavens, which are receptive of the influx of the Lord, through the interior of the mind. These correspond to the operations of the Royal and Select Master's degrees, by which every truth and affection is renewed by the death of another. The divine Word is first received into the memory and the understanding, as natural truth, but when it is worked in the rational, it is like the baser metals that are found to contain gold and silver. The baser ores are then cast away, and the precious metals retained.

Without a knowledge and understanding of the Word of God, as given through the Prophets and

Apostles, no spiritual principle can be formed in the mind.

When the Word has once been introduced into the will, and a spiritual conscience formed, the baser metals are cast away and the finer ores supply their place. When man lives in accordance with the Word of God, a regrowth of the mind and of the whole tissues of the body takes place, and the mind becomes an outward correspondent of inward truths.

Then, the outward man becomes subject to the control of the influxes of the heavens, and the spirit becomes a living temple of the Lord, not made with hands, eternal in the heavens. The gates of this temple are the memory, the scientific principle, and the will; by which reception takes place, first ascending and then descending, ascending when receiving the Word by the memory into science or doctrine, and thence into the will and life, from thence, still ascending to the Royal Arch, when the celestial degree of the will is opened. Here the order becomes changed and the mind receives its orders directly from the Grand Council of the divine attributes of Jehovah, and a perception and knowledge of them as the reward its labors.

Each man must form to himself a plane from the Word. Doctrines may be taught to assist the formation of this plane of science; but, the truths of such doctrines must be clearly seen and understood from the Word of God by each individual mind, or the faith of the man is a mere persuasion.

Every false doctrine in the world has been derived from individuals and confirmed by conventions of men, or general consent of the people, through constant repetition and teaching. With such, all worship is vain, because regeneration is arrested and its growth distorted. The Lord said, "But in vain they do worship me, teaching for doctrines the commandments of men", Math., 15. 9. Men, through self love, the love of the world, and riches, lay hold on the doctrines of the church and pervert them to suit their loves, by which there is a distortion of the Word, and heretical doctrines of the divine attributes, formed in the mind, which are represented by Juballa, Juballo and Juballum. These doctrines, derived from self love, the love of the world, and riches, guard constantly the gates of the temple, night and day, and endeavor to control all the truths, doctrines and affections of the Word, and the twelve principles of faith formed therefrom, which they tempt, but cannot use them for their purpose. These things are clearly and beautifully represented in the second section of this degree.

No. 122. Let no man say, when he is tempted, I am tempted of God : for God cannot be tempted with evil, neither tempteth he any man. But every man is tempted, when he is drawn away of his own lusts and enticed. See James, 1. Chap. 2, to the 15 inclusive. When man is led into temptation, evil spirits seize upon the evils and falsities of doctrine and lusts of the affections, and, like a beseiged city, they first assault the gates of the temple. The South gate represents the science of doctrine, the West the memory of events, and the East gate the affections. The intellectual principle is first assaulted at the South gate, where all the falsities and inconsistencies of doctrine are arrayed to destroy the faith of the man. He is next assailed at the West gate, by bringing up all the events of life, to show the inconsistencies arising from his faith, and when the mind is bewildered and confuted, the lusts of his affections are seized upon at the East gate, and the temple is carried by storm. The working tools of the Craft, which have heretofore been employed in the erection of the temple, are turned against the man.

The spiritual principles of faith can in no wise be comprehended and asssailed by evil, the Lord being always present, guarding them; but the natural goods and truths of the mind are swept away before the infernal crew, like chaff before the wind, when man is led into temptation. Previous to the formation of the spiritual principle in the will, the Lord guards man with unremitting care, using, in his divine Providence, the man's own love of self respect, the opinion of his friends, and desire of riches, to restrain his evils, as long as it is perceived that he is capable of regeneration. But when he has been advanced to the highest good that he is capable of receiving, he is then frequently led into his own evils. If his besetting sin be spiritual pride, drunkenness ensues until he abhors himself. He thus can be restrained in the spiritual world. If the lust of riches is his besetment, then he is led into theft, until he shuns his evils through punishment. With those who are in love of mammon, so long as they cultivate the integrity of business and are useful to the community, they are permitted to enjoy the pleasures of riches, but for awhile they are subject to adversity, to check and restrain their loves. Although there is but little difference in accumulating riches by dishonesty and theft, yet a dishonest man is sometimes permitted to attain to riches that his affections may be restrained by fear of losing his position in society, while the integrity of the business community cramps and restrains his desires.

Thus it is that all the evils of life, when they are opened and brought forth, tend to regeneration, and act as a bond of restraint; but when an increment of spiritual good is formed, through faith, in the will, the man can be let into spiritual temptation; when evil spirits, at once, attack by the evils and falses of his own mind, and carry away, and destroy the natural truths, goods and affections which hinder the birth of the new man. The spiritual principles of the new man retire deeply within the recesses of the will.

The former goods and truths that constituted the body, which is receptive of the spiritual principles of faith, are cast out of the memory through the Western gate of the temple, and there lie buried in its rubbish until low twelve, when every principle of faith is dormant in the mind, during which time the evils of his own mind think to avoid the responsibilities of their own acts by concealment and escape. At this time, the Lord, who is represented by king Solomon, lays open and discovers, through the twelve principles of faith, the spiritual principle of the mind, which is raised to newness of life, represented by the resuscitation of the dead, the heretical doctrines of the divine attributes being first destroyed by their own profanations. See profanations, No. 113.

No. 123. And the man said: " The woman whom thou gavest to be with me, she gave me of the tree, and I did eat." There is a male and female principle in every individual, existing by virtue of the hereditary of the father and mother. These constitute the natural will and intellectual principle of man. With the male, the will is interior, and the intellectual exterior; with the female, the intellectual principle is interior, and the will exterior.

The natural form of the man corresponds to natural truth, and the form of the woman to natural affections. The man receives all things of the exterior world through the medium of the intellect, which is the female principle in him. The woman, on the contrary, receives by the affections, into which her intellectual principles flow, taking shape and form from her affections. Thus, in the woman, the intellect takes the form of the will; and, in man, the affections take the form of his intellectual. In man, the affections are perverted through the falses of the sensual principle, and, in woman, the intellect is falsified through the affections of the sensual. She was, therefore, the first to digress from that path of rectitude, through the lusts of the sensual, perverting the intellectual principle, transmitting those perversions hereditarily to her offspring in man, whereby his intellectual principle becomes deceptive and false. The will, flowing in, partakes of the intellectual. Hence, it is said: "She gave me and I did eat." The tree of good and evil signifies good and false perceptions, and the fruit the goods and evils thereof." Genesis 3.

Thus it is, that the fall of man was accomplished. But the preparation for his regeneration is directly the reverse. The truths of the divine Word are introduced into the memory and scientific principle, by which they are arranged into doctrines, and by habits of life they are implanted in the will.

Regeneration unobstructed, as it was before the fall of man, is purely a natural progression of states, from the sensual and corporeal to the spiritual and celestial angelic states of the body and mind, by which the corporeal and sensual of the body were put off without the process of death. The hereditary principles of the natural intellect derived from the mother, as well as the body, were successively put off, and the man came into the will and intellectual of the father, without sickness or pain. It is possible to put off the body without death even now. Such was the case with Enoch and Elijah, and such would have been the case with our Lord, had not a violent death ensued. With Him, the hereditary and corporeal principles of the mother were put off, leaving only the divine of the Father. This outward life in the world, derived from the mother, flowed inward, and, by the process of remains, was adjoined to his divine attributes, so that He is at once both God and man. These remains were glorified in his resurrection, so that they became divine. See remains, Nō. 28.

A likeness of the glorification of the Lord takes place in the regeneration of man. The putting away of the natural rational principle,

44

which is represented by our Grand Master, Hiram Abiff, took place with our Lord, when he was led into the wilderness to be tempted by the Devil: by which the natural rational principle of the mother was put away, and hence, we hear Him say, at the marriage of Cana, to his mother: "Woman, what have I to do with thee? mine hour is not yet come."—John 2. 4th.

Again He says: " Who is my mother?"---Math. 12. 48—Mark 3. 33, and Luke 8. 21. And yet there is a peculiar sweetness and sympathy in the name of mother, and the natural mind feels almost shocked, when the Lord says on the cross: " Woman, behold thy son !" directing her to a disciple: and to the disciple: "Son, behold thy mother !"—John 19. 26, 27.

The divine principle had taken to itself a body from the Virgin, and, with it, a nativity and hereditary principle of the female. The Virgin clothed, dandled and caressed the holy child, planting within Him the remains of childhood, which had flowed inward, and conjoined · itself to the Divine attributes, by which there was a tender rational principle formed for the divine intellectual. As the Divine came forth, the human of the mother receded, being put off in successive combats and temptations, until the final combat and passions of the cross, in which the celestial degree of the Divine was opened in Him, and the natural degree of the Lord was swallowed up in the divine natural, when he says : "Woman, behold thy son ! Son, behold thy mother ! "

A likeness of the glorification of the Lord takes place with every regenerate man, in whole or in part; with the celestial it is complete ; but with the spiritual, it is in part, which is represented by the death of Hiram Abiff, wherein, the female principle, called the widow's son, is put away by temptation and death. The final opening of the celestial principle, and the bringing forth of the concealed treasures of the will, are represented in the Royal Arch.

The female principle in man is the ground into which the seed or Word of God is cast ; for this reason, woman represents the church.

When man is regenerated, he comes into the the hereditary principles of the father, which cannot be destroyed ; but the evils are put on one side and restrained. When the evils and falses of the natural, derived from the mother, are restrained by a life of faith, the progressive order of regeneration commences. See No. 107. But when the love of self, the world and mammon are unrestrained, a downward progression takes place, by which the soul sinks into hell. The hereditary principles of the mother are not put off, but are the ground and principle of every act. The order of the man is inverted, until his head is turned towards the hells and feet towards the heavens.

No. 124. And lead us not into temptation, but deliver us from evil. Math. 6. 13. The Lord's prayer is a universal expression, in successive order, of the operations of regeneration, and hence it contains the universal truths of the heavens which are infinite in their character. All truth is successive, depending upon something that has gone before, or is to succeed, the arrangement being governed by motives that are true or false. A statement may be true in itself, yet the truth be perverted by a wrong application. The Lord's prayer commences with regeneration, and follows each step successively in its universals.

We can only understand such statement or declaration, contained in the Lord's prayer, as we pass through the states described. The name, "Our Father," signifies a knowledge of the attributes of divine good in the memory, scientific principle and will. These follow each other in successive order, as has been shown in the preceding numbers. A name signifies quality or attributes, hence to hallow the name of Jehovah signifies to receive his qualities into the holy principles of love. To profane his name, signifies to receive the knowledge of the divine attributes into one's own selflove, the love of the world and mammon, by which there are profanation and heretical doctrines relative to the divine attributes formed in the scientific principles of the mind, which are represented by Juballa, Juballo and Juballum. "Thy Kingdom come," signifies the establishment of the divine truths of the Word in the mind. "Thy will be done on earth as it is in heaven," signifies that there should be a correspondence or parallelism between the natural, spiritual and celestial degrees of the mind, by which there is a life of charity on earth corresponding with the divine ends and motives. "Give us this day our daily bread," signifies that there should be a reception of divine truths of the Word in the will sufficient for the state, which we are in. "And forgive us our trespasses as we forgive those that trespass against us," signifies that no sin can be forgiven to any one except through states of the mind.

"And Lead us not into temptation, but deliver us from evil," signifies that evil should be put away by repentance and not by temptation. "For thine is the kingdom and the power and the glory for ever," signifies that the Lord should rule all things, that all power is derived from him, and to Him belongs all praise.

. Evils and falses of the mind are put away in two ways, by repentance and temptation. Profanation is the sin of hypocrisy, wherein a man speaks well, but means evil to his fellow. This sin is called the sin against the Holy Ghost that hath not forgiveness in this world, nor in the world to come. Math. 12, 32. "O, generation of vipers, how can ye, being evil, speak good things?" 12. 34.

In the sin of hypocrisy, the truths and faith of the church are used by selflove, the love of the world, the love of mammon, to accomplish the purposes of hell. Thus there is a conjunction of truth with evil affections, of which there can be no repentance. In this state, the man, after death, can neither be elevated into the heavens nor cast into hell, but is rejected of both. Such spirits wander without society, being unable to escape by sea or land.

They hide themselves in the cliffs of the rocks,

where they repeat their own profanations. Having no passport to the heavens or hells, they are unable to escape from the condition which they are in; for, when they speak the truths of faith, their affections are seen by the angels as vipers within. Being drawn towards the hells by their affections, their thoughts are seen by the devils as the truths of the church. This state of hypocrisy and profanation can only be put away through vastation, sickness and death. "Wo unto the world because of offences: for it must needs be that offences come; but wo to that man by whom the offénce cometh." Math. 18. 1. Luke, 17. 1. No man, who is deeply imbued with selflove, the love of the world and mammon, can be brought into a true faith in the Lord, without passing through a state of profanation, which only can be put away in temptation, through vastation, sickness and death. All the evils of faith which are sins and blasphemies against the son of man, can be put away by repentance; but the sin of profanation hath no forgiveness, of which it is said, if thine eye offend thee, pluck it out. The putting away of profanation in the man that is being regenerated, is represented by the death of Juballa, Juballo and Juballum. The putting away of the hereditary principle of the mother, is represented by the widow's son.

So direful is the effect of profanation upon the spirit, that the Lord is always restraining and guarding the man who is being regenerated, leading the blind by a way they know not, making darkness light before them, and crooked things straight; but the interior spiritual principles of faith are so closely guarded that no profanations can gain admittance; if it were so, no man could be saved. Just in proportion as the love of self, the world and mammon are restrained by the Lord in the man that is being regenerated, he can be delivered from evil through a state of repentance, wherefore we pray, "Lead us not into temptation, but deliver us from evil," which was the case with the twelve Fellow Crafts, or the twelve principles of faith, which were contaminated with the profanations of Juballa, Juballo and Juballum. For profanations, see Master's obligations. See No. 113.

When repentance has taken place, the profanations of the mind are brought to light through faith, when their vastation ensues.

During temptation, man fights against the evils and falses from the truths of the Word confirmed in his life. This he does, as it were, from himself.

Yet the Lord is present, closely guarding the spiritual principle, to see that every evil and falsity is restrained, so that they cannot enter the will during the assimilation and conjunction of the truths of the Word with the affections. King Solomon, who represents the Lord on this occasion immediately issues his edict, that no one shall leave the kingdom by sea or land, without his permission for a space of forty days. Forty is the multiplication of four and ten. Four signifies conjunction, and ten the fulness of affections. Therefore, forty signifies a state of temptation in which the things of faith are more interiorly conjoined with the will.

The various states of the heavens are represented by the four quarters of the earth. The North signifies those who are in nataral good, but without the truths of the Lodge. Therefore the North has ever been considered a place of darkness. The East, from the rising of the sun, represents the divine light which shines through the affections. The sun in the South, at high meridian, represents the divine light of the Word shining in the intellectual principle, by which there is science and doctrine. The sun, setting in the West to close the day, represents the experience of the past, shining in the memory, from which there is wisdom. To one or other of these four quarters of the earth, belong all the principles of faith. Therefore the twelve Fellow Craftsmen are said to be divided into companies of three travelling North, East, South and West. Those, who travel in the westwardly direction, report the tidings of wisdom derived from the memory, by which the profanations of the truths of the Word in the memory are brought to light and destroyed, which are represented by three men of Tyre.

.When man is led into spiritual temptation, the doctrines and scientific principles of faith are at ·once attacked through the profanations of the Word; and when they are overcome, they are cast out of the affections and scientific principles into the memory as dead, where they lie, as it were; concealed among the rubbish of the Temple, until they are finally removed and buried as useless. But the internal memory is still retained, sinking inward, and so is present with every conclusion, although unperceived, by which there is consciousness of eternal life, which is represented by the sprig of acacia.

When the right and left lobes of the cerebellum

are sliced in disecting them, they present, on either side, the beautiful appearance of the arbor vitæ, which masons call the sprig of acacia, which will be treated of in its proper place.

No. 125. The temple of Solomon was built upon Mount Moriah, where the angel appeared to David at the threshing-floor of Ornan, and staid the plague. The symbolic meaning of mountain will not be easily understood without explanation. Things, that belong to a degree, are said to agree or disagree with each other, but things that belong to different discrete degrees of the mind, can neither agree nor disagree, because they flow into each other by influx, and are therefore said to be parallel or correspond with each other, or represent them, and the same is true of different discrete degrees of creation.

The building is said to agree with the plan by which it is constructed; but both the plan and the building do not agree with the spiritual ideas expressed in either; but are a parallelism, representative, or correspondence of the spiritual ideas. Thus there is a parallelism or correspondence between the Creator and the thing created; no one can invent and construct any original piece of machinery or mechanism, unless the mind is previously prepared and adapted to the work. Therefore, the thing invented corresponds to and represents the state, condition and attributes of the mind of the inventor; so that persons, who have passed through like states of mind, may, in future ages, perceive, from the machine that has been invented, the states and conditions of the mind of the inventor. The same thing is true of the Creator and the things created. All things created, represent, correspond to, and are a parallelism of the states, conditions and attributes of the great Creator in the different discrete degrees of the mind, so that as man advances and passes through the discrete degrees of regeneration, all things beheld teach him of the divine attributes of Jehovah.

The universal heavens are bound together by the law of mutual love in the form of one man. This is so vast, that each individual appears to be surrounded with the heavens above, and the earth beneath, with the balmy air, the liquid stream, the lofty mountains and the solid rock. These are the divine principles that flow forth from the attributes of Jehovah, in three discrete degrees of the animal, vegetable and mineral kingdoms. In the heavens, they are life and substance, but, in the earth, they are material and death. The light, heat and electric forces of that world represent the spiritual and celestial degrees of the divine attributes ; but the earth, the water, the mountain and the rock represent the ultimate forces of the celestial and spiritual degrees in the natural. The air, the clouded canopy, and the starry decked heavens, represent the rational principle of the Lord, wherein his celestial attributes shine forth as a mighty sun in its refulgent glory.

Water represents ultimate spiritual truth. Rock signifies the truths of the Word, and, in a supreme sense, the Lord. Mountain signifies the drawing together and ultimation of truths and affections in the natural principle. Therefore, every man's life in the spiritual world, as to its goods, evils and falses in his natural, is represented by mountains, hills, undulations, caverns and valleys, in which he lives. For these are the ultimations and profanations of the divine principles in him. Therefore, the celestial angels live upon the highest mountain, the spiritual in plains by the sea-side and water courses, and the infernal in caverns, in the wilderness and hilly countries, and among the rocks, which are the perversions of the affections and truths of the Word. The names, histories and uses of mountains modify and govern the ideas of their symbolic meaning.

Mount Moriah was the threshing-floor of Ornan, the Jebusite, a place where the wheat was separated from the chaff and the straw, which signifies the good derived from science or doctrine. Traditions also inform us, that this was the very spot upon which Noah built his ark. Mount Moriah, also furnished most of the stones from which the Temple was built. It is quarried underneath, in every direction, for a great distance. The rock is very firm and solid, consisting of a magnesia lime stone, of a beautiful gray, from which large rocks may be obtained, and easily worked. Through the perfect organization of the Craft, such secrecy was maintained, that the Temple and city of Jerusalem were quarried underneath without the knowledge of the inhabitants, a fact which has only been brought to light by modern discoveries. Upon the site where the Temple stood, now stands the Mosque of Omar. Over the spot of the *sanctum sanctorum* of the Temple, is a large stone, thirty or forty feet in diameter, and from seven to ten feet thick, mysteriously supported in an elevated position, which the Mahomedans hold in great veneration from their traditions.

The mountains of Judea have always been held in high reverence. Before the erection of the Temple, high places were sought for worship and sacrifices. Here the most ancient people of the golden age lived. Every mountain, stream and rock had received some name expressive of the divine attributes. Therefore, the representative Word was given in the land of Canaan, which signifies the church. Here all the religions of the earth, which are expressive of the knowledge and worship of the living God, sprang into existence. Here the mighty Arch-Angel descended to the earth. Here the Lord took upon himself flesh, nativity and glorification, and here the sublime institution of Masonry sprang into existence, to bless the rich, the powerful, the humble and lowly, to preserve the true doctrines of regeneration and life of charity, which will come forth in the resplendent glory of the new age.

Mount Moriah signifies the state of the affections, receptive of the divine truths of the Word, which are located in the cerebellum of the brain, from which arise all the perceptions of truth. The first perception, being that of eternal life, is clearly marked by the sprig of acacia in the form of the tissues of the cerebellum. Tree, in the Word, always signifies perception, and perception arises from the affections. Therefore the tissues of the cerebellum, as the mind advances in regeneration, grow into the likeness of the vegetable kingdom. The tissues of the cerebrum are the seat of the voluntary and intellectual mind, and are formed into bundles or sheaves, as the intellectual mind advances.

No spiritual temptation can take place until the intellectual, derived from the Word, is adjoined to the affections in the cerebellum, by which the intellectual of the father comes forth, and assumes control, after the natural rational principle, derived from the mother, has been put away, represented by a state of death and resurrection, wherein the profanations represented by the death of Juballa, Juballo, Juballum, are destroyed, in which there is frequently a vision state of the mind, in which the man's own condition, to a certain extent, is comprehended, from which Mount Moriah is sometimes called the Mount of vision and the Mount of instruction; but its more general signification is the Mount of temptation or bitterness.

It was into the land of Moriah that Abraham was led, for the trial of his faith, in the sacrifice of his son, Isaac, when the angel of the Lord appeared unto him and staid his hand. It was on Mount Moriah that the angel of the Lord appeared unto David with a drawn sword and staid the plague of Israel. It was on Mount Moriah that the combats of our Grand Master, Hiram Abiff, took place, and also the death of Juballa, Juballo, and Juballum. It was in the land of Moriah that the first and final temptation of the Lord took place. " Then the devil taketh him up into the Holy city, and setteth him on a pinnacle of the Temple."—Math. 4. 5. The true idea of Mount Moriah is represented by the Threshing floor of Ornan, the Jebusite. Threshing floor signifies the separation of the wheat from the straw and chaff, or the good from science.

Wheat signifies the good of truth. Straw signifies the scientific principle of the mother. Chaff signifies the natural goods and truths of the rational principle, which protect the spiritual in their formation. Threshing signifies temptation. The Temple was built upon this threshing floor, because it is constructed of spiritual truth, also because it signifies father of nations, or, covenant from the " *H*," which signifies the same as it does in the names of Abraham and Sarah.—Gen. 17, 5, 14. The " *H*" is transferred from the name

45*

Jehovah, which signifies to partake of his qualities or attributes.

All of the letters in the ancient Hebrew alphabet had their representative meaning : the letters in the name Jehovah, signify his attributes, and names commencing with "J," represented that they partook of the true or perverted doctrines of His attributes. From these facts, we are enabled to infer the quality and connection of the perverted doctrines, represented by Jubal, Juballa, Juballo and Juballum, Jebu, and the Jebusites, all of which relate to the doctrine of temptation.

No. 126. "For in the day thou eatest thereof, thou shall surely die." In the spring of the human family during the golden age, the affections in youth were opened to the reception of truth. The intellectual principle was not impaired by sin. Therefore every truth was immediately received into the scientific principle, and thence into the will; so that in early childhood, there were preceptions of truth through the affections. Every affection is an effort to do, and, the will being unimpaired, it rejects the false and receives the truth, which it immediately puts in practice. Every perception of the natural mind arises from the will principle, which is located in the cerebellum, where the tissues of the brain come forth as trees, shrubs and plants. Therefore every perception, in celestial language, is called a tree, a shrub or a plant. Hence, the intellectual principle is in likeness of a garden wherein there is every kind of perception, which is represented by trees. To eat the fruit of a tree, signifies to appropriate the good or evil thereof, so that it becomes a part of the hereditary principle of the man. To appropriate good perceptions aids regeneration; to appropriate evil perceptions, destroys the intellectual and will principle, mixing good and evil, so as to prevent the normal growth or progression of the spirit, which is regeneration. To appropriate good perceptions leads to eternal life, of which every one may partake as long as he only appropriates the good. But to appropriate evil perceptions restrains and prevents the normal growth of the spirit, which is death, for whenever the hereditary principle of the father and mother becomes both good and evil, the fruit of the tree of life can no longer be appropriated. If it were so, the divine mercy of the Lord, through the celestial degree of the spirit, would flow into the hereditary principles of man, giving eternal life to the body, preventing the natural changes of regeneration, whereby the sensual and corporeal principles of the mother are put off, and the man comes into a spiritual state. Thus dying, he would never die, but remain a devil  carnate, bound by the laws of natural gravity to the earth; and thus there could be no heaven formed from the spirits of regenerated men. Therefore the tree of life is said to be guarded by a cherubim with a flaming sword, so that the hereditary principle cannot flow inward and destroy the celestial principle of the mind.

The sensual and corporeal principles of the body cannot easily be renewed, after they have once taken to themselves the hereditary principles of good and evil. Such however was the case with Enoch and Elijah. For this reason, the body can only be put off by death. Dust thou art, and unto dust thou shalt return. The putting away of the body, in natural language, is called death; but that of the spiritual body, in spiritual language, is called eternal death. A few of the operations of natural and spiritual death, we shall now describe.

All life is from the Lord, and therefore it is guarded with the utmost care by the angels. Spiritual death is from the hells, and guarded by the devils. Hence, in the mind of every man, there is a conflict of life and death, which descends into the bodily tissues. When the evils of eternal death descend into the body, there arise all the abnormal growths of the tissues, known to pathological anatomy, which prevent the regeneration of the spirit. But, when the principles of eternal life prevail, the bodily tissues are renewed, and pass through the orderly changes of the affections, so that the body is put off in successive states, and finally removed in old age without pain. For the foregoing reasons, the Lord has never committed the issues of life and death to the physician; but yet the exercise of sound, practical common sense, derived from knowledge and science, is a great benefit to the body and mind.

The states of the body and spirit are readily perceived by the angels that are with a man. When about to be taken by death, each individual is placed under the care of a spirit, who is called the angel of death, who has absolute control of all the circumstances surrounding the man, even to the direction of the mind of the physician and of the nurses, or of the bullet in battle.

When the heart has ceased to beat and the vital

forces of light, heat and electricity have been dissolved, the celestial angels take charge of the body, which is in an unconscious condition. The power of attraction retains every particle of the physical body, while the attractive forces of the spiritual world attract and separate the spirit from the natural principles of the body. When the celestial angels bear it to a place fitted for it in the celestial heavens, there the spirit is vitalized and brought into its own celestial state. If the celestial of the mind has been opened in the bodily life on the earth, the man immediately becomes a celestial angel, and remains in the presence of the Lord; but, if not, he is committed to the care of the spiritual angels, who vitalize the spiritual of the man, and restore within him his own spiritual states. If the spiritual has not been opened, the man becomes a natural spirit, and either descends to the hells or ascends to the heavens, according to to the states and conditions of his regeneration; and hence, it was said by our ancient Grand Master, "if the tree fall towards the South or towards the North, in the place where the tree falleth there it shall be." Ecc. 11, 3. In the putting away of the natural body by a state of death, the vital forces of the light, heat and electricity or the body are so dissipated and absorbed by the electric sphere of the world, that the spirit is but slightly clothed upon by the electric forces of the earth. The spirit does not therefore come in to its full bodily powers, which it was originally designed to have. It therefore cannot be fully clothed upon from the earth, until the electric spheres of the world are purified from the effects of sin by a restoration, through regeneration, of those that live upon the earth. The angelic spirit, therefore, looks forward with hope to the redemption of the world, and his final glorification, which is the last resurrection. In the process of natural death, and also in passing a discrete degree in regeneration, the principles of the mind undergo a transposition from an outward to an inward state, so that the intellectual principles of either the father or mother, which bore rule in regeneration, are transmitted inwardly and buried. This was represented by the burial of our Grand Master, Hiram Abiff, at the foot of Mount Moriah, and afterwards by his burial beneath the sanctum sanctorum, which represents the putting away of the natural rational principle of the mother and the bringing forth of the intellectual principle of the father, which, to a certain extent, is a likeness of the resurrection and glorification of the Lord.   In childhood or infancy, the affections come forward for the reception of remains, by which there is an intellectual principle formed.  These, in childhood, sink inwardly, and the hereditary principle of the mother  comes  forth  by  which  the  natural, rational plane of the mind is formed, which is receptive of the truths of the Word, by which there is a restraint of the hereditary principles of the mother, which are put off in regeneration, together with the profanations of selflove, represented by the widow's son and three men of Tyre.  These, in death, sink inwardly and are buried, the intellectual principle of the father coming forth, which is represented by the resurrection.

In the death of the body and resurrection of the spirit, which takes place immediately after death, as before described, the intellectual principle sinks inward and is buried within the affections, so that a man cannot say one thing and mean another without its being instantly discovered by those about him; for the affections take form and are seen, as the representatives which are, in likeness of the divine principles of the Word, ultimated within him by the habits of life.  Therefore, every spirit appears in a country, with a surrounding landscape, in likeness of the ultimations of divine truth in himself or the society which he is in, which is no more nor less than the life he has lived, relating to the divine Word. Thus the divine principle, so far as it is ultimated in man, is a microcosm of the world, complete in its animal, vegetable and mineral kingdoms. But the divine humanity of the Lord himself, is a man complete in its human principles, from which all human beings are derived by creation, and not by continuity. Therefore no created being can attain to the divine essence.

No. 127. The token of the Entered Apprentice corresponds to truth in the memory, by which there is a plane of sensation formed, giving a natural consciousness of right and wrong, which, like the skin, is the most external plane of mind, by which there is a sensation of pain, when the natural goods and truths of the man are violated in the life. This plane is a kind of conscience, formed exteriorly, which serves as an integument or bond of union, by which man is restrained from rushing into evils through the natural fears arising from selflove, the love of the world and mammon. In reference to this plane of the memory, it is said that one Mason can know an ·

ther in the dark as well as in the light. This
external plane, or bond of conscience, does not
extend inwardly or adjoin itself to the interior
principles of life. But, when the old man and
his deeds decay in regeneration, it cleaves off like
skin from the flesh, retaining no interior principle of life. It is therefore said, that no man can
be raised to a life of charity, by the grip of an
Entered Apprentice, which is the sensation of
right and wrong, arising from the exterior conscience.

Truth, in the memory, when there is no delight
in obedience, corresponds to Judas who betrayed
his Lord, or Rheuben, who went up to his father's
bed. But when there is delight in obedience, it
is a sign of progression. Such become servants,
and remain in the house forever, being attached
to the heavens as good spirits, but, do not become
angels. Those, who obey from the will, are sons,
and those who obey from the intellectual principle, are friends. "If ye love me, keep my commandments."

No. 128. The token of the Fellow Craft corresponds to sensations or delights of the scientific
plane of the intellect, by which there is a delight

in reasoning upon the subject of natural goods and truths, which is the rational plane derived from the mother, in which truths are interwoven and bound in bundles, like the areola and fibrous tissues of the body. For this reason, the natural rational principle corresponds to the flesh and muscles of the body, which is constantly being renewed and put away by an order of progression of the affections. The sensations of the rational principle are felt as the delight of the intellect; but, in them, there is no interior of life. This plane of understanding, which is derived from the mother, decays in regeneration, and, hence, it is said to cleave from the bone. Truth, in the scientific principle, corresponds to the Apostle Peter, and, like him, when it is led into temptation, denies its Lord. Therefore, there can be no resurrection to newness of life by the scientific principle.

No. 129. The Lion of the tribe of Judah, signifies the Lord, who is the power of the resurrection. The Lion's paw signifies the power of divine truth derived from celestial love. The power of divine truth adjoins, in the resurrection, to the affections of truth in the will, by which there is a conjunction of the divine truths of the Word with the celestial good of truth, which is represented by the blue ray of the light, and is the first influx of eternal life in the cerebellum, which is adjoined to external truths of the Word through doctrine or the intellectual principle, which is a new conscience in man, through which he is raised to a life of charity from the will. Much of the good of life, before this period, in man's regeneration, is done through the love of self, the world and mammon, which are put off in the new birth by temptation. This is beautifully expressed by Paul, 1.—Cor. 3. from the 11th to the 18th inclusive. "If any man's work be burned, he shall suffer loss: but he himself shall be saved; yet so as by fire."

Bone signifies truth. Dry bones signify falses and evils. Live bones, in which there is marrow, signify the affections of truth from the celestial good of truth, by which the new birth takes place. "Verily, Verily, I say unto thee, except a man be born again, he cannot see the kingdom of God."—John 3, 3.

To see the kingdom of God, signifies to comprehend and understand the attributes of God. It has been shown in Nos. 110, 111, 112, that no man can attain to a knowledge of the divine attributes except as he advances in the degrees of regeneration. In the first degree of Masonry the knowledges of God are introduced into the memory, by which there is an external bond of conscience. In the Fellow Craft's degree, the knowledges of God are conferred on the scientific principle of the man, in the middle chamber, by which there is perception of the creative power in the scientific mind, which is nearly allied to Geometry.

In the Master's degree, a substitute for the divine attributes of Jehovah is conferred upon the will principle of the man, by which there is a perception of the divine good. The substitute for the Master's word, signifies that there is good in the truth, from which arise a perception and life of charity. The mind perceives, in this state, that whatever is true is also good, and, *vice versa*, that whatever is good is also true.

Therefore, that faith without works is dead, and the reverse of this proposition, that works, without faith, do not save. Therefore, that all zeal must be according to knowledge, and that all knowledge must be brought into a life of charity. Before this period, the natural affections, which belong to the mind, are adjoined to the perception of natural good and truth, forming a natural mind, by which there is an intellectual principle derived from the sensual and corporeal of the mother, which is represented by the widow's son. In this state of the mind, there is an appropriation of the perceptions of good and evil. To the perceptions of evil there are adjoined the love of self, the love of the world and the love of riches. To the perceptions of good, there are adjoined the love of the Lord, the love of the neighbor, and the love of usefulness. Thus the wheat and the tares grow together in the same field.—Math. 13. 25th to the 30th, inclusive,

The evils and falses, thus residing in the mind, are represented by Juballa, Juballo, and Juballum. The harvest represents the putting away of the scientific principle of the natural rational mind, which corresponds to the straw and the chaff, before treated of, as the threshing floor of Ornan, the Jebusite. No. 125. The burning of the tares corresponds to temptation, in which the evil spirits, that are with a man, are let into his natural principle, by which they carry away and destroy the evils and falses thereof.

After the man has once been let into spiritual

temptation and triumphed over death, hell and the grave, in a resurrection to a life of charity, there is no further appropriation of the fruit of the perception of evil; but the more interior spiritual evils still reside in the spiritual man, by which there is a constant warfare, which corresponds to, and is represented by the conflict of the children of Israel and the Canaanites, and also the wars of the children of Israel, and their captivity by the Babylonians, by which the will principle of the father is brought forth, and opened in the Royal Arch degree, into the celestial perceptions of the divine attributes of Jehovah.

No. 130. Masonry teaches that charity is not merely a matter of ritual which is to be learned, but is also to be practised. If a brother or sister be naked, and destitute of daily food, and one of you say unto them, "Depart in peace, be ye warmed and filled; nothwithstanding ye give them not those things which are needful to the body; what doth it profit? Even so, faith, if it hath not works, is dead, being alone." — James 2. 15, 16, 17.

The works of charity, in general, are five, which the Mason represents by five parts of the human or the bonds of mutual love. These works are to be performed by the mouth, the ear, the hand, the knee and the foot. Each of these we shall separately consider.

The mouth signifies speech, by which we are instructed in the truths of doctrine, as given and conferred in the Entered Apprentice degree, in which the candidate is instructed in all the truths of the divine Word. The truth must first be learned, before it can be received into the scientific principles and arranged into doctrines. Therefore, the Entered Apprentice degree is a system of general instruction, sufficient to guide the Mason in all the common avocations of life. The first duty of the Mason is to instruct, to give good counsel, and teach the way of life. This he is bound to do in an humble, honest and sincere manner, entirely free from prejudice and unbiased by selfish motives. He is, at all times, required to unlock the secret treasures of the soul for the benefit of a brother who requires instruction, advice or consolation; for, in the multitude of counsellors, there is safety. Many a wandering step is restrained by the timely warning of a brother, and many a heart is made glad by the oil of consolation. In the hour of distress, the Mason body, which he calls the points of Fellowship, always has a counsellor at hand in whom he can confide. To betray the trust of a Fellow Mason, is an unpardonable crime that brings forth the censure of the entire fraternity, and which forever deprives him of the name of a brother. The importance of enforcing this rule is duly appreciated by all. Integrity is the first bond of Masonry.

All doctrines are taught to be heard, and heard to be obeyed. Therefore, the ear signifies obedience. No man is prepared to teach, until he has learned to be obedient to the truth. All commands are at first forced, then performed from habit; then they are introduced into the scientific principle of the man, and understood as doctrines. There are three ways by which truth is received, first, by commands, which are enforced by punishment; secondly, by habits of life, and lastly, by affection, terminating in action, whereby it is introduced into the will.

Nothing is more common than for individuals, as soon as they have been introduced into a faith, a society or a Lodge, to want immmediately to obtain an office, through which they may gratify their own seifioves of teaching, before they have even learned to obey or have digested the principles they wish to teach. Such do not teach for the good of the whole, but draw about them little circles of friends, who minister to their vanity and ambition ; such, the older members of the society first gently admonish and then retire ; and, not unfrequently the teacher is heard complaining of the absence of those whom he has failed to edify. No man should be elected to an office in a Lodge, until every member is satisfied that the principles of the institution have been well digested and received by the affections into the will; so that the will of the man takes the form of the truth which teaches, and, he is actuated by the principles of mutual love. Such a Master and Wardens will make a Lodge a pleasure to all : giving the proper attention to each individual of the society, and every heart is made glad with the wine of instruction, and every wound is healed by the oil of joy. In such a Lodge, there is no contention heard, sive that noble contention of who can best work and can best agree.

The ten commandments should be taught in early youth, for these are the ground-work of all law and society. Every law, rule and regulation of the society that does not conflict with the commandments, should be strictly obeyed; and every rule be enforced by a proper degree of punishment; strict obedience should be rendered, that hope may be cheered. The ear is the medium of sympathy, by which we listen to the cries of a distressed brother, and by it, we are taught to obey the precepts of charity, which are inculcated in the Lodge.

No. 131. The human has many and wonderful advantages over the forms of the brute creation. The flexibility of the mouth and tongue enables man to adapt the voice to the affections, so as harmoniously to express the lights and shades of thought.

The ear detects the slightest variations of the affections, and the emotions of the soul, flowing into the muscles of the mouth and tongue, give the power of speech. But the most wonderful advantages are manifested in the power of the hand. By it we express, in art, the science of the mind. The magnificent mansion, the engine and the ship are its works. Hence, the hand is the representative of the power and ability of man. By it, we are taught to support a sinking and falling brother with all the means we can command. By the ear we listen to his wants; by the mouth, we warn him of approching danger, but by the hand we hold him up when he is weak, tottering and afflicted. Many an unworthy man has obtruted himself into the fraternity to obtain these benefits; but they are due to the worthy man alone, and from him they are never withheld. As well might the heavens suffer the mansions of the blessed to be invaded by satans, as allow a worthy man irretrievably to fall among brothers? In charity, there is no idea of recompense. He, that thinks of a return, does not perform a deed of charity. Charity is due to every living being, according to the state he is in. To the good and worthy, the liberal hand should ever be opened. The immediate wants even, of the bad, should be supplied; bu he good to be done is his reformation and restoration to society. In this every brother of the Lodge has works of love to perform, and the Lodge that suffers a brother to be lost to society until all of its resources are exhausted, is not entitled to the name of a guardian angel. He, that would barter the benefits of the Lodge for money, would make it the home of the hypocrite, the selfish and the sordid, and its protection the protection of satan and not of heaven. Money is requisite for the uses of the Lodges, but membership should depend on the qualities of the man.

No. 132. The breast contains the heart and lungs, which are involuntary organs of the will and understanding. The lungs adjust themselves to the affections of every thought, so that it is readily expressed by speech and action. The heart receives the innermost affections of the will, flowing from the tree of life, in the cerebellum, conjoined with the pulsations of the cerebrum, which are decomposed by the ganglionic system, partitioned and allotted to the involuntary organs. Thus, it this, that there is co-ordinate action in all the operations of the involuntary organs, as well as the voluntary. But the heart partakes more of the will and the lungs more of the affections of the understanding.

When speaking of the natural man, the breast signifies the conjunction of the natural good and truth, but, after his resurrection to newness of life upon the five points of fellowship, the breast signifies the conjunction of spiritual good and truth which is mutual love, or the lowest bond, that unites the universal heavens in one society, consisting of innumerable parts, the laws and bonds of which cannot be broken, or exposed to the assaults of hell. No devil can comprehend, or understand the least operation of mutual love. Therefore, the heavens are preserved as an entire secret from the hells. Mutual love, when represented by the breast, also signifies secrecy, which cannot be violated without profanation, and the angel so violating it, would be immediately cast out of the heavens. For the foregoing reasons, the secrets of a brother Master Mason, are said, to be as inviolable in the breast of a brother, as they were in his own before communicated, and also, for the foregoing reasons, no man can comprehend, and be admitted by vision into a heavenly state, until he has conquored in spiritual temptations, represented in the Master's degree. For these reasons, the Word of the Lord, which treats altogether of the Lord, the heavens and the church, is written in correspondential and representative language, which at the same time, treats of the celestial, spiritual and natural degrees. The natural degree, only to a limited extent, being understood and comprehended by the natural man; but as he progresses in regeneration, there is an unfolding of the Word.

No. 133. The various positions of the body, before the Lord, signify the states of the affections. To sit, signifies to be in, and consociate with the truth. To stand, signifies to see and understand the truth. To walk, signifies to practice the truth. To postrate the body upon the earth, signifies to confide in the divine mercies. To lie in bed, signifies to confide in doctrines. To kneel down, signifies a state of humiliation, by which there is reception. To kneel on the left knee, signifies to receive the truth into the memory. To kneel on the right knee, signifies to receive the truth into the understanding, by which there is science and doctrine. To kneel on both knees, signifies the reception of the truth into the will, by which there is charity.

Every divine blessing is distributed to man by the Lord, through the angels of heaven, by which there is a consociation of the angels with man. This consociation takes place through the affections. The states of the angels being higher than those of man, they can only flow in through humiliation with man, which is represented by kneeling. It is not the words of prayer that beget consociation, but, the affections manifested in the words. But words enable us to concentrate our own affections, and consociate the affections of those who join us in prayer. When a man prays from a selfish and arrogant spirit, although his prayers may be couched in the most devout words, they are re-

jected by the angels, and heard by the satans.
When a prayer is directed to any spirit or angel in
the heavens, as an intercessor it is rejected of the
angels, and turned to the hells.

For there is but one intercessor, which is the divine human of the Lord, and to look to any other
being, is to impugn His mercies and presence. If
an angel prays for a man in the flesh, his prayer is
received by the Lord : or, if one man prays for
another, his prayer is heard by the angels, and
thus by the Lord ; for they are ministers of his
will, and no life except in Him, and should they
act independently, for a single moment, of His divine will, they would be rejected by the heavens,
and cast down to hell. When we concentrate the
will upon a friend or brother, so far as mutual love
prevails between us, there is reception and consociation which is not affected by distance; and when
we earnestly pray for a friend through mutual
love, the thoughts are concentrated upon him and
he appears to the angels as present with us ; and
is made a partaker of our consociations with them,
and thus with the Lord. But if the mind in prayer
be concentrated upon the angels, there is no correspondence or parallelism between the Lord and
us, and our affections are rejected and turned

away from the heavens. But if our affections be
concentrated upon the Divine human of the Lord,
which is the Son, there is a correspondence and
parallelism with the Lord of the entire heavens, in
which the angels are adjoined and unite with our
prayers. Every man who is being regenerated, is
under the guardian care of some Lodge or society
of angels, among whom every act of the man's
life is known.

To kneel down and offer up our devotions to
the Almighty God, without recollecting a brother
Master Mason, is to pray from ourselves and not
from mutual love. Such prayers are selfish and rejected by the heavens; for no Master Mason can
receive any special mercy without its being distributed to all, through the principles of mutual love.
For if one brother is elevated to wealth and honor,
all are made partakers of his glory, or if one brother
Master Mason be given wisdom and intelligence,
it radiates like the light of the sun to all. Thus
it is, that every Master Mason is bound to his
Fellows in the bonds of love.

For the foregoing reasons, the knee is representative of prayer, in which every Mason is
bound to recollect his Fellows, in which there is
mutual love and Fellowship. The knee, therefore,

47*

in Masonic language, is said to be one of the five points of Fellowship.

No. 134.   The foot is the lowest member, which receives the weight and sustains the entire body. Thus it is with the truths and affections of the man; they have higher and lower principles.   The principles receptive of the celestial heavens are represented by the head.   The principles, truths and affections, flowing in by the spiritual heavens, are represented by the thorax and abdomen, and the natural heavens by the limbs.

In the conception and birth of the child, the body is ultimated from the brain and the limbs from the body, the extremities of the organism being the last to be completed.   Thus, it is that the inferior and ultimate principles subsist and grow from the superior, all of the inferior affections and truths being simultaneously contained in the higher, but brought forth in successive order.   By the hand we perform all the works of art and commerce, by which we are bound to support a worthy, sinking and falling brother.   But by the foot we are admonished to practice all the precepts of charity to the last and lowest extremity, even to the depriving of ourselves of the comforts and conveniences of life, to part with even our hat and shoes to save a brother from ruin, or to relieve his greater necessities.

The heavens are bound *in solido* by universal bonds proceeding simultaneously from the higher to the lower, in successive order, all of which must be perfect in its character to give health and ability to the whole system. Masonry, being a likeness, a correspondence, and representative of the heavens in man in his states of regeneration, must be equally full and complete in its principles of charity, from the highest to the lowest, and the brother who interprets the principles of Masonic charity to mean, and depend upon, his own convenience is like Simon, the sorcerer, yet in the gall of bitterness and the strong bonds of iniquity, and should be equally rejected of all good Masons, as Simon was of Peter. But if a Mason judge another, let it be with a righteous judgment, for therewith shall he be judged.

All charity is performed from truth in the will, which corresponds to the state of a Master Mason. All the works of kindness before this state, proceed from natural good and truth, which in reality are not works of charity, but are conducive to a final state of charity; and therefore should be practiced with zeal and energy, even if they arise from selflove, the love of the world and the love of mammon.

All things appertaining to the conjunction of the intellect with the affections, rise in series of five, ten and fifteen. Ten represents the fulness of all things of charity. Therefore there are ten commandments and ten states of the mind, from which arise the ten blessings enumerated in the sermon on the Mount.—Mathew, 4, 3, 12, inclusive.

All things of the degrees of the intellect rise in series of three, six, nine and twelve, and so on to twenty-seven. Twelve signifies the fulness of faith. But there are two principles of faith that are not introduced into charity: namely, faith in the memory and faith in the understanding. There can be no charity until the truth is done from the will. All acts of kindness, before this period, only tend to salvation. All the various states of the intellectual principle, up to the final conjunction of the will and the understanding, are represented by the first three degrees of Masonry, after which there follow the ten states of charity to be treated of. The ten states of charity, as well as the ten commandments, are common to the female, as well as the male, but the regeneration of the female takes place differently from that of the male. Therefore, she cannot be made a Mason. Her regeneration takes place by the affections, and not by any other process. Her road is different, which we will briefly explain.

Woman was created from a rib of the man, which signifies the ultimate of his spiritual truth. She therefore commences where he leaves off. Her interior principle is truth, and her exterior affections. The interior of man is good, and his exterior truth. If this were not the case with the male and female, there could be no procreation of offspring. Man was created first, and contains within himself the male and female principle. Woman was taken from man and returns to him again, for the twain shall become one flesh. She was made a help-meet for man; but in her fallen condition, she is separated from the male, and must be restored again by regeneration, before there can be any true conjugial love. Previous to the final restitution of the male and female to states of charity, there is no real marriage, but only an apparent one, in which it becomes their duty to live strictly according to the divine law of marriage, that they may be finally restored to the married state through regeneration. Therefore, it is said by Paul, 2d. Timothy, 2d, 15. "Notwithstanding, she shall be saved in child-bearing, if they continue in faith and charity and holiness, with sobriety." Therefore, when the love of offspring has ceased with woman, she can no longer be saved, for in that state, she ceases to be a help-meet to man. True marriage arises from the conjunction of the will and the understanding in acts of charity. Previous to this state, there is a continual striving for mastery between the consociated partners, until one or the other is subdued, when there is the peace of subjugation. For this reason, the man is made the head of the family; if it were not so, salvation would be impossible.

The woman receives truth through the affections, and the man through the understanding. He curbs and restrains his affections by truth, the woman by uses. The man inquires, if it be true. The woman thinks only of its uses, and, so far as she is in the pleasures of life, she thinks or cares but little for the truth, but depends upon her own interior perceptions to see whether the thing proposed is right or wrong, and only argues to confirm it. The philosophical principles of nature are of but little interest to her, further than they administer to her gratification. In the more advanced states of mind, she only inquires within herself, Is the thing good? and she pays but little attention to the truth. The man, on the contrary, investigates and reasons to ascertain the truth or falsity of a statement, and scarcely perceives or asks within himself, Is it good? and not until he is far advanced to the Master's degree, does he say or realize that the thing is good and therefore true.

The woman receives truth through the affections and consociations of the church. Man receives faith through the investigations of the truth, and will leave it, when he perceives that his faith is wrong. But the woman will never retire as long as she is pleased with her consociations, until she arrives at a state of charity, in which the exterior affections are joined with the interior intellectual principle derived from the father, by which the mother is put off as to the affections, when she comes into an intellectual state from the interior principles of truth. Then she rises above the faith and consociations of her youth, and sees that every faith is true, so far as it leads to spiritual good from the Lord. In this state of the mind, the affections, that heretofore have been uppermost in the mind, die and sink inwardly, being buried within the intellectual, when there comes forth a full and rich perception of the truths of the Word. He that would hold an argument with a woman, thinking to convince her of the errors of her faith, has nò knowledge of the states of regeneration, either in himself or in her. She must be led by her affections, and not by argument, until she has arrived at a state of charity, which is the third degree of regeneration, in which there commences to be a true state of marriage, which, in its fulness, is called conjugial love, when she comes into the ten principles of charity, in common with the man. The affections of charity, with him, being the outermost, and the affections of truth, with her, having changed their relative positions of good and truth, in the progress of regeneration. Many trouble themselves about their conjugial partners in the resurrection. Such do err, not understanding the subject, for neither natural marriage nor the resurrection has anything to do with the consociation of the angels, which takes place purely from the conjunction of divine good and truth in the natural of the spirit. When two persons in the world have perfected themselves in the life and principles of charity, coming into a like angelic state of faith, a conjunction of their interiors takes place by conjugial love, and they twain become one flesh. But when they do not obtain to this perfection of faith and charity, they pass into the spiritual world, by the resurrection, entirely free, and are, like the angels of heaven perfected and consociated with their true counterparts through the divine marriage of love and truth. Conjugial love is given only to those who are in like states of faith and charity. The Christian cannot be conjoined with the Jew, the Mahomedan or Heathen; for although they may be brought into states of faith and charity, yet they reside in different quarters of the heavens.

No. 135. "Blessed are the poor in spirit : for theirs is the kingdom of heaven."— Math. 5. 3. To him that hath shall be given, is a universal law. We are more willing to give a good price to the rich than to the poor, and as a man becomes rich, the greater is the field of fortune. The first start in life is the most difficult. So it is with the acquirement of knowledge and all the other virtues. They are slow at first, but increase rapidly.

As we progress, our capacities and desires en-

48

large.  So it is with spiritual life.  As we increase in goodness and truth, our affections and understandings enlarge, and we perceive more clearly that all that is good and true belong to the Lord, and that we are really, in ourselves, poor and destitute.  To such belongs the kingdom of heaven. This is the first start of the mind derived from charity, in which there is salvation and true bliss.

No. 136.  "Blessed are they that mourn: for they shall be comforted."  The states arising from a life of charity follow each other as day and night.  But man is not permitted to see the operations of divine Providence, only as he passes the successive states that follow each other.  When the state that man is in from charity is about to change, there comes a day of visitation, when the sun of the affections declines to darkness, and the night follows.

When man supposes that the goods and truths in him have perished, he betakes himself to a state of mourning, which is a sign to the angels that he is about to be elevated to a higher state of dignity and use.  But, the man who has reached his highest state, so that he cannot be exalted, relapses into a state of lethargy and indifference, in the night of his darkness, which is a sign that he has reached the fulness of his capacity for elevation ; to such, there are no further honors. But with those that mourn, the morning sun rises with splendor and beauty to adorn the day.

No. 137. "Blessed are the meek, for they shall inherit the earth." To learn to subdue the passions, is the first thing that we are taught in Masonry. Moses and the Lord were the most perfect examples upon the earth of meekness. All anger arises from the love of self, in the natural man. The complete subjugation of the passion of anger has been seldom accomplished by the greatest men on earth. But to forgive our enemies, and pray for those that despitefully use us, is the doctrine of the Sacred Scriptures, and most eminently practiced in the Lodge.

The earth signifies and represents the natural principle in man, in which salvation takes place. For all the opposing principles in regeneration, have their seats in the natural. Hence, to overcome the passion of anger in the natural, is to obtain a full and complete triumph over it. With such, the spirit is enabled to take to itself, in its resuscitation after death, its earthly body, consisting of the vital forces of light, heat and electricity, by which there is a much greater state of activity and vital force of the natural. Hence, the meek are said to inherit the earth.

No. 138. "Blessed are they that do hunger and thirst after righteousness, for they shall be filled."

The spirit is sustained from the good of truth and love, which is represented by the food and drink of the body. To hunger spiritually, is ardently to desire good. To thirst, is to desire the truth ; from which springs a life of righteousness. Hence, when a man ardently desires to do good to his neighbor and to act rightly, he is said to hunger and thirst after righteousness, there being a sensation in the natural, very much like hunger and thirst, which no natural food can satisfy. When this state arises in man, the Lord opens to him fields of usefulness commensurate with his desires, which satisfy the longing desires of the soul, and fill the spirit with the delights and joys of heaven.

No. 139. "Blessed are the merciful: for they shall obtain mercy."

In a spiritual sense, mercy is the forbearance and kindness of the Lord towards the hells. For, although the devil and satans have violated every principle of justice, yet, the Lord, in His mercy, extends to them every good, so far as they do not abuse it, by using it against others. In a natural sense, mercy is the forbearance to execute judgment against the guilty, when we are satisfied that no evils to others will come from the relaxation of justice. For mercy considers the universal good of the human family, and is one of the ten principles of charity.

It is the Lord that regenerates and forms the spirit receptive of the will. Man alone does evil. It belongs to him, but goodness to the Lord. Therefore, every gift is of his mercy and not of man. The Lord is constantly regenerating man, and elevating the angels to dignity, honor and glory; all of which they receive and acknowledge to be of his mercy. To be merciful, in a spiritual sense, is always to recollect and acknowledge the Lord's mercy, and to extend the same to others. " Blessed are such, for they shall obtain mercy; in which there is true salvation and bliss."

No. 140.  " Blessed are the pure in heart: for they shall see God."

All purity is derived from the truth : for the truth is pure.  The affections are represented by the heart, and hence, when the pure in heart are mentioned, we understand those whose affections have been purified by the truth, so that they will good to all men.  God signifies the divine attributes of creative power.  To see, signifies to know, to understand, and comprehend, for sight is spiritually predicated of intelligence.  According to the perfection of our intelligence, we are present with, and perceive, the object of our affections. We are here promised, if our affections are pure, that our intelligence shall be so perfected, that we can come into the presence of the Divine in His creative power, so as to see and behold His form, which is the highest state of a spiritual angel.

No. 141.  "Blessed are the peace makers : for they shall be called the children of God."

The states of the mind in regeneration follow each other successively.  True peace can only be given to the pure in heart ; and their first work is to make peace between their fellows.  With a man who is entering upon a life of charity, the first state is one of poverty, the second, a state of mourning, when there appears to be a death of truth and a famine of good. In the third state, he subdues his passions. In the fourth state, there commences a hungering and thirsting after righteousness. The fifth state in one of the perceptions, and a life of mercy. In the sixth state the affections are purified by the truth. From which follows a state of peace, which is preparatory to a more active state of the affections, in which evils and falses are most vigorously resisted. Therefore, a state of peace corresponds to the spring, or the gray dawn of the morning, before the day of vigorous labor.

Peace is derived from the kingdom of God in man, and its blessedness from his divine good. Therefore, those that make peace shall be called the children of God, for they are his offspring.

No. 142. " Blessed are they which are persecuted for righteousness sake : for theirs is the kingdom of heaven. "

Righteousness is an active state of all the divine virtues in man, which follows a state of peace, for no man can really be active and energetic in any cause, as long as there is any opposing principle left in him. The Lord, before this period, protects the various formations of the principles of charity in man ; but, when they are fully formed, he is brought into an active state, and prepared for the final and great struggle in the cause of truth. He loves his neighbor as himself and opposes, with energy and zeal, the evil and the false. The sword of truth is now fairly drawn in battle, and no man within its reach can remain neutral. The battle is set in array, and the opposing forces strive with fierceness for the mastery of the field. The weapons, upon one side, are love and truth, and on the other, persecution and calumny. But as love and truth must ever triumph over hatred and vice, the battle is one for the righteous. Therefore, "Blessed are they that are persecuted for righteousness sake: for theirs is the kingdom of heaven."

No. 143. "Blessed are ye when men shall revile you and persecute you, and shall say all manner of evil against you falsely for my sake."

When men have entered in to combat, and the righteous have triumphed, by truth and love, over the evils and falses of the world, unfurling the standard of truth before their subdued enemies, which have lost all hopes of conquest for the cause of evil, the latter burn with an intense hatred towards the Lord and begin to revile, persecute, and slander falsely his followers who have triumphed over them in the cause of truth, and say all manner of things falsely for his sake. This is a sure sign of conquest and subjugation, from which there is the bitterness of persecution.

No. 144. "Rejoice and be exceedingly glad, for great is your reward in heaven, for so persecuted they the prophets which were before you."

Sing, O Zion, and let thy shouts be heard on the mountain top, for thy delivery has come! Rejoice thou blessed, and sing aloud, for thou hast overcome the world, the flesh and satan, and art for evermore numbered among the Apostles and Prophets.

"O death! where is thy sting? O grave! where is thy victory?"

# INDEX

## INTRODUCTION.

## THE ENTERED APPRENTICE DEGREE.